THE MODERN WORLD-SYSTEM
IN THE *LONGUE DURÉE*

Fernand Braudel Center Series
Edited by Immanuel Wallerstein

Alternatives: The United States Confronts the World
  by Immanuel Wallerstein

The Modern World-System in the Longue Durée
  edited by Immanuel Wallerstein

Overcoming the Two Cultures: Science versus the Humanities in the
  Modern World-System
  Richard E. Lee and Immanuel Wallerstein, coordinators

THE MODERN WORLD-SYSTEM
IN THE *LONGUE DURÉE*

EDITED BY
IMMANUEL WALLERSTEIN

Paradigm Publishers
BOULDER • LONDON

Copyright © 2004 by Paradigm Publishers

Published in the United States by Paradigm Publishers, 3360 Mitchell Lane, Suite C, Boulder, Colorado 80301 USA.

Paradigm Publishers is the trade name of Birkenkamp & Company, LLC, Dean Birkenkamp, President and Publisher.

Library of Congress Cataloging-in-Publication Data

The modern world-system in the *longue durée* / edited by Immanuel Wallerstein.
p. cm.
Includes index.
ISBN 1-59451-036-9 (hard cover : alk. paper) — ISBN 1-59451-037-7 (pbk. : alk. paper)
1. Economic history. 2. Capitalism—History. 3. Economics—Sociological aspects. I. Wallerstein, Immanuel Maurice, 1930–
HC51.M595 2004
330.9—dc22

2004014557

Printed and bound in the United States of America on acid-free paper that meets the standards of the American National Standard for Permanence of Paper for Printed Library Materials.

Designed and Typeset by Straight Creek Bookmakers.

09   08   07   06   05   04
5   4   3   2   1

Contents

Introduction: Scholarship and Reality

Immanuel Wallerstein

That there is an intimate connection between the real world in which we live and the ways we hope to better perceive and learn about that real world has been a premise of the work of the Fernand Braudel Center for the Study of Economies, Historical Systems, and Civilizations since its founding in 1976. When we decided to celebrate the twenty-fifth anniversary of the center with a conference during November 2–3, 2001, it seemed natural and useful to make this connection the centerpiece of our reflections about the current reality of the world and the state of our attempts to learn more about it.

We argue that we are living in a world-system that is a capitalist world-economy. We argue that this system has been in existence for a long while, circa five hundred years. We argue that this system is a historical system, that is, it has rules that govern its operations (which makes it a system) and it is constantly evolving (which makes it historical). This system did not always exist. It follows that, during its existence, there have been some constants or repeated patterns also that the prior history of the system creates the framework within which any particular action occurs. And of course, like all systems, our modern world-system is mortal. It will not last forever. It may well be in its terminal crisis now.

The ideas, the concepts, the knowledge that people and institutions within the system create is part and parcel of that historical system; this knowledge is itself both systemic and historical (just like any other structures of the system). If we are to understand these structures of knowledge, they must be historicized, evaluated, and explained within the framework of this system. We must discover their rules, how these rules came into existence, and how they frame what we might learn about reality.

So, of course, our authors seek to do their analyses within the Braudelian *longue durée*. But since they are also persons of today, they are deeply concerned with where the modern world-system as a whole and its structures of knowledge are heading at this moment and in the relatively near future. These are not exercises in futurology, but attempts to assess what are, what we might be, and the historical choices we are being called upon to make.

We are seeking to universalize the universals by particularizing the particulars. In this deep sense, the effort is neither nomothetic nor idiographic. It is part of a project to overcome the false dichotomy of the two cultures, to reunify the epistemology of knowledge, and to be socially useful in the analysis and transformation of the world-system in which we find ourselves.

*

PART I

The Capitalist World-Economy: From Past to Future

1

Globalism or Apartheid on a Global Scale?

Samir Amin

The confusion created in the dominant discourse between the concept of free market economy and that of capitalism is the root cause of a dangerous relaxation of the criticism leveled against the policies implemented. The market, which naturally refers to competition, is not capitalism. The content of capitalism is specifically defined by the limit to the competition implicit in the monopoly of private property, including the oligopolistic control by certain groups, to the exclusion of others. Market and capitalism are two distinct concepts; the really existing capitalism being the very opposite of what the imaginary market constitutes.

On the other hand, capitalism, abstractly viewed as a mode of production, is based on a market integrated into its three dimensions (market for products of social work, financial market, and labor market). However, the notion of capitalism as a really existing global system is based on the universal expansion of the market in its first two dimensions alone, since the creation of a real-world labor market is obscured by the perpetual existence of national political boundaries, despite economic globalization, which is therefore always truncated. Hence, the really existing capitalism is necessarily polarizing on the global scale, and the unequal development it engenders becomes the most violent and increasing contradiction that cannot be surmounted through its own logic.

The centers are the product of history, which permitted, in certain regions of the capitalist system, the establishment of a national bourgeois hegemony and a state that can equally be referred to as national capitalist. The bourgeoisie and bourgeois states are inseparable in this context and it is only the so-called liberal ideology that can speak of a capitalistic economy—setting the state aside, contrary to all expectations. The bourgeois state assumes national dimensions when it controls the accumulation process, certainly within the limits of external constraints, but that is when such constraints are highly relativized by its own capacity to respond to their action, or even to take part in formulating them.

For their part, the peripheries are defined in negative terms: They constitute regions that are not established as centers in the global capitalist system. They represent countries and regions that do not control the accumulation process locally, which is consequently influenced mainly by external constraints. The peripheries are not stagnant, although their development is similar to the development of the centers in the successive stages of the global expansion of capitalism. The bourgeoisie and local capital are not absent from the local sociopolitical scene and the peripheries are not synonymous with precapitalist societies. But the state's formal existence is not synonymous with the national capitalist state even if the local bourgeoisie amply controls this machinery inasmuch as it does not control the accumulation process.

The coexistence of centers and peripheries in the world capitalist system at each stage of global development is obvious. The question does not lie in this recognition; it consists in knowing whether the peripheries are moving toward the crystallization of new centers. More precisely, it is a question of knowing whether the forces operating in the global system are advancing in this direction or are moving in the opposite direction, beyond the changes affecting such forces in between the development stages of the entire system.

In its globalized expansion, the really existing capitalism has always fostered inequality among peoples. Such inequality is not the outcome of circumstances peculiar to any given country or time; it is the product of the immanent logic of capital accumulation. Racism is the inevitable outcome of this system. In the discourse on the dominant vulgar ideology, the free-market economy naturally ignored the disparity between individuals and between peoples, thereby promoting democracy. In practice, the really existing capitalism is another thing altogether, creating inequality between peoples and breeding fundamental racism.

In the current era of neoliberal globalization, this notion claims that the page of inequality between peoples is being turned. It is purported that the new globalization offers a "chance" to those countries that accept the inherent challenge to learn how to become integrated into the system. These countries can then "catch up with" the former centers. However, the reality is nothing of the sort. The new forms of monopolistic domination of the centers in the whole system account for further polarization and increasing inequality between peoples. The logic of this globalization consists of organizing apartheid on a global scale.

Globalization Is Imperialism

Imperialism is not a stage—not even the highest stage—of capitalism: It has always been inherent in capitalism's expansion. The imperialist conquest of the planet by the Europeans and their North American children was carried out in two phases and is, perhaps, entering a third phase.

Phase I

The first phase of this devastating enterprise was organized around the conquest of the Americas, in the framework of the mercantilist system of Atlantic Europe. The net result was the destruction of the Indian civilizations and their Hispanicization-Christianization: the total genocide on which the United States was built. The fundamental racism of the Anglo-Saxon colonists explains why this model was reproduced elsewhere: in Australia, Tasmania (the most complete genocide in history), and New Zealand. While Catholic Spaniards acted in the name of the religion that was imposed on conquered peoples, the Anglo-Protestants took from their reading of the Bible the right to wipe out the "infidels." The infamous slavery of the Blacks, made necessary by the extermination of the Indians—or their resistance—briskly took over to ensure that the useful parts of the continent were "turned to account." No one today can have any doubt as to the real motives for all of these horrors unless they are ignorant of their intimate relation to the expansion of mercantile capital. Nevertheless, contemporary Europeans accepted the ideological discourse that justified their actions, and the voices of protest—that of Las Casas, for example—did not find sympathetic listeners.

The disastrous results of this first chapter of world capitalist expansion produced, some time later, the forces of liberation that challenged the logic that produced them. The first revolution of the Western hemisphere was that of the slaves of Saint Domingue (present-day Haiti) at the end of the eighteenth century, followed over one century later by the

Mexican revolution of 1910, and fifty years after that by the Cuban revolution. I do not cite either the famous American Revolution or that of the Spanish colonies that soon followed because these revolutions only transferred the power of decision from the metropolis to the colonists so that they could pursue the same project with even greater brutality, but without having to share the profits with the "mother country."

Phase II

The second phase of imperialist devastation was based on the Industrial Revolution and manifested itself in the colonial subjection of Asia and Africa. To open the markets—like the market for opium forced on the Chinese by the English—and seize the natural resources of the globe were the real motives. But again, European opinion, including the workers' movement of the Second International, did not see these realities and accepted the new legitimizing discourse of capitalism. This time, it was the famous "civilizing mission." The voices that expressed the clearest thinking at the time were those of the cynical bourgeois like Cecil Rhodes, who encouraged colonial conquest in order to avoid social revolution in England. Again, the voices of protest—from the Paris Commune to the Bolsheviks—had little resonance. This second phase of imperialism is the origin of the greatest problem that has ever confronted mankind: the overwhelming polarization that has increased the inequality between peoples from a maximum ratio of two to one around 1800, to sixty to one today, with only 20 percent of the earth's population being included in the centers that benefit from the system. At the same time, these prodigious achievements of capitalist civilization gave rise to the most violent confrontations between the imperialist powers that the world has ever seen. Imperialist aggression again produced the forces that resisted its project: The socialist revolutions that took place in Russia and China (not accidentally in the peripheries that were victims of the polarizing expansion of really existing capitalism) and the revolutions of national liberation. Their victories brought about a half-century of respite, the period after World War II, which nourished the illusion that capitalism, compelled to adjust to the new situation, had at last managed to become civilized.

The question of imperialism (and the question of its opposites—liberation and development) has continued to weigh on the history of capitalism up to the present. Just after World War II, the victory of the liberation movements won the political independence of the Asian and African nations, not only putting an end to the system of colonialism but also, in a way, bringing to a close the era of European expansion that had opened in 1492. For four-and-a-half centuries, from 1500 to 1950, that expansion had been the form taken by the development of historical capitalism, to the point where these two aspects of the same reality had become inseparable. To be sure, the world-system of 1492 had already been breached at the end of the eighteenth century and the beginning of the nineteenth century by the independence of the Americas. But the breach was only apparent, because the independence in question had been won not by the indigenous peoples and the slaves imported by the colonists (except in Haiti) but by the colonists themselves, who thereby transformed America into a second Europe. The independence reconquered by the peoples of Asia and Africa took on a different meaning.

The ruling classes of the colonialist countries of Europe understood that a new page of history had been turned. They realized that they had to give up the traditional view that the growth of their domestic capitalist economy was tied to the success of their imperial expansion. This view was held not only by the old colonial powers (primarily England, France, and Holland) but also by the new capitalist centers formed in the nineteenth century (Germany, the United States, and Japan). Accordingly, the intra-European and international conflicts were primarily struggles over the colonies in the imperialist system of 1492. It was understood that the United States reserved for itself exclusive rights to the whole new continent.

The construction of a great European space—developed, rich, having first-class technological and scientific potential and strong military traditions—seemed to constitute a solid alternative on which to found a new resurgence of capitalist accumulation, without "colonies," that is, on the basis of a new type of globalization that was different from the system of 1492. The questions remained of how this new world-system could differ from the old, if it would still be polarizing like the old one, if on a new basis, or if it would cease to be so.

No doubt this construction, which is far from finished and is going through a crisis that could call into question its long-term significance, will remain a difficult task. No formulas have yet been found that would make it possible to reconcile the historical realities of each nation, which weigh so heavily, with the formation of a politically united Europe. In addition, the vision of how this European economic and political space would fit into the new global system, which is also not yet constructed, has so far remained ambiguous, if not foggy. Is this economic space to be the rival of the other great space, the one created in the second Europe by the United States? If so, how will this rivalry affect the relations of Europe and the United States with the rest of the world? Will the rivals confront each other like the imperialist powers of the earlier period or will they act in concert? In the latter case, will the Europeans choose to participate by proxy in this new version of the imperialist system of

1492, keeping their political choices in conformity with those of Washington? On what conditions could the construction of Europe become part of a globalization that would put a definitive end to the system of 1492?

Phase III

Today we see the beginning of a third wave of world devastation by imperialist expansion, encouraged by the collapse of the Soviet system and of the regimes of populist nationalism in the Third World. The objectives of dominant capital are still the same—control of market expansion, looting of the earth's natural resources, the superexploitation of the periphery labor reserves—although they are being pursued in conditions that are new and, in some respects, very different from those that characterized the preceding phase of imperialism. The ideological discourse designed to secure the assent of the peoples of the central triad (United States–Canada, the European Union, Japan) has been refurbished and is now founded on a "duty to intervene" that is supposedly justified by the defense of "democracy," the "rights of peoples," and "humanitarianism." The examples of the double standard are so flagrant that it seems obvious to Asians and Africans how cynically this language is used. Western opinion, however, has responded to it with as much enthusiasm as it did to the justifications of earlier phases of imperialism.

Furthermore, the United States is carrying out a systematic strategy designed to ensure its absolute hegemony by a show of military might that will consolidate all the other partners in the triad. From this point of view, the war in Kosovo fulfilled a crucial function; note the total capitulation of the European states, which supported the American position on the "new strategic concept" adopted by NATO immediately after the "victory" in Yugoslavia on April 23–25, 1999. According to this new concept (referred to more bluntly on the other side of the Atlantic as the "Clinton Doctrine"), NATO's mission is, for practical purposes, extended to all of Asia and Africa. The United States, ever since the Monroe Doctrine, has reserved the sole right to intervene in the Americas; an admission that NATO is not a defensive alliance but an offensive weapon of the United States. At the same time, this mission is redefined in vague terms that include new "threats" (international crime, "terrorism," the "dangerous" arming of countries outside NATO, etc.), which plainly make it possible to justify almost any aggression useful to the United States. Moreover, President Clinton made no bones about speaking of rogue states that might be necessary to attack preventively, without further specifying what he meant by the roguery in question. In addition, NATO is freed from the obligation of acting only on a mandate from the United Nations, which is treated with a contempt equal to that which the fascist powers showed for the League of Nations (there is a striking similarity in the terms used).

American ideology is careful to package its merchandise, the imperialist project, in the ineffable language of the "historic mission of the United States." This is a tradition handed down from the beginning by the founding fathers, sure of their divine inspiration. American liberals, in the political sense of the term, who consider themselves as the Left in their society share this ideology. Accordingly, they present American hegemony as necessarily benign, the source of progress in moral scruples and in democratic practice, which will necessarily be to the advantage of those who, in their eyes, are not victims of this project, but beneficiaries. American hegemony, universal peace, democracy, and material progress are joined together as inseparable terms. Reality, of course, is located elsewhere.

The unbelievable extent to which public opinion in Europe (and particularly the opinion of the Left, in places where it has the majority) has rallied around the project—public opinion in the United States is so naive that it poses no problem—is catastrophic and will have tragic consequences. The intensive media campaigns, focused on the regions where Washington has decided to intervene, partly explain this widespread agreement. But beyond this, people in the West are persuaded that because the United States and the countries of the European Union are democratic, their governments are incapable of ill will, which is reserved for the "bloody dictators" of the East. They are so blinded by this conviction that they forget the decisive influence of dominant capital interests. Thus, once again, people in the imperialist countries believe their conscience is clear.

The Legacy of the Twentieth Century: The South Confronted with the New Globalization

I.

During the post–World War II period, which I call the "Bandung period" (1955–1975), the states of the Third World had instituted policies of (real or potential) autocentric development, almost exclusively on a national scale, in an effort to reduce world polarization, to "catch up." The result of the uneven success of these policies was to produce a contemporary Third World composed of countries very different from each other. Today, we can distinguish the following three groups:

1. The capitalist countries of East Asia (Korea, Taiwan, and Singapore), countries of Southeast Asia (Malaysia and Thailand),

and China, in which growth rates have risen, while in almost all areas of the world they were sinking. Looking beyond the crisis that has gripped them since 1997, we must henceforth count these countries among the active competitors in world markets for industrial products. This economic dynamism generally has been accompanied by a lesser aggravation of social imbalances (a point that requires a case-by-case discussion and the making of finer distinctions), by a lesser vulnerability (because of the intensification of intraregional relations in East Asia similar to those in the European Union), and by effective state intervention (the state retains a determining role in the implementation of national strategies of development, even when they are open to the outside).

2. The countries of Latin America and India, which possess equally great industrial capacities. But regional integration is less marked in these countries (20 percent for Latin America). State interventions are less consistent, and the widening of inequalities, which in these regions are already enormous, is all the more tragic because growth rates remain modest.

3. The countries of Africa and the Arab and Islamic worlds, which on the whole have remained locked into an outdated international division of labor. They are still exporters of primary products, either because they have not entered the industrial era or because their industries are fragile, vulnerable, and noncompetitive. In these cases, social imbalances take the form of an expansion of the destitute and excluded masses. There is not the least sign of progress in regional (intra-African or intra-Arab) integration. Growth is almost nonexistent. Even though the group includes rich countries (oil exporters with small populations) as well as poor or very poor countries, not one of them is an active agent that participates in shaping the world-system. In this sense, they are completely marginalized. These countries might be analyzed in terms of three alleged models of development (based on the export of agricultural products, on mining, or on income from oil) and of the different social hegemonies that emerged from national liberation. We would then see clearly that the "development" in question was hardly more than an attempt to join in the global expansion of the capitalism of the time and that, under these conditions, the appropriateness of the term is doubtful, to say the least.

The competitiveness of their industrial production is not the only difference that separates the active peripheries from the marginalized ones. There is also a political difference. The political powers in the active peripheries, and behind them the society as a whole (for all its social contradictions), have a project and a strategy for carrying development out. This is the case of China, Korea, and to a lesser degree, India, certain countries of Southeast Asia, and a few Latin American countries. These national projects are confronting those of globally dominant imperialism, and the result of this confrontation will shape the world of tomorrow. The marginalized peripheries, on the other hand, have neither their own project (even when a rhetoric like that of political Islam claims that they do) nor their own strategy. It is the imperialist circles that think for them and that have the exclusive initiative for projects concerning these regions (like the association of the EEC and the ACPs countries of Africa, the Caribbean and the Pacific, the "Middle East" project of the United States and Israel, and the vague Mediterranean projects of Europe), which are not opposed by any locally initiated project. These countries are therefore passive subjects of globalization. The increasing differentiation between these groups of countries has exploded the concept of the Third World and put an end to the united front strategies of the Bandung era.

Nevertheless, observers are far from unanimous in their evaluation of the nature of the countries of the former Third World and of the prospects for capitalist expansion there. For some, the most dynamic of the emerging countries are on the road to catching up and are no longer peripheries, even if they are still at an intermediary level in the global hierarchy. For others (including myself), these countries constitute the true periphery of tomorrow. The contrast between centers and peripheries, which from 1800 to 1950 was synonymous with the contrast between industrialized and nonindustrialized economies, is now based on new and different criteria. These can be identified through an analysis of the five monopolies exercised by the triad, to which we shall return.

In any event where industrialization has made the most marked progress, the peripheries always contain huge reserves, by which I mean that very large, although varying, proportions of their labor forces are employed (when they are employed) in activities having low productivity. This is because the policies of modernization—that is, the attempts to catch up—impose technological choices that are themselves modern (in order to be efficient, perhaps even competitive), choices that are extremely expensive in terms of the use of scarce resources (capital and skilled labor). This systemic imbalance is further aggravated whenever the modernization in question is accompanied by a growing inequality in the distribution of income. Under these conditions the contrast between the centers and the peripheries remains extreme. In the former, this passive reserve, that does exist, is a minority (varying from time to time according to circumstances, but almost always less than 20 percent).

In the latter it is always a majority. The only exceptions are Korea and Taiwan which, for various reasons, (including the geostrategic factor that has been extremely favorable for them [they had to be helped to confront the danger of "contamination" by Chinese communism]), have enjoyed a growth unparalleled elsewhere.

What about the marginalized regions? Are they a phenomenon without historical precedent? Or, on the contrary, are they the expression of a permanent tendency of capitalist expansion—a tendency that was slowed (for a time), after World War II, by power relations that were less unfavorable to the peripheries as a whole? In the latter case, it was this exceptional situation which, despite the differences among the countries making up the Third World, was the basis for their "solidarity" in their anticolonial struggles, their demands regarding prices of primary products, and their political will to modernize—a will to industrialize that the Western powers tried to thwart. It is precisely because the different countries achieved varying degrees of success on these fronts that the cohesion and solidarity of the Third World were eroded.

In this respect, some countries are qualified as being marginalized, the word suggesting that these countries are "out" of the global system, or at best integrated into it only superficially, and therefore that their development implies that they are "more" integrated. In fact, all the regions of the world (including so-called marginalized Africa) are equally integrated into the global system, but they are integrated into it in different ways. The concept of marginalization is a false concept that hides the real question, which is not "To what degree are the various regions integrated?" Rather it is: "In what way are they integrated?"

Africa was integrated into the global system from the initial building of the system—in the mercantilist phase of early capitalism (1500–1800)—and then during the colonial period (1880–1960). The results of this mode of insertion into world capitalism proved catastrophic for Africans. First, it delayed—by a century—any commencement of an agricultural revolution. A surplus could be extracted from the labor of the peasants and the wealth offered by nature without making investments for modernization (no machines or fertilizer), genuinely paying for the labor (reproducing itself in the framework of traditional self-sufficiency), or even guaranteeing the maintenance of the natural conditions of wealth reproduction (pillage of agrarian soils and forests). Simultaneously, this mode of natural resources development tapped into the framework of the unequal international division of labor of the time, thereby excluding the formation of any local middle class. On the contrary, each time the latter started to form, colonial authorities hastened to suppress it.

As a result, today most so-called less developed countries (LDCs) are located in Africa. Today, the countries that make up this "Fourth

World" are, in large part, countries destroyed by the intensity of their integration during an earlier phase of the global expansion of capitalism. Bangladesh, the successor state of Bengal that was the jewel of British colonization in India, is also an example of this destruction. There are only a few countries that are poor and nonintegrated or less integrated in the global system. Perhaps yesterday we could count North Yemen or Afghanistan among them. Their integration, which is presently underway, like the integration of others yesterday, produces nothing more than a "modernization of poverty"—shantytowns taking on the landless peasants. The weaknesses of the national liberation movement and of the inheritor states of colonization date back to this colonial fashioning. Therefore, these weaknesses are not the products of a pristine precolonial Africa, which disappeared in the storm—contrary to the ideology of global capitalism, which endeavors to derive its legitimacy by harkening back to it with the usual racist discourse. The criticisms of independent Africa, which address its corrupt political middle classes, its lack of economic direction, and the tenacity of its rural community structures, forget that these features of contemporary Africa were forged between 1880 and 1960.

II.

Let us suppose that the present dominant tendencies remain the principal active force determining the evolution of both the system as whole and its various component parts. In this case, what might be the evolution of the relations between what I call the active army of labor (the totality of workers engaged, at least potentially, in competitive activities on the world market) and the passive reserve (the others, that is, not only the marginalized and the unemployed but also those employed in low-productivity activities, who are condemned to poverty)?

According to some observers, the countries of the triad will pursue the evolution initiated by their choice of neoliberalism, and consequently, a large reserve army of labor will be reconstituted on their own territory. In order to maintain their dominant position on a world scale, these countries may reorganize themselves chiefly around their five monopolies, thus abandoning whole segments of "traditional" industrial production that become commonplace and are relegated to the dynamic peripheries (but kept under control by the exercise of these monopolies). In that event, this reconstituted reserve army would be all the larger. In the peripheries concerned, we would also find a dual structure characterized by the coexistence of an active army (employed in the "commonplace" segments of industrial production) and a reserve army. So in a way, the evolution would bring the two groups (center/peripheries) closer together, even though the hierarchy was maintained by the five monopolies.

A great deal has been written on this subject and on the profound revisions it implies in the very concept of labor, in the concept of the relative homogeneity produced by a national productive system, and even in the concept of the contrast between the centers and the peripheries. The "end of labor" that has been announced in accordance with this line of thought, the so-called new network society, and the recomposition of social life by and around the interaction of projects (what is sometimes called the "society of projects," as opposed to the Fordist industrial society) (Castells 1996) are some of the problems which futurology places on the agenda. In whatever form they are expressed, these propositions no longer envisage the possibility that societies can remain even relatively homogeneous, thanks to the generalization of a dominant form of social relations. Everywhere, in the centers as well as the peripheries, there would necessarily be economies and societies advancing at different rates of speed. In different places, there would be a "first world" of the wealthy and the well-off, enjoying the comforts of the new society of projects, a "second world" of heavily exploited workers, and a "third (or fourth) world" of the excluded.

Political optimists may say that the juxtaposition on the territories of the centers and peripheries of an active army and a reserve army will create the conditions for a renewal of significant class struggles, capable of radicalization and internationalism.

My reservations about these hopes are based on two observations that may be summed up as follows:

1. In the centers, it will probably be impossible to reconstitute a large, permanent reserve army and to refocus the economy on activities connected with the five monopolies (defined below). The political system of the triad will hardly permit it. In one way or another, then, violent explosions will cause the movement to branch off from the paths laid out by the neoliberal option (which will become untenable). It will turn either to the Left, in the direction of new and progressive social compromises, or to the Right, in the direction of national populisms with fascist tendencies.

2. In even the most dynamic peripheries, for the reasons given above, it will be impossible for the expansion of modernized productive activities to absorb the huge reserves presently occupied in low-productivity activities. The dynamic peripheries will therefore remain peripheries, that is, societies riddled with all the major contradictions produced by the existence of modernized enclaves

(even large ones), surrounded by vast areas that are only slightly modernized. These contradictions will keep them in a subaltern position, subservient to the five monopolies of the centers. The thesis (developed by Chinese revolutionaries, among others) that only socialism can solve the problems of these societies remains true. True, that is, if by socialism we mean not a formula that is completely worked out and supposedly definitive, but a movement articulating the solidarity of all, carried out in accordance with people's strategies that ensure the gradual, organized transfer, by civilized means, of vast reserves into modern enclaves. This requires de-linking understood as the subordination of external relations to the logic of this popular, national stage of the long transition.

It is important to add that the notion of competitiveness is misused in the dominant discourse. There, it is reduced to a microeconomic concept (the myopic view of the director of an enterprise), whereas it is the productive systems (which are historically national) whose efficiency as a whole gives their component enterprises the competitive capacity in question.

On the basis of the observations and reflections set forth here, it can be seen that the world outside the central triad is made up of three levels of peripheries.

3. *First level.* The former socialist countries: China, Korea, Taiwan, India, Brazil, and Mexico, which have succeeded in building national productive systems (and are therefore potentially, if not actually, competitive).

4. *Second level.* The countries that have embarked on industrialization but have not succeeded in creating national productive systems: the Arab countries, South Africa, Iran, Turkey, and Latin American countries. In these countries, one can occasionally find competitive industrial establishments (thanks in particular to their cheap labor), but no competitive systems exist.

5. *Third level.* The countries that have not entered into the industrial revolution (roughly speaking, the ACPs). These are potentially competitive only in domains where natural advantages are the controlling factor: mines, oil, and tropical agricultural products.

It has been impossible in all countries in the first two levels to absorb the "passive" reserves, which vary from 40 percent (in Russia) to 80 percent (in India and China). In Africa, the proportion is close to or greater than 90 percent. Under these conditions, to talk about a strategic objective of becoming competitive is to engage in meaningless discussion.

The Renewed Monopolies of the Imperialist Centers

I.

The position of a country in the world pyramid is defined by the level of competitiveness of its products on the world market. Recognizing this truism in no way implies that one shares the commonplace view of popular economics that this position is achieved by the application of "rational" economic policies whose rationality is precisely measured by the yardstick of its obedience to the alleged "objective laws of the market." I suggest that, to the contrary, the competitiveness in question is the complex product of a cluster of conditions operating in the whole field of reality: economic, political, and social. Furthermore, in this unequal combat, the centers take advantage of what I call their "five monopolies," articulating the action of all for maximum effect. These five monopolies therefore challenge social theory in its totality. In my opinion, they are as follows:

1. The monopoly in various areas of technology, which demands gigantic expenditures that only the state—the big, rich state—can conceive of sustaining. Without this support, which is never mentioned in liberal discourse, and especially the support of military spending, the monopoly in most of these areas could not be maintained.
2. The monopoly of the control of global financial flows. The liberalization of the establishment of major financial institutions operating on the world financial market has given this monopoly an unprecedented effectiveness. Not so long ago, the major portion of the saving of a nation could circulate only in the space—generally national—governed by its financial institutions. Today, this is no longer the case: Savings are centralized by the intervention of financial institutions whose field of operation is now the whole world. They constitute financial capital, the most globalized segment of capital. Nevertheless, this privilege is based on a political logic that ensures the acceptance of financial globalization. This logic could be challenged by a simple political decision to de-linking, even if it were limited to the domain of financial transfers. Moreover, the free movement of globalized financial capital takes place within a framework defined by a world monetary system. This system is based on the dogma of the free appreciation of currency value by the market (in accordance with the theory that money is a commodity like any other) and on reference to the dollar as the de facto universal currency. The first

of these conditions is without scientific basis, and the second functions only because there is no alternative. The national currency of a particular country can satisfactorily fulfill the function of an international currency only if the conditions of international competition produce a structural surplus of exports from that country, ensuring that it will finance the structural adjustment of the others. In the nineteenth century, that was the case with Great Britain. It is not the case today of the United States, which, on the contrary, finances its deficit by the loans it forces upon others. Nor is it the case of the rivals of the United States. Germany's surpluses disappeared after unification, and Japan's are utterly inadequate to meet the financial needs of the structural adjustment of others. In these conditions, financial globalization, far from being a "natural" development is, on the contrary, extremely fragile. In the short run, it engenders only a permanent instability, and not the stability necessary for the process of adjustment to operate efficiently.

3. The monopoly of access to the natural resources of the planet. The dangers that the mindless exploitation of these resources pose henceforth for the planet—dangers that capitalism, which is based on nothing more than a short-term social rationality, cannot overcome—reinforce the significance of the monopoly of already developed countries, whose only concern is to prevent others from adopting their own wasteful practices.

4. The monopoly in the field of communication and media, which not only homogenize the world culture at the lowest level but also open up new means of political manipulation. The expansion of the modern media market is already one of the major factors in the erosion of the concept and practice of democracy in the West itself.

5. Finally, the monopoly of weapons of mass destruction. This monopoly, which was limited in the postwar period by the bipolar structure of world power, has again become the absolute weapon that American diplomacy reserves for its sole use, as in 1945. Although proliferation entails the obvious danger of spinning out of control in some unforeseen way, in the absence of democratic world control of a truly global disarmament, there is no other means by which this unacceptable monopoly can be combated.

Taken together, these five monopolies define the framework within which the globalized law of the value expresses itself. Far from being the expression of a "pure" economic rationality, which can be separated from its social and political setting, the law of value is the condensed expression of all these conditioning factors. I maintain that these factors cancel out the significance of the industrialization of the peripheries, devaluing the productive labor incorporated in its products while overvaluing the alleged added value attached to the activities through which the new monopolies operate to the benefit of the centers. Therefore, they produce a new hierarchy in the distribution of income on a world scale, which is more unequal than ever, subordinate the industries of the peripheries, and reduce them to the status of subcontractors. This gives polarization a new foundation that will determine its forms in the future.

II.

The system of global and international institutions is being currently reorganized with a view to reinforcing the above-mentioned monopolies of which the triad's centers benefit.

The World Trade Organization (WTO) was established precisely to strengthen these "advantages" of transnational capital and establish their legitimacy for the ruling of the global economy. The so-called rights of industrial and intellectual property are conceived with a view to perpetuating the monopoly of transnationals, guaranteeing their superprofits, and creating additional enormous obstacles for further autonomous industrial development in the peripheries. The scandal that major pharmaceutical multinationals claim a right to free and exclusive access to the market everywhere in the world, to the prejudice of any attempt to produce cheaper medical drugs locally is a good example of the pattern of "apartheid on a global scale." The people of rich countries will have access to efficient medical care, while others (the people of the South) are denied this right to life. Similarly, the offensive of the WTO, which is aimed at integrating agriculture in the global deregulated open market, will destroy any attempt by countries of the South to ensure food security, and will throw hundreds of millions of peasants in the South into poverty.

The logic that commands these policies of systematic overprotection for northern monopolies denies the validity of the dominant discourse with respect to the advantages of the so-called free trade, free access to markets. These policies brutally contradict that discourse, which is therefore nothing but "propaganda," that is, lies. This logic is clearly formulated in the strategy of the WTO, which aims to develop an international business law which is given priority over any national legislation. The scandalous project of a Multinational Agreement on Investment, prepared in secret by the Organization for Economic Cooperation and Development (OECD) countries, is part of this plan.

In contrast to this project of legalizing apartheid on a global scale, what is needed is a global international law of peoples (not a law for business, as if business interests constituted the exclusive legitimate rights). Only in that frame can we hope to develop a new, higher law that will guarantee that everyone on the planet is treated with dignity, which is the prerequisite for their active, creative participation in building the future. A complete, multidimensional body of law that deals with the rights of the human being (both men and women, in full equality), with political rights, social rights (to life, work, and security), the rights of communities and of people, and finally, with relations between states is certainly an agenda that will take decades of reflection, debate, actions, and decisions.

The principle of respect for the sovereignty of nations must remain the cornerstone of international law. If the framers of the Charter of the United Nations chose to proclaim that principle, it was precisely because it had been denied by the fascist powers. In his poignant address before the League of Nations in 1935, Emperor Haile Selassie made it clear that the violation of that principle—a violation that the democracies of the time had accepted in cowardly fashion—tolled the knell for the organization. That today it is the democracies themselves which violate this fundamental principle is not an attenuating circumstance but, on the contrary, an aggravating one. Moreover, it has already marked the beginning of the end of the United Nations, which is treated as a bureau for rubber-stamping decisions taken elsewhere and carried out by others. The solemn adoption of the principle of national sovereignty in 1945 was logically accompanied by the prohibition of recourse to war. States are authorized to defend themselves against anyone who violates their sovereignty by aggression, but they are condemned in advance if they are the aggressors. Yet NATO member countries have been the aggressors in former Yugoslavia.

No doubt the interpretation of the principle of sovereignty given in the United Nations Charter was absolute. Today, democratic public opinion no longer accepts that this principle authorizes governments to do whatever they want to the human beings placed under their jurisdiction, a change in attitude that represents definite progress in the moral conscience of humankind. But how are we to reconcile these two conflicting principles? Certainly not by eliminating one of the terms—either the sovereignty of states or human rights. The path chosen by the United States and followed by its subaltern European allies is certainly the wrong one and also conceals the true objectives of the operation, which have nothing to do with respect for human rights, notwithstanding the media blitz that tries to make us think so.

The United Nations should be the place where international law is elaborated. There is no other that can be respected. To accomplish this task, the organization must be reformed. Thought must be given to the ways and means (including institutional innovation) of enabling real social forces to be represented beside the governments (which represent them very imperfectly at best). The organization must set the goal of integrating into a coherent whole the rules of international law (respect for sovereignty), rules concerning the rights of individuals and people, and those concerning economic and social rights, which are forgotten in the standard liberal list and which necessarily require that markets be regulated. That is enough to provide an agenda heavy with questions that I shall not attempt to deal with here, as the answers would inevitably be too brief. There is no doubt that the process will be long. But there is no shortcut: The history of humanity has not yet reached its end; it will continue to progress at a pace in accordance with its possibilities.

NATO is the other major "international" institution instrumental in the implementation of apartheid on a global scale plan of transnational capital, supported by the governments of the triad.

World geopolitics constitutes the framework within which all development strategies unfold. This is the way it has always been, at least so far as the modern world is concerned—that is, the world capitalist system since 1492. The power relations that give the geopolitics of the successive phases of capitalist expansion their configuration facilitate the development (in the ordinary sense of the term) of the dominant countries and constitute a handicap for the others. The present time is characterized by the deployment of a United States project of hegemony on a world scale. Furthermore, this project occupies the whole stage alone. There is no longer any counterproject aiming to limit the space controlled by the United States, as was the case during the period of bipolarism (1945–1990). In addition to its original ambiguities, the European project has itself entered a phase where it is receding into the background. The countries of the South (the Group of 77, the Non-Aligned Nations), which during the Bandung period (1955–1975) had the ambition of forming a common front to oppose Western imperialism, have given up that idea. Even China, which is going it alone, scarcely has any ambition other than to protect its national project (which is itself ambiguous) and does not pretend to be an active partner in shaping the world.

The hegemony of the United States rests on a major pillar: its military power. Built up systematically since 1945, and covering the entire planet, which is divided into regions (each belonging to a U.S. military command), this hegemony was forced to accept the peaceful coexistence imposed by Soviet military might. When the Cold War was over, in spite of the collapse of the U.S.S.R. whose alleged threat had served as a pretext for the establishment of the U.S. military system, Washington chose not to dismantle that system, but, on the contrary, to strengthen and extend it to the regions that had hitherto escaped its control.

The military is the preferred instrument of the hegemonist offensive. U.S. hegemony, which in turn guarantees the hegemony of the triad over the world-system, demands that its allies agree to follow in the American wake, like Great Britain, Germany, and Japan, acknowledging the necessity of doing so without any emotional crises or any hand-wringing over "culture." But this means that all the speeches that the European politicians feed their audiences about the economic power of Europe have no real significance. By placing itself solely on the terrain of mercantile disputes with no project of its own, Europe is beaten in advance. Washington knows this very well. Today, NATO speaks in the name of the "international community," thereby expressing its contempt for the democratic principle that governs that community through the United Nations. In the American debates concerning the global strategy in question, human rights and democracy are rarely mentioned. They are invoked only when it is useful for the implementation of the global strategy. Hence the dazzling cynicism and the systematic use of the double standard are apparent.

It is not difficult to know both the objectives and the means of the U.S. project. They are set forth in a language whose chief virtue is candor, even if the justification of the goals is drowned in the self-righteous talk characteristic of the American tradition. The American global strategy has five objectives: (1) to neutralize and subjugate the other partners in the triad (Europe and Japan) and to minimize their capacity to act outside the orbit of the United States; (2) to establish military control through NATO and to "Latin Americanize" the pieces of the former Soviet world; (3) to exercise sole control over the Middle East and Central Asia and their oil resources; (4) to break up China, ensure the subordination of the other big states (India, Brazil), and prevent the formation of regional blocs that might be in a position to negotiate the terms of globalization; and (5) to marginalize the regions of the South that do not represent any strategic interest.

WTO and NATO, replacing the United Nations, are the main instruments of the new "global order" (disorder), that is, the new apartheid global imperialist system. Other institutions of the global system also play some role in that frame, while only supportive of WTO and NATO overall strategies. This is the case of the World Bank. This institution, often pompously presented as the major "think tank" formulating strategic choices for the global economy, is certainly not that important. The World Bank is hardly more than a kind of ministry of propaganda for the G-7 in charge of producing slogans and discourses, while actual responsibility for making economic strategic decisions is left to WTO and for political decisions to NATO. The International Monetary Fund (IMF) is more important, although its importance is not as much as is usually stated. As long as the principle of flexible exchange rates governs the international monetary system, and as long as the IMF is not accountable for the relations between major currencies (dollar, mark, euro, yen), the IMF operates only as a kind of supreme currency authority for the South, governed by the North.

III.

In the framework of globalized capitalism, the comparative competitiveness of the productive systems in the triad and in the peripheral worlds, and the major trends of their evolution, are important factors in the prospect for the medium long term. Taken as a whole, they produce economies almost everywhere that function at several speeds: Certain sectors, regions, and enterprises (especially among the giant transnationals) are registering strong growth rates and realizing high profits; others are stagnating, declining, or breaking up. The labor markets are segmented so they can be adjusted to this situation.

Once again, is this really a new phenomenon? Or, on the contrary, does functioning at different speeds constitute the norm in the history of capitalism? If that was the case, it was only an exception that this phenomenon was attenuated during the postwar phase (1945–1980) because at that time the social relations necessitated systematic interventions by the state (the welfare state, the soviet state, and the national state in the Third World of Bandung). The state facilitated the growth and modernization of the productive forces by organizing the requisite transfers between regions and sectors.

It is not easy to sort out from the tangled reality those phenomena that are part of significant long-term trends and those that depend on the particular circumstances of crisis management. In the present phase, the two groups of phenomena are both very real. There is the aspect of "crisis and management of the crisis," and there is the aspect of "ongoing transformation of systems." The main point I want to emphasize is the following: Transformations in the capitalist system are not the product of metasocial forces to which we must submit as to laws of nature (accepting that there is no alternative), but the product of social relations. Accordingly, there are always different possible options corresponding to different social equilibriums.

Thus we are confronted with a new question of development, which makes it more imperative than ever to go beyond the limited vision of catching up that was dominant in the twentieth century. To be sure, the new question of development includes a dimension, if not of catching up, at least of expanding the productive forces. And in this sense, certain lessons from the past remain valid for the future. But it also obliges us to give much greater importance to what is required for the construction, on a world scale, of another society.

Conditions for an Alternative to Globalized Apartheid

I.

There are no capitalist expansion laws asserted as a quasi-supernatural force, just as no historical determinism existed prior to history itself. The trends inherent in the concept of capital always meet resistance by forces opposed to their effects. Real history is the outcome of the conflict between the logic of capitalist expansion and those arising from the social forces' resistance to its expansion.

For example, the industrialization of the peripheries in the course of the postwar period (1945–1990) is not the natural outcome of capitalist expansion but rather that of conditions posed to the latter by victories of the national liberation process imposing this industrialization, to which the globalized capital was adjusted. For instance, the declining efficiency of the nation-state, as a result of capitalist globalization, is not an irreversible determinant of the future. On the contrary, the natural responses to such globalization can give unexpected clues to global expansion, for better or for worse, depending on the circumstances. For example, environmental concerns in conflict with the capital logic (since the latter is naturally a short-term concept) could bring about substantial changes in capital adjustment. Many more examples can be cited.

The effective response to the challenges can be found only if it is understood that history is not commanded by the inevitable deployment of "pure" economic laws. It is produced by social responses to the tendencies expressed by such laws that in turn define the context of social relations in which these laws operate. The "antisystemic" forces—the possible designation for this organized, coherent, and effective refusal of unilateral and total submission to the exigencies of these so-called laws (which, in fact, constitute the law of profit peculiar to capitalism as a system)—influence real history as much as the "pure" logic of capitalist accumulation. They command the possibilities and forms of expansion then deployed in the contexts organized by said forces.

The proposed humanist response to the challenge of globalized expansion of capitalism is by no means utopian. On the contrary, it is the sole realistic project possible in the sense that the beginning of an evolution in its direction must quickly rally powerful social forces capable of imposing logic. If there is to be a utopia, in the common and negative sense of that term, it is actually that of the proposed management of the system limited to its regulation by the market.

To identify the conditions of this humanist alternative, it is essential to start with the diversity of aspirations motivating social mobilization and social struggles and perhaps to classify these aspirations under five

headings: (1) aspiration for political democracy, rule of law, and intellectual freedom; (2) aspiration for social justice; (3) aspiration for respect
for various groups and communities; (4) aspiration for improved ecological management; and (5) aspiration for a more favorable position in the
global system.

It can easily be recognized that the protagonists of the movements
meeting these aspirations are seldom identical. For instance, it is imag-
ined that the concern to offer the country a higher position in the global
hierarchy, which is defined in terms of wealth, power, and autonomy of
movement, will constitute a major concern among the ruling classes and
authorities even if this objective might win the sympathy of the population as a whole. Aspiration for respect—in the full sense of the term,
respect for equal treatment—can mobilize women, or a cultural, linguistic, or religious group subjected to discrimination. The movements inspired by such aspirations may be transclassicist. On the other hand, the
aspiration for greater social justice, defined at will (in conformity with
the wishes of the movements motivated by such aspiration)—for improved material well-being, a more pertinent and effective legislation or
a system of social relations and a radically different system of production—will almost inevitably find expression in class struggles. This can
take the form of a claim by the peasantry or by one of its groups for
agrarian reform, property redistribution, a legislation favorable to ten-
ant farmers, more favorable prices, and so on. It may be expressed in the
context of union rights, labor legislation, or even a demand for state
policy that would enhance its effective intervention in favor of workers
as far as nationalization, joint management, or, more radically, labor
power. But it can also appear in the form of demands by groups of
professionals or entrepreneurs claiming tax relief. It can be channeled
through claims concerning all citizens, as testified by the movements
pressing for the right to education, health, or housing and, *mutatis mutan-
dis*, the right to suitable environmental management. The democratic
aspiration can be limited and definite, particularly when it inspires a
movement against an undemocratic authority. At the same time, it may
be integrative and can therefore be conceived as the lever helping to
promote all the social demands.

A current distribution chart of these movements would certainly
show vast inequalities in their presence in the field. But we know that
this chart is not static because in the event of a problem, there is almost
always a potential movement to find an appropriate solution. However,
it would smack of naive optimism to imagine that the result of the chart
of forces operating in these very diverse fields will promote the coherence of a joint movement mobilizing societies to press for enhanced
justice and democracy. Chaos stems as much from the nature as from the

order. Similarly, one would be naive to overlook the ruling authorities' reaction to such movements. The geographical distribution of these powers and the strategies they develop to meet challenges facing them at both local and international levels respond to considerations other than those underlying the aspirations in question. In other words, the possibility of drift on the part of the social movements, their exploitation and manipulation also constitute some of the realities that could eventually render them powerless or compel them to adopt a different perspective.

There is a global political strategy for world management. Its objective is to ensure the maximum disintegration of potential antisystemic forces by contributing to the decline of the state system and creating as many Slovenians, Chechens, Kosovars, and Kuwaitis as possible! The use of demands for recognition and even their manipulation are welcome. The question of community—ethnic, religious, or other forms of identity—therefore constitutes one of the major concerns of our era.

The basic principle of democracy, which implies real respect for national, ethnic, religious, cultural, and ideological diversity, cannot be circumvented. <u>Diversity cannot be managed in any fashion other than the sincere practice of democracy. Otherwise, it becomes an instrument that opponents can use for their own purposes.</u>

In Bandung, the national liberation movements often succeeded in uniting the various ethnic groups and religious communities against the imperialist enemy. Whereas the ruling classes in the first generation of African states were often transethnic, few power systems were able to manage such diversity democratically and consolidate the achievements, if there were any. In this regard, their meager propensity for democracy produced results as deplorable as their management of other problems facing their societies. With the ensuing crisis, the ruling classes in desperate straits, and helpless, often played a decisive role in resorting to community withdrawals as a means of prolonging their control of the masses. However, even in many authentic bourgeois democracies, community diversity is often far from being managed correctly.

The success of culturalism measures up to the inadequacies inherent in the democratic management of diversity—culturalism being understood in the assertion that the differences in question might be primordial, should have priority (in relation to the class differences), and are sometimes supposed to be transhistorical; in other words, based on historical invariants (this is often the case of religious culturalisms which easily lead to obscurantism and fanaticism).

An essential criterion will therefore be proposed for enhanced understanding of the jumble of demands for recognition at social and other levels. The aspects considered progressive are the claims intended to fight against social exploitation and that press for increased democracy in all of its dimensions. On the other hand, all the claims presented "without a social program" (because that is said to be unimportant!), purportedly "not opposed to globalization" (because that may also be insignificant!), and presented, *a fortiori*, as falling outside the concept of democracy (accused of being Western) are clearly reactionary and they absolutely serve the interests of the dominant capital. All the same, the latter is aware of the existing situation and supports such claims even when the media take advantage of their barbarous content to denounce peoples who are victims of the system, using or even manipulating such movements.

The humanist alternative to apartheid on a global scale cannot be sustained by nostalgia; nor can it be based on the assertion of diversities inherited from the past. This will not be effective unless it comes within a framework oriented toward the future. This entails going beyond the truncated and polarizing capitalist globalization—constructing a new postcapitalist globalization based on real equality among people, communities, states, and individuals.

Inherited diversities create problems because they exist. But in concentrating on them, one loses sight of other diversities that are otherwise more interesting—those that the future invention necessarily generates in its movement. The concept associated with such diversity proceeds from the idea of emancipatory democracy and the uncompleted modernity that accompanies it. The creative utopias that may crystallize peoples' struggles for equality and justice always find their legitimacy from multiple systems of values. The systems of social analysis—utopias' necessary complement—are inspired by social theories, which are themselves diverse. The strategies proposed with a view to moving effectively in the suitable direction cannot themselves be the monopoly of any organization. These diversities in the future invention are not only inevitable, they are also welcome.

II.

The alternative to global apartheid is therefore a pluricentric world. In this world, economic and political relations among regions and countries that have inherited the destructive effects of polarization produced by the expansion of capitalism are systematically organized through a complex set of negotiations, policies, and regulations aimed at:

1. Renegotiating market shares and the rules of access to them. This project, of course, challenges the rules of the WTO, which, behind the talk of fair competition, is exclusively concerned with defending the privileges of the oligopolies active on a world scale.

2. Renegotiating the systems of capital markets, with a view to putting an end to the domination of financial speculation and orienting investment toward productive activities in the North and South.
3. Renegotiating monetary systems, with a view to putting in place regional arrangements and systems that would ensure the relative stability of exchange rates, supplemented by the organization of their interdependence. This project challenges the IMF, the dollar standard, and the principle of free and fluctuating rates of exchange.
4. Establishing a worldwide system of taxation—for example, by taxing income derived from the exploitation of natural resources and redistributing of these funds for designated purposes around the world according to appropriate criteria.
5. Demilitarizing the planet, beginning with the reduction of weapons of mass destruction in the arsenals of the most powerful countries.

This program for the reconciliation of globalization with local and regional autonomies (what I call a pattern of de-linking appropriate to the new challenges) would include making a serious review of the concept of aid and addressing the problem of democratizing the United Nations system. That system could then begin effective work on disarmament (which would be made possible by the formulas for national and regional security associated with the reorganization of regions) and could prepare the way for the establishment of a globalized tax system (related to the management of the natural resources of the planet). It could also supplement the United Nations with the beginnings of a "world Parliament" capable of reconciling the demands of universalism (rights of individuals, of collectivities, and people; political and social rights, etc.) with the diversity of historical and cultural heritages.

Of course, there is no chance of gradual progress toward the realization of this "project" as a whole without, at the level of nation-states, social forces and projects that can carry forward the necessary reforms (which are impossible within the limits imposed by liberalism and polarizing globalization). Whether it is a question of reform in a particular sector or of larger visions of democratization of societies and their political and economic management, these preliminary stages are indispensable. Without them, the vision of world reorganization that could bring it out of crisis and make development "take off" again will inevitably remain completely utopian.

This last consideration obliges us to make room for proposals for immediate action, around which real political and social forces can be mobilized—first at local levels, even if they have a broader aim—to globalize the struggle. I am thinking here of the many types of regulation that could be implemented rapidly in every domain: economic (e.g., taxation of financial transfers, abolition of the "fiscal paradises" that are tax shelters for foreign capital, cancellation of debt), ecological (protection of species, prohibition of harmful products and methods, initiation of a globalized system of taxes on the consumption of certain nonrenewable resources), social (labor legislation, investment codes, participation of peoples' representatives in international bodies), political (democracy and individual rights), and cultural (rejection of the commodification of cultural goods).

The program for the medium term that I have suggested is not merely designed to modify the forms of market regulation so as to protect the weak (classes and nations). Its political components are no less important. The key ideas in that component are disarmament and the elaboration of a new system of international law governing individuals, people, and states. The challenges and the alternatives are therefore either neoliberal globalization, which in fact naturally leads to global apartheid, or polycentric negotiated globalization along the lines briefly described above.

Reference

Castells, Manuel. 1996. *The Rise of the Network Society*. Malden, MA: Blackwell Publishers.

*

2

Through the Obstacle(s) and on to Global Socialism

Christopher Chase-Dunn

The Fernand Braudel Center at Binghamton University has led the way to a new transdisciplinary historical perspective on human social change and has educated a whole generation of scholars to go forth and multiply the insights that this perspective generates about the past and the future of our species. One branch of this fruitful tree, comparative world-systems theory, attempts to explain the continuities and new departures of social change by formally comparing the modern world-system with earlier, smaller, regional intergroup networks (Chase-Dunn and Hall 1997). This approach facilitates even greater temporal depth on both the past and the future. The idea of social evolution, washed clean of its unscientific corollaries (teleology, the inevitable, and progress), provides a useful handle for clearing away the "fog of globalization" and for delineating future human possibilities more clearly.[1]

One way to celebrate the twenty-fifth anniversary of the Fernand Braudel Center is to chart the possible courses ahead that could establish a collectively rational and democratic global commonwealth. Comparative world-systems theory (CWST) retools the conceptual apparatus

G-20 protest: Two women gag themselves with Canadian currency Wednesday during a demonstration outside a Group of 20 meeting in Montreal. Protesters are accusing the financial officials of
protecting only the interests of the world's richest nations.

AP photo

Figure 2.1.

that was developed by Fernand Braudel Center scholars. These concepts
were originally invented for the purpose of analyzing and telling the
story of the modern Eurocentric system (core/periphery hierarchy, interstate system, capitalism as including peripheral capitalism, etc). In CWST
the concepts are opened up and the links among them are loosened.
World-systems are defined as nested interaction networks of regularized
exchange. The idea of a core/periphery hierarchy is defined generally as
any kind of power hierarchy among polities or regions, and is turned
into a question rather than an assumption: "Do all world-systems have
core/periphery hierarchies?" The interstate system is defined more broadly as inter*polity* systems so that tribes and chiefdoms may be studied. The
analysis of hegemonic ascent and decline is expanded to include the rise
and fall of large chiefdoms and corewide empires.

This comparative perspective, which combines archaeology and ethnography with world history, allows us to see important patterns that
are visible once one systematically juxtaposes smaller, older systems with
larger, more recent ones. First, it becomes apparent that core/periphery

hierarchies themselves evolve as techniques of power are invented that allow for the exploitation and domination of distant people. States, markets, empires, religions, military infrastructure, and organizations— all are important institutions that allow greater integration and more efficient long-distance exploitation and domination. Small-scale world-systems have very little in the way of core/periphery hierarchy (Chase-Dunn and Mann 1998).

The other important insight that becomes clearer once we use the world-system to analyze social evolution is the phenomenon of "semi-peripheral development." This means that semiperipheral groups are unusually prolific innovators of techniques that both facilitate upward mobility and transform the basic logic of social development. This is not to say that all semiperipheral groups produce such transformational actions, but rather that the semiperipheral location is more fertile ground for the production of innovations than is either the core or the periphery. This is because semiperipheral societies have access to both core and peripheral cultural elements and techniques, and they have less already invested in existing organizational forms than core societies do. Thus, they are freer to recombine elements into new configurations and to invest in new techniques, and they are usually more highly motivated to take risks than are older core societies.

Knowledge of core/periphery hierarchies and semiperipheral locations is necessary for explaining how small-scale interchiefdom systems evolved into the capitalist global political economy of today. The process of the rise and fall of powerful chiefdoms (called "cycling" by anthropologists [Anderson 1994]) was occasionally punctuated by the emergence of a polity from the semiperipheral zone that conquered and united the old core region into a larger chiefly polity or an early state. This phenomenon is termed the "semiperipheral marcher chiefdom" (Chase-Dunn and Hall 1997, 83–84; Kirch 1984, 199–202).

Much better known is the analogous phenomenon of "semiperipheral marcher states," in which a relatively new state from out on the edge of a core region conquered an interstate system to form a new corewide empire (Mann 1986; Collins 1981). Almost every large conquest state you can think of is an instance of this. A less frequently perceived phenomenon that is a quite different type of semiperipheral development is the "semiperipheral capitalist city-state." Dilmun, early Assur, the Phoenician cities, the Italian city-states, Melakka, and the Hanseatic cities of the Baltic were examples of this semiperipheral development. These small states in the interstices of the tributary empires were agents of commodification long before capitalism became predominant in the emergent core region of Europe, itself still semiperipheral in the larger Afro-Eurasian world-system.

Semiperipheral Development

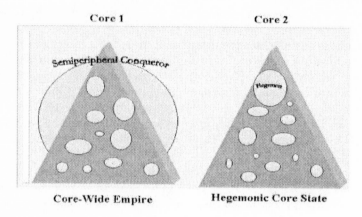

Figure 2.2. Core-Wide Empire versus Hegemonic Core State

The semiperipheral development idea is also an important tool for understanding the real possibilities for global social change today, because semiperipheral countries are the main weak link in the global capitalist system—the zone where the most powerful antisystemic movements have emerged in the past and where vital and transformative developments are likely to occur in the future.

The hegemonic sequence (the rise and fall of hegemonic core states) is the modern version of an ancient oscillation between more and less centralized interstate systems. All hierarchical systems experience a cycle of rise and fall, from "cycling" in interchiefdom systems to the rise and fall of empires, to the modern sequence of hegemonic rise and fall. In state-based (tributary) world-systems, this oscillation typically takes the form of semiperipheral marcher states conquering older core states to form a universal empire (see figure 2.2).

One important consequence of the coming to predominance of capitalist accumulation has been the conversion of the rise and fall process from semiperipheral marcher conquest to the rise and fall of capitalist hegemons that do not take over other core states. The hegemons rise to economic and political/military preeminence, but they do not construct a corewide world state. Rather, the core of the modern system oscillates between unipolar hegemony and hegemonic rivalry (see figure 2.3).

Hegemonic Sequence

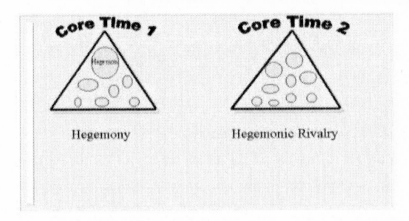

Figure 2.3. The Modern Hegemonic Sequence

One implication of the CWST is that all hierarchical and complex world-systems exhibit a "power cycle" in which political/military power becomes more centralized followed by a phase of decentralization. This is likely to be true of the future of the world-system as well, though the form of the power cycle may change. Our species needs to invent political and cultural institutions that allow adjustments in the global political and economic structures to take place without resorting to warfare. This is analogous to the problem of succession within single states, and the solution is obvious—a global government that represents the interests of the majority of the people of Earth and allows for political restructuring to occur by democratic processes.

Capitalist accumulation usually favors a multicentric interstate system because this provides greater opportunities for the maneuverability of capital than would exist in a world state. Big capitals can play states off against one another and can escape movements that try to regulate investment or redistribute profits by abandoning the states in which such movements attain political power.

The three hegemonies of the modern world-system have been the Dutch hegemony of the seventeenth century, the British hegemony of the nineteenth century, and the U.S. hegemony of the twentieth century. World-systems analysts see a strong analogy between the decline of British

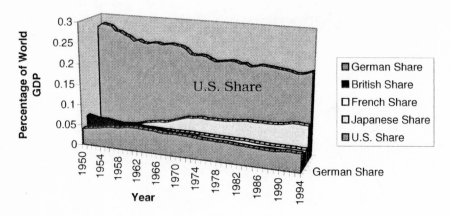

Figure 2.4. Declining U.S. Economic Hegemony

hegemony after 1870 and the trajectory of the United States after the 1970s. Figure 2.4 shows the declining U.S. share of world GDP since 1950.

The modern world-system has experienced waves of economic and political integration (structural globalization) (Chase-Dunn, Kawano, and Brewer 2000). These waves of global integration are the contemporary incarnations of the pulsations of widening and deepening of interaction networks that have been important characteristics of all world-systems for millennia. But since the nineteenth century these have occurred in a single global system. Figure 2.5 shows the waves of global trade integration in the nineteenth and twentieth centuries.

The theorists of global capitalism contend that the most recent wave of integration has created a single integrated global bourgeoisie that has overthrown the dynamics of the hegemonic sequence (hegemonic rise and fall and interstate rivalry).[2] While most world-systems theorists believe that the U.S. hegemony continues the decline that began in the 1970s, many other observers interpret the demise of the Soviet Union and the relatively greater U.S. economic growth in the 1990s as ushering in a renewal of U.S. hegemony. In figure 2.5, the U.S. share of global GDP can be seen to have turned up in the early 1990s.[3] The theorists of global capitalism contend that the U.S. state (and other core states) are now instruments of the integrated global-capitalist class rather than of separate and competing groups of national capitalists.

I agree with Wally L. Goldfrank (2000) that both models (global capitalism and the hegemonic sequence) continue to operate simultaneously and to interact with one another in complicated ways. Despite the rather high degree of international integration among economic and political elites, there is likely to be another round of rivalry among core

Average Openness Trade Globalization

(5-year moving average)

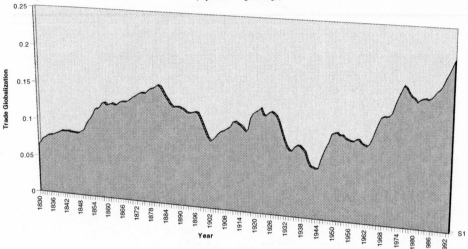

Figure 2.5. International Trade Relative to the Size of the Global Economy, 1830–1994

states. Global elites achieved a high degree of international integration during the late nineteenth-century wave of globalization, but this did not prevent the world wars of the twentieth century.

Admitting to some aspects of the "global capitalism" thesis does not require buying the whole cake. Some claim that information technology has changed everything and that we have entered a new age of global history in which comparisons with what happened before 1960 are completely inappropriate. The most important slice of the cake is global class formation, and this needs to be analyzed for workers and farmers as well as for elites (Goldfrank 1977). Figure 2.6 illustrates the idea that a portion of all objective classes in the world class structure are transnationally integrated. Research is currently under way to compare the nineteenth- and twentieth-century global elites regarding their degree of international integration as well as changes in the patterns of alliances and connections among the wealthiest and most powerful people on Earth (Chase-Dunn et al. 2001).

The hegemonic sequence is not usefully understood as a cycle that takes the same form each time around. Rather, as Giovanni Arrighi (1994) has so convincingly shown, each "systemic cycle of accumulation" involves a reorganization of the relationships among big capitals and states. And the evolutionary aspects of hegemony not only adapt to changes in scale, geography, and technology, but they also must solve problems

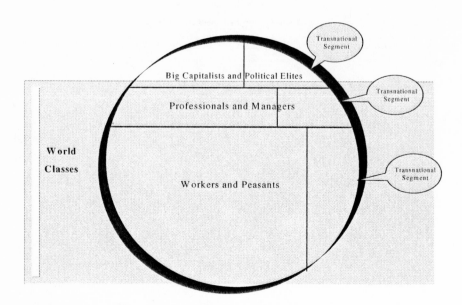

Figure 2.6. Transnational Segments of World Classes

created by resistance from below (Arrighi and Silver 1999; Boswell and Chase-Dunn 2000). Workers and farmers in the world-system are not inert objects of exploitation and domination. Rather, they develop new organizational and institutional instruments of protection and resistance. So the interaction between the powerful and less powerful is a spiral of domination and resistance that is one of the most important driving forces of the developmental history of modern capitalism.

The discourse produced by world-systems scholars about "the family of antisystemic movements" has been an important contribution to our understanding of how different social movements act vis-à-vis one another on the terrain of the whole system (Arrighi, Hopkins, and Wallerstein 1989). It is unfortunate that public discourse about globalization has characterized recent protest movements in terms of "antiglobalization." This has occurred because, in the popular mind, globalization has been associated primarily with what Phil McMichael (2000) has termed the "globalization project"—the neoliberal policies of the "Washington consensus" and the hegemony of corporate capitalism. This is the political ideology of Reaganism-Thatcherism—market magic, deregulation, privatization, and allegedly no alternative to submitting to the "realities" of global capitalist competition.[4]

The term "antiglobalization" is a disaster because it conflates two different meanings of "globalization" and it implies that the only sensible form of resistance to globalization involves the construction of local institutions to defend against the forces of global capitalism. Structural globalization means economic, political, and cultural (international and transnational) integration. This should be analytically separated from the political ideology of the "globalization project" (Chase-Dunn 1999).

The "globalization project" is what the demonstrators are protesting, but the term "antiglobalization" also implies that they are against international integration and global institutions. Our usage of the term "antisystemic movements" needs to be carefully clarified so that it does not contribute to this confusion.

Local protectionism will undoubtedly be an important component of the emerging resistance to corporate globalization and neoliberal policies. But one lesson we can derive from earlier efforts to confront and transform capitalism is that local resistance cannot, by itself, overcome the strong forces of modern capitalism. What is needed is globalization from below. Mainly, global politics has been the politics of the powerful because they have had the resources to establish long-distance connections and to structure global institutions. But waves of elite transnational integration have been accompanied by upsurges of transnational linkages, strategies, and institutions formed by workers, farmers, and popular challenges to the logic of capitalist accumulation. Globalization from below means the transnationalization of antisystemic movements and the active participation of popular movements in global politics and global citizenship.

An analysis of earlier waves of the spiral of domination and resistance demonstrates that "socialism in one country" and other strategies of local protection have not been capable of overcoming the negative aspects of capitalist development in the past, and they are even less likely to succeed in the more densely integrated global system of the future. Strategies that mobilize people to organize themselves locally must be complemented and coordinated with transnational strategies to democratize or replace existing global institutions and to create new organizational structures that facilitate collective rationality for all the people of the world.

The rest of this chapter will concentrate mainly on matters of strategy and tactics for the antisystemic movements. I am not suggesting that all the problems of ultimate goals have been resolved. The model of world socialism based on global institutions and market socialism delineated in *The Spiral of Capitalism and Socialism: Toward Global Democracy* (Boswell and Chase-Dunn 2000) is only the beginning of a conversation about political and organizational goals (see also Wallerstein 1998). But for now, I want to discuss some tactical issues that are already pressing themselves upon the transnational movements that are challenging global capitalism.

The major transnational antisystemic movements are the labor movement, the women's movement, the environmental movement, and the indigenous movement. Of these, the environmental movement and the women's movement have had the most recent success in forming transnational linkages and confronting the difficult issues posed by regional, national, and core/periphery differences. But the labor and indigenous movements have made recent efforts to catch up. Transborder organizing efforts and support for demonstrations against corporate globalization show that the AFL-CIO is interested in new directions. One important task for world-system scholars is to study these movements and to help devise initiatives that can produce tactical and strategic transnational alliances.

Let us imagine that the family of antisystemic movements has managed to organize a working alliance (perhaps with the help of the World Party, an organization dedicated to building a global socialist commonwealth) (Wagar 1992; Boswell and Chase-Dunn 2000). This assumption is not meant to trivialize the practical and theoretical difficulties that will be involved in the emergence of such an agent of human sanity, but I wish to discuss some additional problems that will probably need to be confronted down the road.

Besides attending to its own contradictions, what difficulties would such an alliance be likely to face in the coming decades? I see three major obstacles in the path:

1. A return, within the next two decades, to a condition of hegemonic rivalry among core states and competing groups of capitalists that will again pose the danger of warfare among "the great powers," except with a potential for mass destruction that could result in either a major global die-off or even the end of complex life on Earth.
2. Possible environmental catastrophes caused by the continuing process of capitalist industrialization, energy utilization, and new technologies (especially biotechnology).
3. Increasing global inequalities and consequent multiple challenges to the hegemony of global capital and U.S. power.

All of these problems are predictable from what we know of the cyclical regularities and secular trends of capitalist development in the world-system (Chase-Dunn and Podobnik 1995). Each of them poses great dangers, and also some opportunities, for the family of antisystemic movements. We must try to prevent or ameliorate the worst aspects of each of these likely disasters. We also need to consider the best routes to take if truly disastrous events occur.

This complicates an already thorny program. The calculus of tradeoffs between reforming existing institutions versus radically restructuring or replacing them will need to include considerations about reducing the likelihood of, or the worst consequences of, the obstacles. The issue of organizational goals needs to be informed by not only a consensual political philosophy but also a structural understanding of the cyclical processes and secular trends of the world-system as they are likely to emerge in the next decades. Long-term goals need to be clarified and their short- and mid-term pursuit needs to take into account the dynamics of the capitalist world-system.

Avoiding War among Core States

Here is an example of this sort of problem. W. Warren Wagar's fictional scenario, *A Short History of the Future* (1992), tells the story of the next fifty years under the title "Earth, Incorporated." It is a story of continued expanding domination by huge capitalist corporations, continued technological development, ecological degradation, and the emergence of a capitalist proto-world-state, but not yet the dismantling of the military structure of the interstate system. The U.S. hegemony continues to decline. Immigration and the emergence of greater class and color consciousness in the United States eventually result in the election of a Chicano woman as president. Heartland Republicans start a civil war, but the U.S. Army, now staffed by a large majority of nonwhite personnel, quickly puts down the opposition. The United States begins to support semiperipheral states that are resisting the hegemony of the global corporations, so the world government (under the control of the "megacorps") decides upon a nuclear first strike to take out the leftist U.S. regime. Thus begins a three-year nuclear war that destroys most of the cities of the Northern Hemisphere. In the aftermath, the World Party is able to put together a global socialist commonwealth.

If something like Wagar's scenario is at all probable, the antisystemic movements need to work to prevent such a catastrophe. It is ethically unacceptable to simply wait for global capitalism to destroy itself and then pick up the pieces. Wagar gets the timing of the onset of world war wrong because he believes that world wars occur during economic downturns. But Joshua S. Goldstein's (1988) research on Kondratieff waves and war cycles shows that wars among core states usually occur at the end of the K-wave upswing, when states have lots of resources with which to wage war. This means that the next window of vulnerability to world war will occur in two or three decades.

If it is true that another period of hegemonic rivalry will include a substantial risk of renewed warfare among core powers, such an extremely risky situation could be avoided by a revitalization of U.S.

leadership (hegemony) because the single superpower configuration is militarily stable. Without a bipolar or multipolar military configuration, there will be no war among core powers. Continuing U.S. economic decline would arguably eventuate in the inability of the United States to serve as a world policeman, and would likely result in the rearming of possible hegemonic contenders (Japan and Germany). If this can be prevented for another twenty or thirty years, the system will have gotten through the obstacle of hegemonic rivalry until the next interregnum of the power cycle.

A truly democratic global peacekeeping government should be the eventual goal of the family of antisystemic movements. But the problem is that the emergence of an effective global state within the relevant time frame (the next two or three decades) is highly unlikely. It would require that the existing core states devolve a substantial portion of their sovereignty to the global state, and there would be considerable resistance to this. A comparable situation in the European Union, while it is far more advanced than at the global level, shows how slowly consolidations of this kind move forward.

A more feasible alternative (within the relevant time frame) would involve the perpetuation or renewal of U.S. economic hegemony that is sufficient to prevent the reemergence of potential core military challengers. Some scenarios that focus on new lead industries (information technology and biotechnology) foresee the strengthening of the economic basis of U.S. hegemony (e.g., Rennstich 2003). But mobilizing the antisystemic movements to support a renewal of U.S. hegemony may be as unlikely as the rapid emergence of a global democratic state.

A good compromise would be a condominium of global governance that includes the United States as well as possible contenders and challengers (China, Germany, Japan, and Russia). In this scenario, the United Nations would be reformed so that it more realistically represented the core states as well as the people of the world. Right now, Germany and Japan are not formal members of the UN Security Council. The Security Council needs to be expanded to include Germany and Japan, and to better represent the noncore countries. This, and the beefing up of the UN peacekeeping capability, could be accomplished without threatening the sovereignty of the core states. This would be a combination of proto–global democracy and partial renewal of U.S. hegemony that would get us through the next obstacle of hegemonic rivalry unscathed. It would move in the direction of a more democratic global government as well. This is what I meant about needing to include the calculus of emergent systemic crises in the organizational strategies of the antisystemic movements and the necessity of compromises between mid-term and long-term goals.

Environmental Crises

Ecological disaster could arrive in smaller or larger, more catastrophic, dimensions. Peter Taylor (1996) portrays the emerging "global impasse," the ecological impossibility of the noncore countries developing the same level of energy and resource utilization as already exists in the United States. If the Chinese eat as many eggs and drive as many cars per capita as citizens of the United States do, the global biosphere will fry. Clean water is going to become scarce within the next twenty-five years. Global warming may produce destructive consequences.

The revolution in biotechnology involves such radical recombinations that grave mistakes are almost certain to occur as these new technologies are applied to agriculture, pest control, and biosphere engineering. The learning curve will be steep and fraught with upsets as we develop saner and safer ways to reinvent nature and ourselves. As with warfare, the antisystemic movements must try to prevent catastrophes at the same time that we invent institutions that can make our collective life sustainable. Preparation for these developments means coordinating with extant world parties such as Greenpeace to educate people about the causes of capitalist ecological degradation and feasible movement toward sustainable and democratic development.

Growing Inequalities

Growing inequalities (both within and among countries) were an important source of globalization backlash in the late nineteenth century (O'Rourke and Williamson 1999) and are already shaping up to be an important driving force in the coming world revolution. Mike Davis's (2001) analysis of late Victorian drought-famine disasters in Brazil, India, and China shows how these were partly caused by newly expanded market forces impinging upon regions that were subject to international political/military coercion. He also documents how starving peasants created millenarian movements that promised to end the domination of the foreign devils or restore the rule of the good king. Islamic fundamentalism is a contemporary functional equivalent.

Huge and visible injustices provoke people to resist, and in the absence of true histories and theories, they use whatever ideological apparatus is at hand. The world-systems perspective has the potential to serve as the basis for a scientific understanding of social change that can be used by the antisystemic movements to organize an effective response to corporate globalization that constructs new institutions for democratizing the global political economy. But this will require popular communication of the main lessons of the world-systems perspective.

The phenomenon of semiperipheral development suggests that social organizational innovations that can transform the predominant logic of accumulation will continue to emerge from the semiperiphery. The Russian and Chinese revolutions of the twentieth century are understood as efforts to restructure capitalist institutions and developmental logic that succeeded mainly in spurring the U.S. hegemony and the post–World War II expansion of capitalism. The Soviet and Chinese efforts were compromised from the start by their inability to rely on participatory democracy. In order to survive in a world still strongly dominated by capitalist states, they were forced to construct authoritarian socialism, a contradiction in terms.

We can expect that democratic socialism will come to state power in the semiperiphery by electoral means, as already happened in Allende's Chile. Brazil, Mexico, and Korea are strong candidates, and India, Indonesia, and China are possibilities. Democratic socialism in the semiperiphery seems to be a good strategy for fending off many of the worst aspects of corporate globalization. The transnational antisystemic movements will want to support, and be supported by, these new socialist democracies.

The ability of capitalist core states to destabilize democratic socialist regimes in the semiperiphery is great, and this is why support movements within the core are so important. Information technology can certainly be a great aid to transborder organizing. Issues such as sweatshop exploitation can help to make students aware of core/periphery inequalities and to link them with activists far away. The emergence of democratically elected challengers to global corporate capitalism will strain the ideologues of "polyarchy" and facilitate debate about narrow definitions of democracy.[5] The emergence of a World Party to educate activists about the world historical dimensions of capitalism and the lessons of earlier world revolutions will add the leaven that may move the coming backlash against corporate globalization in a progressive direction. Awareness of the obstacles will help political campaigns and organizing efforts make tactical and strategic decisions and will provide a structurally informed basis for the building of a democratic and collectively rational global commonwealth.

Notes

1. Stephen K. Sanderson admirably separates the scientific core of evolutionary explanations from the confusing baggage that has accompanied much earlier work on long-term social change (1990). He also clarifies the concept of progress. If we are

explicit about the desiderata in our notion of progress and do not engage in wishful thinking, then we may ask empirically whether or not a particular social change constitutes progress.

2. See, for example, Sassen 1991; Robinson 1996; and Robinson and Harris 2000.

3. While some interpret the U.S. upturn in the 1990s as the beginning of another wave of U.S. "leadership" in the global economy, based on comparative advantages in information technology and biotechnology, Giovanni Arrighi sees the 1990s as another wave of financialization comparable to the *belle époque* or "Edwardian Indian summer" that occurred in the last decades of the nineteenth century. Much of the economic expansion in the U.S. economy was due to huge inflows of investment capital from Europe and East Asia during the 1990s (1994).

4. Giovanni Arrighi has recently argued that the globalization project that emerged in the 1970s was, importantly, a reaction to the world revolution of 1968 that appropriated the antistate ideology and many of the tactics of the New Left (2003).

5. Bill Robinson examines the struggle over the concept of democracy (1996). He defines polyarchy as a system in which a small group actually rules, and mass participation in decision making is confined to leadership choice in elections carefully managed by competing elites. Usually, polyarchy prevents the emergence of more egalitarian popular democracy that would threaten the rule of those who hold power and property. The notion of popular democracy stresses human equality, participatory forms of decision making, and a holistic integration of political, social, and economic realms that are artificially kept separate in the polyarchic definition of democracy.

References

Anderson, David G. 1994. *The Savannah River Chiefdoms.* Tuscaloosa: University of Alabama Press.

Arrighi, Giovanni. 1994. *The Long Twentieth Century.* London: Verso.

———. 2003. "Hegemonia e movimentos anti-sistemicos." Pp. 107–22 in *Os Impasses da Globalizacao,* ed. T. Dos Santos. Rio de Janeiro: PUC-Rio.

Arrighi, Giovanni, Terence K. Hopkins, and Immanuel Wallerstein. 1989. *Antisystemic Movements.* London: Verso.

Arrighi, Giovanni, and Beverly J. Silver. 1999. *Chaos and Governance in the Modern World-System: Comparing Hegemonic Transitions.* Minneapolis: University of Minnesota Press.

Boswell, Terry, and Christopher Chase-Dunn. 2000. *The Spiral of Capitalism and Socialism: Toward Global Democracy.* Boulder, CO: Lynne Rienner.

Chase-Dunn, Christopher. 1999. "Globalization: A World-Systems Perspective." *Journal of World-Systems Research* V, no. 2. Available at: http://jwsr.ucr.edu.

Chase-Dunn, Christopher, and Thomas D. Hall. 1997. *Rise and Demise: Comparing World-Systems.* Boulder, CO: Westview.

Chase-Dunn, Christopher, John Gulick, Andrew Jorgenson, Shoon Lio, and Thomas Reifer. 2001. "Global Elite Integration: In the Nineteenth and Twentieth Centuries: Families, Firms, Organizations and Cities." Unpublished research proposal submitted to the National Science Foundation.

Chase-Dunn, Christopher, Yukio Kawano, and Benjamin Brewer. 2000. "Trade Globalization since 1795: Waves of Integration in the World-System." *American Sociological Review* LXV, no. 1 (February): 77–95.

Chase-Dunn, Christopher, and Kelly M. Mann. 1998. *The Winto and Their Neighbors: A Small World-System in Northern California.* Tucson: University of Arizona Press. Available at: www.irowc.ucr.edu/cd/books/cdbooks.htm#wintu.

Chase-Dunn, Christopher, and Bruce Podobnik. 1995. "The Next World War: World-System Cycles and Trends." *Journal of World-Systems Research* I, no. 6. Available at: http://jwsr.ucr.edu.

Collins, Randall. 1981. "Long Term Social Change and the Territorial Power of States." Pp. 71–106 in *Sociology Since Midcentury,* ed. R. Collins. New York: Academic Press.

Davis, Mike. 2001. *Late Victorian Holocausts.* London: Verso.

Goldfrank, Walter L. 1977. "Who Rules the World: Class Formation at the International Level." *Quarterly Journal of Ideology* I, no. 2: 32–37.

———. 2000. "Introduction: Repetition, Variation, and Transmutation as Scenarios for the Twenty-First Century." Pp. 1–12 in *Questioning Geopolitics,* eds. G. Derlugian and S. Greer. Westport, CT: Praeger.

Goldstein, Joshua S. 1988. *Long Cycles: War and Prosperity in the Modern Age.* New Haven, CT: Yale University Press.

Kirch, Patrick. 1984. *The Evolution of Polynesian Chiefdoms.* Cambridge: Cambridge University Press.

McMichael, Philip. 2000. *Development and Social Change,* 2nd ed. Thousand Oaks, CA: Pine Forge.

Mann, Michael. 1986. *The Sources of Social Power,* Vol. 1. Cambridge: Cambridge University Press.

O'Rourke, Kevin H., and Jeffrey G. Williamson. 1999. *Globalization and History: The Evolution of a 19th Century Atlantic Economy.* Cambridge, MA: MIT Press.

Rennstich, Joachim. 2003. "The Future of Great Power Rivalries." Pp. 143–61 in *Emerging Issues in the 21st Century World-System, II: New Theoretical Directions for the 21st Century World,* ed. W. Dunaway. Westport, CT: Praeger.

Robinson, William I. 1996. *Promoting Polyarchy.* Cambridge, UK: Cambridge University Press.

Robinson, William I., and Jerry Harris. 2000. "Toward a Global Ruling Class? Globalization and the Transnational Capitalist Class." *Science & Society* LXIV, no. 1 (Spring): 11–54

Sanderson, Stephen K. 1990. *Social Evolutionism: A Critical History.* Cambridge, MA: Blackwell.

Sassen, Saskia. 1991. *Global Cities.* Princeton, NJ: Princeton University Press.

Taylor, Peter J. 1996. *The Way the Modern World Works: World Hegemony to World Impasse.* New York: Wiley

Wagar, W. Warren. 1992. *A Short History of the Future.* Chicago: University of Chicago Press.

———. 1996. "Toward a Praxis of World Integration." *Journal of World-Systems Research* II, no. 2. Available at http://jwsr.ucr.edu.

Wallerstein, Immanuel. 1998. *Utopistics.* New York: New Press.

3

Europe: The Asymptote of Political Integration

Bart Tromp

I

Since the emergence of what Immanuel Wallerstein has baptized as "the modern world-system" in the fifteenth century, its core has been the scene of incessant conflicts and wars between the states and protostates of Europe for almost five centuries.[1] Or, to put it in another way: War on this continent has been one of the central factors in the dissolution of Europe as a Christian empire and its corollary, the formation of states and the emergence of an interstate system.

The contrast with the half century behind us could not be more striking: In those years, former antagonists not only lived peacefully together but they became participants in a process without precedent, the integration of European states into a novel political formation, the European Union, as it has been officially known since the Maastricht Treaty (1992).

This political formation is sui generis. It is neither a federation nor a confederation of states. Nevertheless, it has distinct supranational dimensions in which the sovereignty of member states (their formal power) as well as their autonomy (their factual power) has been severely curtailed. Postwar development in western Europe has resulted in an entity that is more than a mere association of individual states but less than a supranational federation. Like Dunsinane's forest, it is always on the move, in terms of the number of member states as well as in the fields that are being covered by an ever-expanding set of European rules, agreements, and commitments. It is now one of the three great economic blocs in the world-economy and the only one that has a formal structure.

It is sometimes expected that this entity will, in due time, also become one of the major military-political players in the world. But in this respect, not much attendance is given to the peculiarities of European integration. Too easily, it is still assumed that economic power will be more or less automatically transformed into political might, or even that "Europe" can be seen as Germany writ large (Borrego 1999, 190).

In this chapter, I argue first that the peculiarities of the development of European cooperation show a possible fatal shortcoming with regard to the potential emergence of Europe as a major political actor; secondly, that this process will be much more precarious in the coming years than is generally expected. This will be not only a result of these internal shortcomings but also a consequence of several secular processes identified in world-systemic analyses. The title of this chapter summarizes my central argument.

II

After World War II, two conceptions of European cooperation became evident. The first, designed by the European Union of Federalists (EUF), formed in 1946 by members of wartime resistance movements, sought the constitution of Europe as a political federation. This conception goes back to the manifest the Italian journalist and antifascist Altiero Spinelli (1907–1986) wrote during his internment during World War II on the island of Ventotene in the Gulf of Gaeta (Bainbridge 2001, 457). The attempts of the EUF resulted in the foundation of the Council of Europe in 1949. This became an important European institution, especially with regard to democracy, human rights, and the rule of law in Europe. It is, however, an intergovernmental organization—not even a protofederal one. So the federal road to European unification had already resulted in failure before the end of the 1940s.

The second conception, on the other hand, has turned out to be greatly successful. Postwar European integration started with the Treaty

of Paris (April 1952), in which France, West Germany, Italy, the Netherlands, Belgium, and Luxembourg agreed to pool coal and steel production under a high authority and, for this purpose, to establish a European
Coal and Steel Community (ECSC), which came into operation in July
1952. The premise behind the ECSC was not so much economic, but
political. It was believed that by placing the production of coal and steel
under a common, supranational body, war between the old antagonists
Germany and France would become not only unthinkable but also ma-
terially impossible. The goal of the ECSC, however, was not only negative—avoidance of war in Europe—but also positive: The ECSC was to
be the first concrete foundation of a European federation, according to
the Schuman Declaration, in which the French minister of foreign affairs,
Maurice Schuman, presented the proposal for the ECSC on May 9, 1950
(Henig 1997, 22).

Jean Monnet, who drafted the Schuman Plan, wrote that the method,
the instruments, and the goal of the plan could be found in this passage:

> Par la mise en commun de productions de base et l'institution d'une
> Haute Autorité nouvelle, dont les décisions lieront la France,
> l'Allemagne et les pays qui y adhéreront, cette proposition réalisera les
> premières assises concrètes d'une fédération européenne indispensable
> à la préservation de la paix. (1976, 353)

Thus, at the outset, "Europeanization" in this second concept was
conceived as a road toward a political federation, but planned as a series
of supranational institutions, of which the ECSC was to be first, each
operating in a specific sector. Interdependence between those sectors
would stimulate their functional cooperation, as the successful integration reached in one sector would generate demand for integration of the
next one. Such "spillover" effects form the essence of the neofunctional
theory on European integration (Haas 1958).

The "functional" notion of integration was not seen as infringing on
the sovereignty of the member states. Indeed, its undeclared promise
was that the whole process was of an apolitical, technical nature, although eventually—which was unspecified—the logic of this process
should result in some kind of supranational Europe, the functional equivalent of a political federation. According to the neofunctionalists, a supranational agency like the European Economic Community (EEC) would
"slowly extend its authority so as to progressively undermine the independence of the nation-state" (Pinder 1986, 43). Spinelli—then a former
member of the European Commission (1970–1976)—summarized this
perspective skeptically in the late 1970s: "At a certain point quantity
would become quality: the originally functional institution would become

a fully-fledged political power" (1977, 79). It was never clearly explained if, how, and when the necessary transformation of a series of administrative supranational organizations into a political body would take place.

So the approach to full integration started with the foundation of the European Coal and Steel Community in 1951. But during the 1950s, it was gradually abandoned for a different strategy: that of creating a common market with the free movement of goods, persons, services, and capital among the member states. The scheme of integration by sector was discontinued; only in the case of nuclear energy was agreement reached to found a second sectoral supranational body, the European Atomic Energy Community (Euratom, 1958).

Agricultural policy was not organized within the framework of another community, but it was nevertheless treated as a further extension of sectoral integration by giving the provision a special place and a separate chapter in the Treaty on the European Economic Community (EEC) in 1958. This put as its central goals "an ever closer union among the peoples of Europe," the elimination of "the barriers which divide Europe," and "the constant improvement of the living and working conditions" of the people of Europe and set as its central instrument the creation of a common market through the abolition of tariffs and other restrictions of free trade among the member states.

The contrast between ECSC and Euratom and the EEC is rather strong if one considers how they have been organized. While ECSC and Euratom were set up as planning agencies in the French *étatiste* tradition—tellingly, Jean Monnet, the architect of the Schuman Plan, had also been the architect of the postwar Commissariat Général du Plan which he then headed—the primary goal of the EEC was to abolish governmental regulations, such as tariffs, which were the most important barriers to free trade among the member states at the time. This contrast can be seen as that between forms of positive and negative integration—a distinction to which I will return in more detail. However, this change did not mean a shift from a functional to a political conception of European integration.

The functional approach has been successful to a great extent because the six original members agreed, from the beginning, upon a particular understanding of how common agreements should be reached: the "Community approach." This has been characterized as "the principle . . . that the detail of problem solving is subordinate to the attainment of a shared political will" (Henig 1997, 32). The implication of such an agreement to agree was that working out details became an assignment for technocrats, not a question of politics. This mechanism made general agreements in the form of treaties possible, but it also postponed dealing with their disadvantages and unintended consequences indefinitely—or until the moment they became evident as well as politically acute.

The functional road to integration was unproblematic as long as it was acceptable to the two broad, but contradictory, views on European integration of political elites in the member states. The first was the view that integration would, in due but unspecified (and remote future) time, lead to some kind of supranational political entity. The second, on the other hand, saw European integration as nothing more than a mechanism to preserve and strengthen the sovereign nation-state (Milward 2000).

The building of a common market fitted perfectly into both views. Thus, as long as the common market and its completion were the *grand projet* of Europe (since 1958), all other questions on the broader architecture of the EEC (or the European Community, as the EEC was renamed in the Maastricht Treaty, because many noneconomic goals had been inserted in the treaty since 1958) could be happily postponed.

Only when this project had been theoretically finished with the implementation of the Single European Act, that is, the completion of the single market (1992), was it no longer possible to evade the question of how to proceed further and in what direction. The answer was the Treaty on the European Union, or the Maastricht Treaty (1992), which called for the construction of a European Monetary Union (EMU), an intricate compromise to compensate France for accepting the unification of Germany. Germany (as well as the other member states in the DM-zone, for instance, the Netherlands) had to offer its hard currency, the deutsche mark, on the altar of European cooperation, or more precisely, that of Franco-German friendship. However, it insisted on an independent position of the European Central Bank (ECB). The ESCB (European System of Central Banks), consisting of the ECB and the national central banks, defines and implements monetary policy for the Union. Its primary objective is to maintain price stability (i.e., to fight inflation), and it takes no instruction from political authorities. This frustrated France's main ambition: political control over the new European currency.

It has yet to be seen whether the EMU will strengthen the political dimension of the European Union. On one hand, there are those who insist that the centralized monetary policy will have spillover effects toward the convergence of the social and economic policies of the member states. On the other hand, this traditional functionalist view is rejected by neoliberals (for instance, *The Economist*) who deem it perfectly possible that the existing situation, a common market with a common currency, can be a stable terminal station of European integration, in spite of the lack of a historical precedent for a viable monetary union that has not been soundly founded on a political union.

The Maastricht Treaty also set up a Common Foreign and Security Policy as well as cooperation in the fields of Justice and Home Affairs. These two policies, now known as the second and third pillars of the EU, were not organized like the first pillar (the ECSC, European Atomic Energy Community, and European Community are the first pillar) along supranational lines, but as intergovernmental institutions. Together, these three pillars form the European Union. The competencies of Europe have thus been expanded considerably. But at the same time, the framework of decision making has been made much more complicated. Intergovernmental elements have increased relative to supranationalism and the distinction between both is becoming blurred.

Clearly, the Maastricht Treaty could not stand in its original form. Apart from organizational and constitutional questions that had not been consistently handled, or not handled at all, its output in terms of expected moves into the direction of "an ever closer (political) union" (as the first sentence of the Preamble to the Treaty of Rome, 1957, put it) had been disappointing in the eyes of several member states.

The subsequent treaties of Amsterdam (1997) and Nice (2000) were the result of intergovernmental conferences, convened in order to review the earlier treaties. But from Maastricht onward, it appears that the community method is suffering severely from the law of diminishing returns. Ever-smaller steps have been made in the same direction, but without solving the institutional and political problems that have been created by the expansion of the EU in terms of membership and tasks. Meanwhile, the agreements on common foreign and security policies have in no way resulted in a common policy of the EU on major issues such as the break-up of Yugoslavia and the subsequent wars there. Recent agreements on the establishment of a military capacity of approximately 60,000 men have also made little progress. While the third pillar has fared better than the second on major issues, such as immigration from outside the EU, it has not yet been possible to frame a common policy.

Thus, it seems that the latent contradiction between Europe as a supranational political entity and Europe as a series of utility mechanisms to strengthen the national state is becoming more and more manifest. The road to political unification is beginning to resemble an asymptote: It appears to be moving more and more slowly toward the goal of unification, without ever reaching it.

III

The process of Europeanization can also be seen in a completely different framework, to which I dedicate a short aside.

In this framework, the central question is whether the formation of a political European Union can perhaps follow the trajectory that in earlier centuries has led to the formation of amalgamated states in Europe out of smaller political units.

If we look at the dynamics of those processes, this does not seem probable. Typically, state formation took shape as a major political unit that forced smaller adjacent units to fuse together one way or another. Thus London and the South of England in the formation of the United Kingdom, Prussia in Germany, Île de France in France, Holland in the United Provinces, and Savoy-Piedmont (the Kingdom of Sardinia) in Italy.

The only contemporary state that, theoretically, could take the lead in the enforcement of political unity in Europe along such lines is Germany. But for a host of reasons, it is extremely improbable, if not completely out of the question, that Germany will try to do so. And if it tried, it would be unlikely to succeed. The most important factor is that the political strength of Germany relative to that of its greatest competitors, Britain and France, is too slight. Just as after the foundation of the Second Reich in 1871, Germany is again too powerful to be seen as equal to other European states, but not powerful enough to dominate over them.

IV

Half a century of Europeanization along the lines of functional integration and the community method has resulted in a deep fault line. It is based on the difference and the asymmetry between negative and positive integration. The economist Jan Tinbergen first made this distinction (1965, 76).

Negative integration refers to the elimination of all national measures that restrict the freedom of goods, persons, services, and capital inside Europe. This is still the core business of Europe. The central treaty of the European Union is the treaty on the establishment of the European Community. The central communitarian institutions of the European Union, the European Commission, and the European Court of Justice exercise their power predominantly to further negative integration. They forbid and fine state intervention that can be interpreted as contrary to negative integration. The European Commission can issue "Commission directives" and decisions or initiate court proceedings in the case of violation of the EC competition rules (Scharpf 1999, 60). The logic of European integration is such that liberalization of the common market takes precedence over state intervention.

"Positive integration," defined by Tinbergen as "the creation of new institutions and their instruments or the modification of existing instruments," means the adoption of measures aimed at reconstructing a system of regulation at the European level (1965, 76). While negative integration is, so to speak, written into the "day-to-day running of Europe," positive integration depends on the achievement of consensus among the many actors involved in European decision making, even if decision making by majority is formally possible in several fields. This means that a fundamental asymmetry between negative and positive integration exists (Scharpf 1999). In essence, negative integration automatically removes the power and authority of states to redress what are regarded as detrimental effects of markets; this loss, however, is not compensated for at the European level unless all member states agree to take a specific measure to that purpose.

What does this mean in the long run? The extension and expansion of the common market is now a self-perpetuating process, firmly grounded in the primary law of the treaties and overseen and implemented by the European Commission and the European Court of Justice. One of the most frequently quoted phrases in works on community law is Lord Denning's characterization of its impact on the national legal systems of the member states:

> "[W]hen we come to matters with a European element, the Treaty is like an incoming tide. It flows into the estuaries and up the rivers. It cannot be held back." (Quoted in Loman et al. 1992, 19)

This means that the legal foundation to forbid national rules is based on the primary law of the European Union (the treaties), while the legal foundation for issuing rules on the European level has to be created—de facto by consensus—in secondary law, such as directives. Europe state intervention to promote goals other than market liberalization and to compensate for the iniquities of the market is severely restricted. At the European level, there is no equivalent of state intervention to redress such iniquities. The predominance of negative over positive integration indeed contributes "to the erosion of institutions, normative standards and public support for existing democracies" (Greven 2000, 36).

The asymmetry between negative and positive integration is crucial in assessing the evolution of the European Union in the next twenty or twenty-five years. The same holds true for the democratic deficit of the EU. Democratic legitimacy and accountability also suffer from erosion at the national level, while reconstruction at the European level remains incomplete. Nevertheless, the democratic deficit refers predominantly to the asymmetry between the powers of the European executive bodies and the European and national parliaments. When the national states lose competencies, which are transferred to the European level, this not only means a loss of sovereignty but also a loss of democratic account-ability at the national level. Some of the competencies that are trans-ferred to the European level seem to leak away. Of the others, some are submitted to the control of the European parliament. Many are not. So the loss of democracy at the national level is not even formally compen-sated for at the level of Europe. This is even more so the case with decision making by the European Council, as it is not accountable to the European parliament. Formally, its members are accountable to their national parliaments. But for several reasons—one being the secrecy of European Council meetings—this formal accountability is a fantasy. As a result, one can see the evolution of the European Council of the heads of state or of government of the member states of the European Union and the president of the European Commission into a body of its own, out of reach of the frameworks of national and European democracy.

In a certain sense, none of this is surprising. The founders of the process of European integration never conceived of it as a process of democratization. The ECSC was planned as an administrative body; the Common Assembly of national parliamentarians was added to its insti-tutional structure as an afterthought "to meet the charge of technocra-cy," like an annual shareholders meeting, and, indeed, with only the competencies of shareholders (Duchêne 1994, 210). The evolution of Europe has been path-dependent in regard to this original democratic deficit. After fifty years of Europeanization along the lines of the com-munity method, the picture is bleak from a perspective that uses politi-cal democracy as a yardstick at the level of national states. The European parliament lacks the power of a national parliament and does not have effective control over the European Commission, and has none at all over the European Council. There are no European political parties and European elections are not much more than national by-elections. The European Commission, the European Council, and the various councils of ministers that make up the government of the European Union are not democratic institutions in the way that governments of the member states are. The European Union is not built on a political constitution; it is built on a system of treaties that gives predominance to the four free-doms constituting the common market (the free movement of goods, services, people, and capital), and is relatively silent on the freedoms of citizens (cf. Greven 2000, 37).

The path of functional integration has, indeed, led to the establish-ment of a European system of governance in a class of its own. Its body politic is not constituted by citizens, but by political and administrative elites, and its political space is at best semipublic. Its legitimacy is almost completely dependent on "output legitimacy," that is, performance, as "input legitimacy" (democracy, the participation of citizens in a European public space) is virtually nonexistent (Scharpf 1999). But deficiency in democracy can never completely be compensated for by performance as a factor of legitimacy. Besides, authority based only on output legitimacy is exceedingly vulnerable to performance failure (Beetham and Lord 1998, 127–28). Greven concludes:

> The EU cannot become a democracy by following the road thus far taken. If it is to continue to develop a regime of legitimate governance, it urgently requires a new model of democracy that will be acceptable beyond the limits of national political space. (2000, 55)

The success of the common market has not been followed by similar developments in the domain of foreign and defense policy, nor in that of social policy. Perhaps the best test for the prospect of a serious and unified European foreign policy would be the willingness of both the United Kingdom and France to relinquish their permanent seats in the Security Council of the United Nations in exchange for a permanent seat for the European Union. As long as they can act in the international arena as permanent members of the Security Council, outside the framework of the European Union and its presumed "common security and foreign policy," the latter can never develop into a truly integrated European policy. Along the same lines, one can argue that a second condition for the EU is the abandonment by both the United Kingdom and France of their nuclear weapons or their integration into a European nuclear command.

The general conclusion so far must be that the functional road to European integration has run its course, as negative integration is eroding more and more national standards and market restrictions, while the road to positive integration at the European level is an uphill battle. Political democracy at the national level is eroding, while at the European level it remains incomplete. Moreover, the intergovernmental second and third pillars do not offer an alternative for further integration, precisely because they are intergovernmental. So the process of Europeanization is suffering from declining levels of effectiveness as well as legitimacy. The contradictions that have been built into the second concept of European integration, the contradiction between the promise of political integration on the one hand and the realities of economic integration on the other, have become more and more visible. Also, it has become increasingly clear that the traditional ways of handling these contradictions—the community method and the establishment of new, intergovernmental pillars—are not fit to solve them.

V

The intended enlargement of the European Union in the coming years will mean the aggravation of these inner contradictions. The institutions for decision making, set up with six members in mind, are already unduly strained by the current number of member states (fifteen). They will not function with four times the original number of members. The Intergovernmental Conference (IGC), which ended with the Treaty of Nice, dismally failed to propose and accept the institutional reforms necessary for a European Union with some twenty-five members. Accession negotiations are now taking place with twelve candidate countries, ten of them former communist countries in Eastern Europe. It is expected that the first candidates will become members around 2004. (Note: On May 1, 2004, Cyprus, the Czech Republic, Estonia, Hungary, Lithuania, Malta, Poland, Slovakia, and Slovenia formally joined the European Union.)

While most of these countries have made a more or less successful transition to democracy and capitalism, it will nevertheless be impossible for them to implement the so-called *acquis communautaire* upon accession. Acceptance (and implementation) of this *acquis* is formally the *conditio sine qua non* for admittance. The acquis communautaire includes the European treaties, all European legislation enacted, the judgments of the European Court of Justice, and joint actions taken in the second and third pillars of the European Union. It is now estimated to cover roughly 87,000 pages of European laws, regulations, and jurisprudence.

The inability of most candidates to completely implement the acquis rests on a fundamental weakness: Their governmental and judicial institutions do not yet possess the necessary autonomy, competence, capacity, and independence. It will probably take ten to twenty years to improve this situation (WRR 2001). But it appears that the fact that the candidates do not meet the conditions for full membership will be ignored in most cases, as long as they formally accept the acquis and claim transition periods only for a few distinct fields. This indulgence is based on the unspoken consideration that it will be politically impossible not to admit them and thereby to destroy the expectations of joining Europe that have been so instrumental in motivating these countries to make the transition from communism to democracy and a market economy. There is also the hope that admitting them will give these states a better chance to make up their deficiencies than if they had remained outside the European Union.

At first sight, such a course of events seems comparable to the way the candidature of Greece was dealt with in 1979. The European Commission delivered a negative *avis* (opinion) on the grounds that neither Greece's economy nor its political and administrative system met the conditions for membership. But the commission was overruled for political reasons by the Council of Ministers, which judged that membership would consolidate Greek democracy.

The situation now, however, could not be more different in that particular case. Then the European Community could afford to accept the admittance of a small, corrupt state like Greece, even though it turned out to be a dire financial trap. But the accession to the European Union of six to ten new members, with more than 130 million inhabitants, that fail the crucial criteria of admittance is quite another matter. The Common Agricultural Policy (CAP), for example, has been in need of structural reform for a long time. Proposals for such reforms have been undermined time and again by member states that profit from the existing CAP. The probability of enacting such reforms will, however, decline dramatically when East European countries, with their huge, inefficient, and backward agricultural sectors, become members of the EU and get a stake in upholding the status quo. Without such reforms in agriculture, the EU budget will be severely strained (George and Bache 2001, 322). Then there is the fact that most of these new members will be the frontier states of the European Union, while they are not and will not be able to control these frontiers. Without radical institutional reforms, the inner contradictions of Europe and the problems of democracy and efficacy will reach the form of an existential crisis of the European Union; the accession of some ten new member states will, in this respect, act as a catalyst.

Following the limited reforms achieved in Nice (2001), it was decided to convene a European Convention that would be given the task to prepare the next IGC by proposing a set of institutional arrangements to enable the EU to function adequately with twenty-five or more members. Already, the convention has been compared to the assembly that gathered in 1787 in Philadelphia and produced the U.S. Constitution. Clearly, it is assumed that this body has to bridge the structural contradictions of the EU and to prepare a constitution that is not limited to incremental institutional reform. So, in a sense, the European Convention and the coming IGC are seen as a last chance for Europe. But if one looks at the composition and powers of the convention, it is more of a problem than a key to its solution. Its composition repeats the technocratic, top-down, and undemocratic approach that is so characteristic of Europe as it has evolved in half a century. It is not an elected body, and as such, certainly not legitimate as a *constituante*. Its 105 members have been appointed by various national and European political bodies, thus, again only representative of political elites. And its formal powers are as scant as the questions it has to address are far-reaching and complex: The convention can only advise. It is the Intergovernmental Conference that will decide in the end. (Note: This IGC was held in October 2003.)

VI

So far I have discussed the development of European integration in terms of the logic of the integration process. But both the original steps in the direction of European cooperation and all major political decisions on the direction of this process have been reached in the context of world politics and the evolution of the world-economy (cf. Henig 1997).

In the beginning, it was the Cold War. For the United States, the answer to the perceived communist threat meant not only transatlantic military cooperation, as in NATO, but also the necessity of a strong Western European economy, which required transnational economic collaboration. So the United States used the Marshall Plan to pressure the European states to cooperate in the economics of reconstruction.

The Cold War also gave urgency to the creation of the European Coal and Steel Community as an instrument to forestall any possibility of another intra-European war between Germany and France by making their war-production facilities completely interdependent. In this sense, European integration was an element of America's postwar hegemony and as such, it was not questioned as long as the postwar reconstruction of the Western European economies was in progress.

From the late 1970s on, the most important external factor influencing the integration process was the position of the European economies relative to the world-economy as a whole, in which the competitive advantage was seen to be resting with Eastern Asian and North American transnational corporations. When the Soviet Union disintegrated in 1991, after it had lost control over Eastern Europe, the foundation of European cooperation (the essential threat of the Soviet Union) disappeared and necessitated the search for new mechanisms to hold Europe together. This was even more true as the unification of Germany required new anchors to guarantee its position in Europe. The Maastricht Treaty and the European Monetary Union can partly be explained by this need.

While European integration is sometimes seen as the unfolding of a kind of inner logic, this best describes the method of integration. Steps forward have been seen as an answer to endogenous processes, and have often been taken as an answer to outside developments. If this is true of the past fifty years, there is no reason to doubt this will also be the case in the near future, even if it is not yet clear what kind of outside developments will emerge. However, it seems to me that there are at least three structural threats or "challenges" to Europe from the outside.

In the debate on the "withering away of the state" as a result of globalization, as predicted, for instance, by authors such as Guéhenno (1994) and Ohmae (1995), Immanuel Wallerstein has taken a distinct position. There is no such thing as globalization, in the sense of a fairly recent phenomenon, according to him, and the existence of states is a necessary prerequisite for the operation of a capitalist world-economy. Far from finding signs of a demise of the state as produced by the growth of transnational corporations and their networks, he argues that, for the first time in the five hundred years of the existence of the inter-state system, states are indeed declining in strength. This has, however, nothing to do with globalization or whatever transformation of world-economic structures there may be. It follows from the declining legitimacy accorded to states by their own populations. Wallerstein thinks this is the consequence of the diminishing performance of states relative to the expectations of their people. Liberal reformism as well as its equivalents on the Left are less and less seen as successful roads toward gradual amelioration, and rightly so. For this, pessimism is a realistic appraisal of the prospect of a gradual progress in life, chances for the great major-ity of the world population. As the state has always been seen as instru-mental to such progress, this loss of hope undermines its legitimacy, which is essential to its existence.

> This is not because of a transformation of the world-economic struc-tures but because of a transformation of the geoculture, and first of all, because of the loss of hope by the popular masses in liberalism and its avatars on the left. (Wallerstein 1999, 73–75)

Such a general trend would not affect only the political capacities of the individual member states. It would be an even bigger threat to the legitimacy of the EU, as its capacity to perform is at stake, and with it, the only form of legitimacy Europe has: output legitimacy. It is therefore crucial that the union should find a way to overcome the problems of positive integration and restore a public capacity to act.

The second major threat is uncontrolled immigration. Europe is a magnet for people from the adjacent peripheral states and for refugees from all over the world and it will—certainly after the enlargement of the EU—progressively become more difficult to stem or control the flow of both illegal and legal immigrants from a variety of countries and cultures. William McNeill sees this growth of polyethnicity within states as the most critical problem for the existing states in the core of the world-economy.

> A persistently polyethnic, culturally diverse society creates strains upon democratic ideals of active citizenship, national unity, and equal rights. In particular, it challenges our inherited assumptions about the ratio-nal autonomy of individual voters, since group loyalty and pursuit of ethnic advantage can easily overshadow the residual and less clearly perceived common interests of all citizens. (McNeill 1994, 133)

He thinks that the "most critical question of the next century for rich nations" is whether states will be capable of using the principle of the political rights of citizens to override the ring of ethnic loyalty among the newcomers.

This is a theme with implications that will strike the EU much more forcefully than its member states, simply because there is neither a European state nor a European nation. Moreover, the member states have not been willing or able to harmonize their policies in this field and to develop, let alone enforce, a common, European approach to immigration.

A third structural threat, or challenge, to Europe follows from the peculiar world-political configuration that has now, more or less, crystallized; a configuration with one hegemonic power that has, for the time being, no realistic challenger(s), but is not as powerful as it used to be: the United States of America. The relative decline of its geopolitical power has led to the propensity to operate unilaterally in global politics and to depend more and more on military instruments instead of on multilateralism and international cooperation under American leadership. In this situation, the member states of the EU will, in due course, have to define their relation to the United States in new terms. They will then have to choose between two possibilities.

On the one hand, Europe can give up its pretense of eventually becoming some kind of supranational political entity that can act on more or less equal terms with the United States. Its member states then would become not so much allies as vassals of the United States in political and military terms; the EU as an unstable set of cooperative arrangements with a free-trade zone as its center and raison d'être. The picture Margaret Thatcher paints of the future of the United Kingdom vis-à-vis the United States in her *Statecraft* (2002) would, in this perspective, fit Europe as a whole. The other possible road is toward a sovereign political federation, based on a European constitution, and with a fully democratic system of government. Following Lijphart, such a democratic system should have proportional representation and a parliamentary government, as parliamentarism and proportional representation are more successful for democracy than presidential and majoritarian forms of government and election, and parliamentarism and proportional representation unite most European democracies and set them apart from most democracies elsewhere (Lijphart 2002).

It is remarkable that the only possible way to meet these three challenges or threats seems to be, following the argument of this essay, the creation of positive integration (one way or another) at the European level, even if it is by no means certain that the realization of such positive integration is sufficient to overcome these threats.

VII

It follows from this analysis that the project of European integration faces major challenges in the next twenty years. It will not be possible to overcome these challenges by proceeding along the lines of the last fifty years. Europe is in a situation of unstable equilibrium, which means that a bifurcation becomes probable. On the one hand, the threats and inner contradictions I have identified could lead to the stagnation of the European project. This does not mean that the EU will fall apart. It could mean that the common market will be maintained, but that on important social and environmental questions, Europe will become a "dead letter regime" (Little 2001, 304) and positive integration will be more and more difficult, just as political cooperation will stay an à la carte choice for the member states. Whether such a reversion to a free-trade zone would be a stable arrangement remains to be seen.

On the other hand, there is the possibility that the perception of these threats will galvanize the political elites of Europe into instituting supranational political integration. The most probable road in this direction could be the formation of a small group of member states, perhaps the original six, that would take the lead, even though there will be a penalty in doing so. This choice has to be made in the next two years, certainly before the accession to the EU of almost a dozen new members. Perhaps this choice will not be made in a conscious way. But by doing nothing, by following the well-trodden road of the last half-century, the decision will, nevertheless, be made—by default.

Note

1. This chapter was written during my stay at the Netherlands Institute for Advanced Study in the Humanities and Social Sciences (NIAS), Wassenaar, January–April 2002. I would like to thank Monika Sie Dhian Ho for her critical remarks and Anne Simpson (NIAS) for her help in editing the English text.

References

Abromeit, Heidrun. 1998. *Democracy in Europe: Legitimising Politics in a Non-State Polity.* New York: Berghahn Books.

Bainbridge, Timothy. 2001. *The Penguin Companion to European Union,* 2nd ed. London: Penguin.

Beetham, David, and Christopher Lord. 1998. *Legitimacy and the European Union.* London: Longman.

Borrego, John. 1999. "The Hegemonic Moment of Global Capitalism." Pp. 174–211 in *The Future of Global Conflict*, eds. V. Bornschier and C. Chase-Dunn. London: Sage.

Duchêne, François. 1994. *Jean Monnet: The First Statesman of Interdependence*. New York: Norton.

George, Stephen, and Ian Bache, eds. 2001. *Politics in the European Union*. Oxford: Oxford University Press.

Greven, Michael Th. 2000. "Can the European Union Finally Become a Democracy?" Pp. 35–62 in *Democracy Beyond the State? The European Dilemma and the Emerging Global Order*, eds. M. Th. Greven and L. W. Pauly. Lanham, MD: Rowman & Littlefield.

Guéhenno, Jean-Marie. 1994. *La fin de la démocratie*. Paris: Flammarion.

Haas, Ernest B. 1958. *The Uniting of Europe: Political, Social, and Economic Forces, 1950–1957*. London: Stevens.

Henig, Stanley. 1997. *The Uniting of Europe: From Discord to Concord*. London: Routledge.

Lijphart, Arend. 2002. "Hoe moet de Europese Unie geregeerd worden? Doe maar gewoon," in M. Sie Dhian Ho, ed., "Democratisering van de Europese Unie," *Beleid and Maatschappij*, 29, 1, 4–7.

Little, Richard. 2001. "International Regimes." Pp. 299–317 in *The Globalization of World Politics: An Introduction to International Relations*, 2nd ed., ed. J. Baylis and S. Smith. Oxford, UK: Oxford University Press.

Loman, J. M. E., Kamiel Mortelmans, Harry Post, and Stewart Watson. 1992. *Culture and Community Law: Before and after Maastricht*. Deventer: Kluwer.

McNeill, William. 1994. "The Fall of the Great Powers: An Historical Commentary." *Review* XVII, no. 2 (Spring): 123–45.

Milward, Alan. 2000. *The European Rescue of the Nation-State*, 2nd ed. London: Routledge.

Monnet, Jean. 1976. *Mémoires*. Paris: Fayard.

Ohmae, Kenichi. 1995. *The End of the Nation State: The Rise of Regional Economies*. New York: The Free Press.

Pinder, John. 1986. "European Community and the Nation-State: A Case for a Neo-Federalism?" *International Affairs* LXII, no. 1 (Winter): 41–54.

Scharpf, Fritz W. 1999. *Governing in Europe: Effective and Democratic?* Oxford: Oxford University Press.

Spinelli, Altiero. 1977. "Reflections on the Institutional Crisis in the European Community." *West European Politics* XV, no. 1 (January): 77–89.

Thatcher, Margaret. 2002. *Statecraft: Strategies for a Changing World*. New York: HarperCollins.

Tinbergen, Jan. 1965. *International Economic Integration*, 2nd ed. Amsterdam: Elsevier.

Wallerstein, Immanuel. 1999. *The End of the World as We Know It: Social Science for the Twenty-first Century*. Minneapolis: University of Minnesota Press.

Wetenschappelijke Raad voor het Regeringsbeleid—WRR. 2001. *Towards a Pan-European Union*. The Hague: SDU.

$*$

4

Using, Producing, and Replacing Life?: Alchemy as Theory and Practice in Capitalism

Claudia von Werlhof

I am going to contribute to the *longue durée* analysis of the modern world-system by introducing to you a new theoretical concept. It is not only of longue durée but also interdisciplinary, very practical, and concrete at the same time: alchemy. The theory and practice of alchemy can be seen as not only a main link between capitalism and precapitalism in general but also as a concept that explains, more specifically, the narrow relationship between capitalism and patriarchy. Capitalism from this point of view can be seen as the latest stage of patriarchy. Last, the concept of alchemy can give us a clear insight into the "short durée" which is left to the modern world-system today. This opens our eyes to the alternatives that must take into account all the existing contradictions simultaneously.

I have made efforts to show how and why the world is seen "upside down," and how this can be changed. First, I tried to show this with respect to the role of unpaid labor, and especially housework, in the world-system. I came to the conclusion that this type of "underground" economy is the permanent fundament without which there would be no accumulation at all (Werlhof 1985; Mies et al. 1988). In the meantime, my analysis has gone further. The look at the other side of political economy has to be completed by a look at the other side as a whole, if not the underground, of modern technology, culture, and religion. It is my hypothesis that a well-defined concept of alchemy could be the very key for a new historical and interdisciplinary analysis of these other aspects of modern society. It is not possible to analyze capitalism without analyzing modern sciences and machine-technology, as well as Christian beliefs and other cultural traditions, including their historical roots that, all together, are interdependently forming our societies.

If the underground economy tells us something about what I call the "permanence" of the process of original accumulation, that is, the connection between economic exploitation and private or public political violence, the underground technology, the collective subconscious belief system, and the hidden culture of alchemy show us something about the permanence of processes of capitalist destruction instead of production (Werlhof 2000a). This means that capitalist transformation of people and nature cannot, because of its alchemical character, end in technological progress and a better matter, but is necessarily promoting the annihilation of the world, since its beginnings on the basis of both nature's and women's sacrifice (Werlhof 1997a, 2000b). Considering capitalism as something like an alchemical mode of production enables us to better understand why the actual and future demise of the modern world-system is already occurring. When we include a well-defined concept of alchemy in our analyses we can more clearly see what was difficult to see before. For example:

- Why it was wrong to center all hopes on technological progress, especially machine technology;
- how this myth of modern technology and the fascination it provokes, especially in men, including the technology of terror and war, can be fully included into the critique; and
- why sexism is not at all an outcome of racism or the same as racism, but rather, is something much older, deeper, and absolutely (not only relatively) necessary within this system.

Let me conclude my introduction by saying that the third largest project in my life is already on the table: It is the question of nature and nature's other side, nature as an underground flow of so-called energy, soul, spirit, morphogenetic fields, and of phenomena beyond time and space. If we continue to look at nature as if it were only dead matter, a material or mechanical process that has to be dominated by people or that can even be replaced by a man-made world, we will fail to solve any of the immense problems accumulated so far worldwide. Nor will we find the way to a new society that we will have to invent soon. A new relationship with nature can only become real if we cooperate with it under its own conditions. And these conditions are no longer known because what we know of nature is only what we imagine or force it to be.

Creation and Transformation or Transformation and Creation?

From the alchemy point of view, the problem is not how to transform creation, but how to create through transformation. This means that creation is not presupposed, but is the problem itself. Everything in alchemy is about life. The main question is: How is life created? In patriarchal alchemy, the question is: How can men create life? The process that leads to the creation of life is transformation. There must be a great deal of transformation before creation is possible.

To look at the world in this way can be understood as a general method that reminds us to never forget the other side or the underground of production: What has to be done before production can start? What has to be there so that production can continue? The alchemist always goes to the bottom, because in the last instance he or she wants to produce or create nothing less than life itself. And from this perspective he or she looks at everything.

The Origins of Alchemy

The word *alchemy* goes back to the Greek word *chemein* (to flow) and to the Arabic word *keme* (the black mud of the Nile). The annual flooding of the Nile left behind thick layers of black mud on its banks, which made them fertile. Through nature's chemistry of transforming water and earth by mixing them, new life was created. Alchemy originally must have begun with observing this natural phenomenon, then attempting to understand it, help it along, and imitate it. This is most likely the phase of the prepatriarchal alchemy of gardeners and peasants, of men and women who wished to help this process along and cooperate with natural phenomena without changing the principles behind them (e.g., the early idea of the garden of Eden is equated to the garden of humankind). Evidence of alchemical practices and theories exists in China, India, Africa, the Middle East, and throughout Europe, especially in Eastern and Southeastern Europe (see Eliade 1980; Jung 1985; Binswanger 1985; Bologne 1995; Gebelein 1996; Biedermann 1991).

Alchemy is known to us through the histories of technology and religion. It has existed throughout the world in many forms. Most certainly, alchemy had its origins in ancient matriarchal cultures and, over time, became more and more patriarchalized and perverted, that is, turned into its opposite. The principles of nurturing and cooperation of early alchemy are entirely different from those of patriarchal alchemy.

Patriarchal Alchemy: A New Technology and Theology

My attempt to look at alchemy from the point of view of the distinction between matriarchal and patriarchal alchemy is, so far, unique (Werlhof 2001b). If matriarchal alchemy, which seems to be unimaginably old, is the result of the first conscious human attempt to understand the "great work" of nature, patriarchal alchemy obviously has developed step-by-step in a totally different direction. As far as I can understand this process, which needs to be defined by different developments and periods, patriarchal alchemy continues to be interested in the process of life creation. But now, it no longer wants to observe and imitate anymore, but to lead, even against nature, thereby becoming more and more independent from natural processes and—in the last instance—finally trying to replace them. Patriarchal alchemy is not only a technology but also a theology. The alchemist sees himself as someone who does not only work close to nature, God, and the female (as the one who brings life into being), but as one who tries to *be* nature, God, and the female himself by replacing them (or at least their importance) through his technology. In its patriarchal forms, alchemy always tries to "dissolve" matter (*mater* equals mother) and, after various transformation and combination processes, tries to get hold of its "essence," its "substance," its "quintessence." In the case of metal, this essence is gold, and generally, it is called the "philosopher's stone," be it in the form of a tincture, an elixier, or a powder which is supposed to be nothing less than the essence of life itself, including the power of life as such, abstracted out of matter. The alchemist then—like a god or goddess—is able to give, prolong, and improve life. He would appear as the divine creator, able to use life for its production and even replacement. He would have all of the power on Earth.

This is patriarchal alchemy's main difference from all the other forms of an older alchemy in which one tries to promote and protect life or fertility, and does this by respecting and cooperating with nature.

Why "Patriarchal"?

If one tries to analyze society from the perspective of what happens to women in contrast to what happens to men, it becomes clear that the pretended sex- or gender-neutrality of this society is a myth. Therefore *patriarchy* has been used to explain why modern capitalist society is so sexist and violent toward women. But the debate on patriarchy—its relationship with capitalism, its past and its future—has, in my eyes, not come to any other conclusion than that patriarchy means male dominance or the rule of men. But the rule of what? And what does this have to do with capitalism (Mies 1988)?

The result of my research into the meaning of patriarchy is the following: Patriarchy does not only mean rule, but also "origin" through rule or ruling men, called "fathers." (The Greek word *archein* means both; *pater* is related to the invention of abstract institutions and hierarchies.) Instead of *matriarchy*, which means "in the beginning the mother," we now have to understand that patriarchy means "in the beginning the father," the ruler, or God as the Creator. In this sense, patriarchy is a theory about how society, nature, and men should be or become. Patriarchy is a utopian concept in the sense that the origin, which always means the origin of life, has to come from a father in the sense of a ruling elite, person, or institution. It implies that this state of things is desirable and achievable one day, so that it could include the real, maternal origin, and/or no longer need the latter until now "normal" origin, because this has been replaced by a male creation.

At this point, patriarchy and patriarchal alchemy can be seen as one single project: The project of a technological transformation that aims at the invention of a male creator and the male creation of life in contrast to the old order of nature where creation is the province of the female sex. It is obvious that such a revolutionary project first of all needs rule, domination, hierarchies, and violence forever—until its supposed realization—and that it needs theology or belief systems where the madness and delusion of the whole project appear as normal and natural, as a method of "improving" humanity, society, and nature, and even as a way to a new paradise in eternity. The technological project of turning the world upside down is then defined as "progress" and "evolution," whereas the world and the people, especially women and nature, appear as low, evil, sinful, impure, worthless, and somehow insignificant. From now on, "salvation" is needed, not only of the world, but also from the world (Kippenberg 1991). One believes that worldly and earthly existence must be overcome and that one must try to get rid of the entire bodily sphere, not to mention women, the senses, and all life-celebrating emotions (Schütz-Buenaventura 2000).

This is why the ongoing violation and destruction of nature, women, people, and living conditions still do not cause panic. It is because most people still believe that the destruction of the low and sinful world will be followed by a new paradise in which those things and beings would have improved or wouldn't be needed anymore (see Unseld 1992). People believe that the progress of civilization will have replaced nature and her beings by a "better matter" or even a metaphysical world.

Most people—and I do not only speak of those who work with artificial intelligence at MIT trying to invent "living" machines, or those who work in genetic engineering trying to invent new biological life in the name of so-called evolution—have become unable to recognize the nihilism of a society that uses and promotes the newest "development of productive forces" to finally realize a much older project (Weizenbaum 1978; Chargaff 1988; Werlhof 1997b). It may be that they do not recognize what is really going on because, over thousands of years, they have become used to this type of thinking. If Josef Schumpeter calls the techno-economical process a "creative destruction" (1962), we can, if we want to, see every day that there is destruction. But where is it replaced by creation?

The Practice of Patriarchal Alchemy: Nature's and Women's Sacrifice

Through my extended as well as more concrete definition of patriarchy, it is possible to understand the logic and permanence, if not growing importance, of patriarchal alchemy until today. Patriarchal alchemy has accompanied patriarchal development. One could say that alchemy has become the method of patriarchy, be it in politics, technology, culture, philosophy, religion, science, or economics. This sharply contradicts the general belief that alchemy is part of the past, that it has always been a failure, and that it has been a ridiculous attempt by superstitious or naive people to influence the world. No modern scientist sees himself in a direct line with alchemists of former times. This is understandable: *Patriarchal* alchemy has, until now, been a failure. But modern science does not know why!

My hypothesis is that modern science and technology are, whether or not they want it, based on procedures that follow the same principles of patriarchal alchemical practice dating from ancient times.

If everything in alchemy is about life, this means that everything is about women and nature because the real forces of creation—or forces of production—are expressed through them. The alchemist, therefore, tries to imitate procreation processes. From this perspective, he looks at the rest of society and social production in general. The idea is that if you know how life is to be generated, you know everything else, too. The early alchemist is a realist: Without women there is no human life. Women themselves are the productive force of life. Without females there is no animal life and without plants and their growth, there is no life at all.

In contrast to the older alchemy which is oriented toward mothers and plants, in patriarchal alchemy, the question goes further and changes direction: How is it possible to control, organize, and even get hold of this productive force that is able to create life? The phenomenon that we call sexism started with patriarchal alchemy long before racism had become a problem. Sexism does not only start with a special way in which women are integrated into the general workforce, but with the way women have become the sex object of a technological project that not only uses their labor-force but also their bodies and bodily forces: their "gynergy" as Mary Daly calls it (1970).

This is the big difference between sexism and racism, which one cannot grasp when looking at the social relations of production alone and/or when defining productive forces independently from immediate life processes in women and nature (Werlhof 2001a). Even then, when observing women only in the labor force or the history of their inclusion into the patriarchal system, an alchemical technology can always be felt, smelled, seen, and experienced. Because, independent from the existence of racism or not, women everywhere are treated from the point of view of their bodily potential in many more ways than merely as a labor force. The roots of sexism are much older and deeper than the roots of racism.

In patriarchal alchemy, women are systematically sacrificed. The same is true for nature in general. In the language of patriarchal alchemy, this proceeds as follows: The alchemist has, first of all, to produce the so-called *materia prima, massa confusa,* or *nigredo:* the black matter. This matter is the outcome of a process in which the alchemist tries to go back to the origins of matter, of life itself (originally, the black and fertile soil). For this purpose, he has to "blacken" all matter, mostly by using fire. In this way, he produces the *nigredo* that is supposed to be the all-inclusive substance of matter. In other words, the alchemist starts with bringing death to matter. This gloomy process is called *mortificatio* (from Latin *mors,* or death) (Bologne 1995). It is no coincidence that blacksmiths and all forms of pyrotechniques played a special role in alchemy (Eliade 1980), and that women, defined as witches, were burned.

After the mortification, the black matter has to be "dissolved and combined" (in Latin: *solve et coagula*). This means that now the individual elements are separated from the materia prima and from one another by using purification techniques in isolating the different elements from one another (like sulphur, mercury, and lead). The "pure" elements or "white" substances are later recombined with one another. In this way, patriarchal alchemy produces new, allegedly improved, substances and materials that, as such, mostly do not occur in nature.

The central principles in this procedure are force and violence. The alchemist completes his *opus magnum,* or great work through the so-called chemical or holy marriage of the substances. Holy marriage is a metaphor taken from matriarchal culture. Whereas originally, it was the coming together of the goddess and her hero in a great celebration of Eros (from which all life springs and is confirmed), in patriarchal alchemy, the holy marriage appears as a forced combination of artificially abstracted substances characterized as either "male" or "female" (Weiler 1993; Jung 1985). For example, the blacksmith often was responsible for circumcision, thus producing "pure" sexes (Wolf 1994). Therefore, the ceremony is no longer one of mixing the natural polarity of materials as a great work of nature. Instead, it is the forced putting together of artificial opposites (Ernst 1993), from which the so-called great work of the alchemist springs. From this established act of bringing together, something entirely new is supposed to originate, in particular, new life (heterosexual reproduction), called *rubedo,* the "reddening" or "redness." This life is based on the special sacrifice of women's gynergy and matter (mater). The alchemist behaves like the priest who leads the holy ritual and completes it with the sacrament without which there could be no creation. Thus, the alchemist sees himself as the true creator, and even as the procreator, of a completely new kind of life.

The patriarchal alchemist is the first to define what is male or female. But this social construction of gender still remains relatively close to the reality of women's gynergy. Mircea Eliade, for example, tells us that alchemists sometimes forced their *soror mystica* (their mystical sister or their wife) to jump into the oven in order to make sure that the alloying of metals would be a success (Eliade 1980). But alchemists also tried to produce life, even human life, directly. From Gnostic sects in ancient Egypt up to the famous alchemist and physician of the sixteenth century, Paracelsus, alchemy attempted to produce the so-called *homunculus* (the little man) by combining male sperm with female blood (Paracelsus 1990). The homunculus often is depicted as sitting in a test tube. He would be, so to speak, the first successful test-tube baby, a creation of the alchemist experimenter—something that has, indeed, never happened.

These principles of alchemical practice show different things:

1. The practice of patriarchal alchemy as the dirty history of the "pure" substances reminds us of the general political principle of "divide and rule." It is the general principle of patriarchal poli-

tics, economics, science, and technology. Also in alchemy, the "raw" material first undergoes the process of division: abstraction, filtering, and isolation. The combination of abstracted substances—as the rule over matter—anticipates machine technology, which though appearing much later, acts the same way (Mumford 1977; Bammé et al. 1983). Machine technology shares with alchemy this principle of separation and purification (see the experiment in sciences), or "whiteness" (see the "white race," white sugar, white flour, and cleanliness or hygiene). Today, the same process leads to the production of so-called raw materials as resources. From this point of view, alchemy and modern chemistry have much more in common than the latter would admit. The rationality of alchemical thinking is as close to machine-technology as its irrationality is close to a theology of God as a male producer of life. This proves the modernity instead of traditionality of patriarchal alchemy, and patriarchy in general.

2. Patriarchal alchemy must be a failure because the alchemist tries to separate mind from matter, converting the latter into something deteriorated, subdued, and "female" in a patriarchal sense. In contrast, the supposedly separate mind, the philosopher's stone, from now on appears to belong to something "higher," "holier," and "male" in a patriarchal sense. "Pure mind," the mind without matter, seems to be the pure power of life in the hands of the alchemist. But neither the production of this hierarchy, nor the production of pure substances can lead to the creation of life. Because pure substances are essentially dead, abstracted out of life and matter so that no life is likely to grow when these substances are brought together, matter without mind is dead and is a mind without matter, too. Patriarchal alchemy, therefore, is in principle barren (Colburn et al. 1996). This is why modern chemistry has begun mixing pure substances with "impure" living ones, and genetic engineering called "algeny" by Jeremy Rifkin even mixes living substances with other living ones—nevertheless maintaining the general procedure of abstraction and isolation (Rifkin 1983).

3. Unlike earlier prepatriarchal alchemy with its principle of cooperation with nature, what we see in patriarchal alchemy is an attempt at the usurpation of the female fertility, pregnancy, and birth process, not only in theory but also in reality. This attempt is supposed to improve these processes, and, in the last instance, to replace them with something else: A male creation of new life. It seems as if the artificial birth machine, the "mothermachine," the industrial production of life as a commodity, or the pregnant

ruler—as it was shown in pictures of the ancient Pharao Echna-
ton already—and the final abolition of women and nature are the
alchemical ideals of a utopian paradise (Corea 1985; Shiva 1992;
Wolf 1994). The "black magic" of using, producing, and even
trying to replace life, be it plant or animal life, and especially
trying to replace the mother, therefore, is not new thinking at all.
This is why relatively few people are astonished by the new
experiments in reproductive technologies up to genetic engineering and cloning. It is maybe more astonishing that people seem
to believe in the success of these technologies because, until now,
patriarchal alchemy was a failure.

4. In sum, the term alchemy should not only be considered as a
   metaphor, but also as a theoretical concept of its own. The concept of alchemy can be used as a key to a new knowledge about
   the historical roots of our present precarious situation. In this
   context, it would be interesting to find out why the use of the
   term alchemy usually causes many (negative) emotions. This
   proves that there are some very real things about alchemy, such
   as: alchemy is a belief system until today; alchemy is a method of
   patriarchal male individuation that has been generalized today;
   or alchemy is an ongoing tradition that weakens instead of
   strengthens people's relationship with the world and its energies. All this has to be clarified, including, of course, the analysis
   of those forces, structures, and relations that have never (or only
   partially) been controlled by patriarchal alchemy and that would
   be urgently needed to overcome the alchemical project of patriarchy as a whole. But even if the historical project of alchemy turns
   out to have been a huge delusion, we cannot overlook how much
   misery, destruction, and death it has created thus far, and we
   should not underestimate how much social power worldwide is
   still behind it.

A Periodization of Alchemy: From Matriarchal Alchemy via Modern (Hidden) Alchemy to Alchemy without Matter?

The very old knowledge of matriarchal alchemy has been used for many
different purposes, slowly perverting the old wisdom into its opposite.
What I call patriarchal alchemy is at least 5,000 years old, which is
exactly the time when the first patriarchal empires appeared in the world.
The knowledge of and respect for nature must have given way to an
attitude of more and more independence from nature and the desire to
rule over it. The same has occurred with women, as we know.

In modern times, the general production process seems to be independent from women and nature. If in former times alchemy tried to imitate the processes of the creation of life, repeating the same pattern in the production of things, it is the other way around today: One tries to produce life the way one produces things—in a seemingly sex-neutral or sexless setting. After the transformation of women as so-called witches into housewives, the process of "housewifeization," it appeared that women were not necessary anymore for work or life in society (Mies et al. 1988). Modern patriarchal alchemy had already replaced them with its institutions and technologies. Feminist research shows us that women have been made invisible while remaining necessary; they have become the hidden underground of society. From our perspective, the modern housewife is the alchemically perverted patriarchal appearance of the woman and the mother-child relationship (Werlhof 2003). We must explain, from this perspective anew, how patriarchy alchemically transformed the world in order to create the female housewife, the male proletariat, and the nuclear family as the household within the modern world-system. The same analysis must be done for the alchemical transformation of society in order to create new races and ethnicities (or methods of ethnic cleansing).

Today, these "creations" are transforming and disappearing. It may be that future households will be larger and that a general norm no longer exists with respect to marriage and heterosexuality. But two things will remain: One, the attempt to use women as an experimental substance for the production of life by men (nearly) independent from nature; and two, the alchemical project of a social production of the human race which eliminates the direct participation of men on the basis of their sexuality, with the final aim of replacing the female sex. Until now, what has counted is that without women there can be no life, be this hidden from social conscience or not. Women's productivity, "the production and reproduction of immediate life," is needed as much now as in former times, even if the processes of pregnancy and giving birth have already been split asunder in the best—or worst—alchemical tradition (Marx and Engels 1976, 191). But exactly because of these experiments with artificial life production, women today appear to be visible once again: Their consent is needed for each step in the new reproductive and genetic biotechnologies. And there is nothing in sight that shows that any artificial life can ever "be made" in a way to replace normally born life.

What has been growing instead of disappearing is the importance of alchemical thinking and acting in today's world. This is true for all fields of (new) technologies as well as for the economy in which the apparently self-creating potential of capitalist money—speculation, interest, money's "children"—is playing a far larger role than capitalist production itself in the meantime (Binswanger 1985). This shows, too, how far patriarchal alchemy has already gone from matter (mother) to the supposed pure (male) mind: as if alchemy without matter at all would be possible. Maybe in the future, information alone or pure thought will be sufficient to create a further step in the development of alchemy. What a progress cyberalchemy would be!

There is also a growing culture of self-realization by a sort of constructivist "self-alchemization": Everyone tries to be creative, to invent him- or herself in total abstraction of origin, sex, age, bodily appearance, or profession. This "doing gender," for example, does not want to get rid of an artificial, alchemically produced "sex or gender" but goes forward to even more arbitrariness, expressing the wish of creating oneself as a sort of flexible materia prima or pure substance—alchemically produced pure human capital ready for the creative combination or (un)holy marriage with another one.

What could have been a huge opportunity for the women's movement, as the whole patriarchal contempt for women, life, and nature is revealed so unequivocally today, has in this way partly been wasted, if not perverted into a patriarchal movement of women against women (Bell and Klein 1996).

Closed Modern Society: The "Social Machine" as an "Alchemical System"

If patriarchal alchemy, as a manner of thinking and acting, has been expanded to all spheres of society, it is justified to speak of the existence of an "alchemical system" (Werlhof 2001b). Alchemy has progressed by means of generalization and globalization. Its methods of usurpation/ negation, mortification/degradation, abstraction/isolation, perversion/ improvement, transformation/creation, and speculation/nihilism seem to leave us without any alternative. In contrast to all the talk about an "open society," we should speak of modern society as a "social machine" which is closed against the realities of life and nature (Soros 1998; Mumford 1977; Ullrich 1977). After 5,000 years of the alchemical implementation of the patriarchal project, most people in our countries subconsciously and collectively continue to believe in it. They believe it is power—that we can destroy and create and destroy again what we have created (e.g., private property, machinery, and natural resources). They don't see that this destruction comes back like a boomerang. They believe in violence. Their god is violence.

Therefore, let us here and now begin to celebrate the liberation of our earth, bodies, matter, minds, and souls from the destructive faith in patriarchy, patriarchal alchemy and the globalization of pure capital.

References

Bammé, Arno, et al., eds. 1983. *Maschinen-Menschen, Mensch-Maschinen, Grundrisse einer sozialen Beziehung.* Reinbek: Rowohlt.

Bell, Diane, and Renate Klein, eds. 1996. *Radically Speaking: Feminism Reclaimed.* London: Zed.

Biedermann, Hans. 1991. *Lexikon der Magischen Künste: Die Welt der Magie seit der Spätantike.* Munich: Heyne.

Binswanger, Hans C. 1985. *Geld und Magie.* Stuttgart: Weitbrecht.

Bologne, Jean-Claude. 1995. *Von der Fackel zum Scheiterhaufen: Magie und Aberglauben im Mittelalter.* Solothurn/Düsseldorf: Walter.

Chargaff, Erwin. 1988. *Unbegreifliches Geheimnis, Wissenschaft als Kampf für und gegen die Natur.* Stuttgart: Klett-Cotta.

Colburn, Theo, et al. 1996. *Our Stolen Future: Are We Threatening Our Fertility, Intelligence and Survival?* New York: Dutton.

Corea, Gena. 1985. *The Mother Machine: Reproductive Technologies from Artificial Insemination to Artificial Wombs.* New York: Harper & Row.

Daly, Mary. 1970. *Gyn/Ökologie.* Munich: Frauenoffensive.

Eliade, Mircea. 1980. *Schmiede und Alchemisten.* Stuttgart: Klett-Cotta.

Ernst, Wernst. 1993. "Zu einer Phänomenologie von 'Fest'-Setzung und 'Gegen'-Stand." Pp. 195–205 in *Vernetztes Denken Gemeinsames Handeln,* ed. H. Reinalter. Vienna: Kulturverlag.

Gebelein, Helmut. 1996. *Alchemie: Die Magie des Stofflichen.* Munich: Diederichs.

Jung, Carl G. 1985. *Erlösungsvorstellungen in der Alchemie.* Düsseldorf: Walter.

Kippenberg, Hans G. 1991. *Die vorderasiatischen Erlösungsreligionen in ihrem Zusammenhang mit der antiken Stadtherrschaft.* Frankfurt: Suhrkamp.

Marx, Karl, and Friedrich Engels. 1976. *Collected Works,* vol. V. Moscow: Progress Publishers.

Mies, Maria. 1988. *Patriarchy and Accumulation on a World Scale: Women in the International Division of Labor.* London: Zed.

Mies, Maria, Veronica Bennholdt-Thomsen, and Claudia von Werlhof. 1988. *Women, the Last Colony.* London: Zed.

Mumford, Lewis. 1977. *Mythos der Maschine.* Frankfurt: Fischer.

Paracelsus. 1990. *Die Geheimnisse, Ein Lesebuch aus seinen Schriften.* Edited by W.-E. Peuckert. Munich: Knaur.

Rifkin, Jeremy. 1983. *Algeny.* New York: The Viking Press.

Schumpeter, Josef A. 1962. *Capitalism, Socialism, and Democracy.* New York: Harper Torchbooks.

Schütz-Buenaventura, Ilse. 2000. *Globalismus contra Existentia: Das Recht des ursprünglich Realen vor dem Machtanspruch der Bewusstseinsphilosophie.* Vienna: Passagen.

Shiva, Vandana. 1992. *Monocultures of the Mind.* London: Zed.

Soros, George. 1998. *The Crisis of Global Capitalism: Open Society Endangered.* New York: Public Affairs.

Ullrich, Otto. 1977. *Technik und Herrschaft: Vom Hand-Werk zur verdinglichten Blockstruktur industrieller Produktion.* Frankfurt: Suhrkamp.

Unseld, Godela. 1992. *Maschinenintelligenz oder Menschenphantasie? Ein Plädoyer für den Ausstieg aus unserer technisch-wissenschaftlichen Kultur.* Frankfurt am Main: Suhrkamp.

Wallerstein, Immanuel. 1988. "The Ideological Tensions of Capitalism versus Racism and Sexism." Pp. 3–9 in *Racism, Sexism, and the World-System,* eds. J. Smith et al. New York: Greenwood Press.

Wallerstein, Immanuel. 2000. "The Racist Albatross: Social Science, Jorg Haider, and *Widerstand,*" presented at the "Von der Notwendigkeit der Beeinflussung—Sozialwissenschaften und Gesellschaft." (March). Vienna University.

Weiler, Gerda. 1993. *Eros ist stärker als Gewalt: Eine feministische Anthropologie I.* Frankfurt: Campus.

Weizenbaum, Joseph. 1978. *Die Macht der Computer und die Ohnmacht der Vernunft.* Frankfurt: Suhrkamp.

Werlhof, Claudia von. 1985. *Wenn die Bauern wiederkommen . . . Frauen, Arbeit und Agrobusiness in Venezuela.* Bremen: Periferia Verlag/Edition CON.

———. 1997a. "Ökonomie, die praktische Seite der Religion: Wirtschaft als Gottesbeweis und die Methode der Alchemie." Pp. 95–121 in *Ökonomie (M)macht Angst,* eds. U. Ernst et al. Frankfurt: Peter Lang.

———. 1997b. "Schöpfung aus Zerstörung? Die Gentechnik als moderne Alchemie und ihre ethisch-religiöse Rechtfertigung." Pp. 79–115 in *Genetik: Einführung und Kontroverse,* ed. W. Baier. Graz: Leykam Buchverlag.

———. 2000a. "'Globalization' and the 'Permanent' Process of 'Primitive Accumulation': The Example of the MAI, the Multilateral Agreement on Investment." In G. Arrighi and W. Goldfrank, eds., *Festschrift for Immanuel Wallerstein, Part II, Journal of World-Systems Research* VI, no. 3 (Fall/Winter): 728–47. Available at: http://jwsr.ucr.edu.

———. 2000b. "Patriarchat als 'Alchemistisches System': Die (Z)ErSetzung *des* Lebendigen." Pp. 13–31 in *Optimierung und Zerstörung: Intertheoretische Analysen zum menschlich-Lebendigen,* ed. M. Wolf. Innsbruck: STUDIA Universitätsverlag.

———. 2001a. "Marx's Own Contradiction, The Main Question until Yoday: Why Did He Not Propagate an Ecological Technology?" Unpublished paper, Innsbruck.

———. 2001b. "Loosing Faith in Progress: Capitalist Patriarchy as an 'Alchemical System.'" Pp. 15–40 in *There Is an Alternative: Subsistence and Worldwide Resistance to Corporate Globalization,* eds. V. Bennholdt Thomsen. London: Zed.

———. 2003. "(Haus) Frauen, 'Gender' und die Schein-Macht des Patriarchats." In *Widerspruch: Beiträge zu sozialistischer Politik,* no. 44, 23. Jg./1 Halbjahr: 173–189.

Wolf, Doris. 1994. *Was war vor den Pharaonen? Die Entdeckung der Urmütter Ägyptens.* Zürich: Kreuz.

5

Hegemony and
Antisystemic Movements

Giovanni Arrighi

Between 1982 and 1988, Terence K. Hopkins, Immanuel Wallerstein, and I wrote a series of essays on antisystemic movements that were reprinted in a book published the very year of the fall of the Berlin Wall (Arrighi et al. 1989). Three years later, we published an article that interpreted the events of 1989–1991 as a continuation of the main tendencies highlighted in that book, *Antisystemic Movements* (Arrighi et al. 1992). The purpose of this chapter is threefold. First, it aims to assess to what extent the arguments advanced in these writings remain valid. Second, it will use Antonio Gramsci's notions of "Piedmontese function" and "passive revolution" to amend some of the shortcomings of those arguments (Gramsci 1971). Finally, it shows how world hegemonies can be conceived as consisting of passive revolutions in Gramsci's sense.

The Great Rehearsal

The thesis advanced in *Antisystemic Movements* can be summed up in five propositions. First, opposition to oppression has been a constant of the modern world-system. Nevertheless, before the middle of the nineteenth century this opposition was short-term and "spontaneous," and as such, largely ineffectual at the level of the system. In the late nineteenth and early twentieth centuries, in contrast, opposition to oppression became organized in relatively permanent institutions with short- and long-term political objectives. This innovation had important repercussions on the dynamic of the world capitalist system, as specified by the second and third propositions below (Arrighi et al. 1989, 29–30).

Second, as instituted in the late nineteenth and early twentieth centuries, antisystemic movements were of two main varieties: movements that defined oppression in class terms and aimed at replacing capitalism with socialism (social movements); and movements that defined oppression in ethnonational terms and aimed at self-determination (national liberation movements). In spite of differences in their definition of the problem and in the social basis of their support, both kinds of movements saw the attainment of state power as the primary, mid-term objective in the pursuit of their respective long-term objectives of ending class and ethnonational oppression. And both kinds of movements tended to split over whether to seek state power through the legal path of political persuasion or the illegal path of insurrectionary force. This tendency was particularly strong in the social(ist) movement, which, during and after World War I, split into two increasingly antagonistic factions—a social-democratic and a communist faction (Arrighi et al. 1989, 30–32).

Third, divisions and antagonisms notwithstanding, this "family" of movements was eminently successful in attaining the intermediate objective of obtaining state power. Social-democratic parties came to power in a relatively large number of core countries, communist parties in a significant number of semiperipheral and peripheral countries, and nationalist parties in most peripheral countries. Antisystemic movements thus became collectively an increasingly consequential element in world politics. At the same time, however, they were distinctly less successful in moving toward their ultimate objectives. They did wrest many "concessions" from the world's ruling strata, but they failed in lessening inequalities between classes and ethnonations. Worse still, they often turned their institutional underpinnings into new instruments of class and/or ethnonational oppression (Arrighi et al. 1989, 33–34, 100–102).

Fourth, the new "family" of antisytemic movements that shook the world around 1968 was simultaneously a reaction against the recuperative powers of prosystemic forces under U.S. hegemony and against the poor, even negative, performance of the world's old Left movements—their "weakness, corruption, connivance, neglect and arrogance." The explosion of movements was a major contributing factor to the systemic crisis of the 1970s. Although the movements were soon checked everywhere, the changes in power relations effected by the movements were not reversed. Four main changes in particular persisted: (1) a reduced capacity of both world war states to police the Third World; (2) a reduced capacity of dominant status groups in core countries (older generations, males, "majorities") to exploit/ exclude subordinate status-groups (younger generations, females, "minorities"); (3) a reduced capacity of managerial strata to enforce labor discipline in the workplace and associated global search for "safe havens" of such discipline; and (4) a reduced capacity of states to control their respective civil societies and associated crisis of "bourgeois" and "proletarian" dictatorships alike (Arrighi et al. 1989, 103–6).

Finally, these changes in power relations in favor of subordinate groups and classes did not result in an improvement in the material welfare of the majority of each subordinate group. On the contrary, since the reproduction of material welfare under capitalism is premised upon the political and social subordination of the actual or potential laboring masses, the lessening of this subordination tended to reduce material welfare. This tendency, we suggested, probably underlay the cultural and political backlash of the late 1970s and of the 1980s against everything 1968 had stood for (Arrighi et al. 1989, 107–8).

Looking beyond this backlash, and having drawn a parallel between 1848 and 1968 as "great rehearsals," we had a hard time answering the question: "1968, rehearsal for what?" We projected probable realignments in the alliances of the interstate system, increased economic turbulence, a geographically widened class struggle, an increasing inability of states to control civil societies, and a persistent reinforcement of the claims to equality by all disadvantaged status groups. But we concluded the last essay in the series with a frank admission and a warning:

> We have no answer to the question: 1968, rehearsal for what? In a sense, the answers depend on the ways in which the worldwide family of antisystemic movements will rethink its middle-range strategy in the ten or twenty years to come. . . . The risks of drifting are very clear. The tenants of the status quo have not given up, however much their position is weakened structurally and ideologically. They still have enormous power and are using it to reconstruct a new inegalitarian world order. They could succeed. Or the world could disintegrate, from a nuclear or ecological catastrophe. Or it could be reconstructed in the way people hoped, in 1848, in 1968. (Arrighi et al. 1989, 115)

1989: The Continuation of 1968

These theses were advanced before 1989. When in 1989 the Soviet Empire began to unravel leading to the collapse of the USSR and of the

Second World, we had little difficulty in fitting the event in our scheme of things as "the continuation of 1968." Indeed, we redefined 1968 as only the beginning of a rehearsal that continued until 1989. In the double rejection that 1968 represented—of the present world-system and of the old Left antisystemic movements—the forces of the 1968 upheaval still persisted in holding onto two illusions of the old Left: the idea that the collapse of the system was imminent and that "there existed some alternative policy, easy at hand, which if adopted and pursued by the 'movement' would bring about 'revolution' and therewith true and full 'national development'. . . . The two decades between 1968 and 1989 swept away these remaining illusions" (Arrighi et al. 1992, 237).

> In that sense the 1989 finale of the 1968 world revolutionary rehearsal was far worse than the initial outburst, but also far better for the world's antisystemic forces. It was far worse because it lacked the incredible degree of joy and optimism that suffused the revolutionaries of 1968. . . . But it was better too, in that the last vestiges of the old left illusions seemed shattered, leaving space to reconstruct. No doubt the reconstruction would require that not only the old ideological scaffolding but its debris (the blather about the market as magic) had to be cleared away. Still, it had at least become possible to do so. (Arrighi et al. 1992, 238)

Once again, however, we had very little to say about the *what, who,* and *how* of the possible reconstruction. We reiterated the challenges and opportunities that the decline of the states as significant organizing centers of the global economy's development posed to antisystemic forces. We pointed out that "What movements and social groups expect in terms of democracy, human rights, equality, and quality of life has become extraordinarily high, just as the states find it increasingly difficult to meet these demands. This is the crunch the world-system is facing as the twentieth century comes to an end" (Arrighi et al. 1992, 232–36). And we again underscored: "The key problem for putative antisystemic movements in the 1990s is the search for a new or renewed ideology, that is, a set of strategies that offers some reasonable prospect for fundamental social transformation" (Arrighi et al. 1992, 239).

But all we had to say about this set of strategies is that they were absent and that their absence translated into an embarrassing silence of antisystemic movements North and South, concerning the three spontaneous claims of oppressed persons and groups: the right to total otherness; the right of power confrontation other than as part of a social project; and the right of instant egalitarianism. The old antisystemic movements had contested these claims on the ground that they were the bearers of a viable, and much more efficacious, alternative. But once the

new antisystemic movements had rejected this alternative as being neither viable nor efficacious without putting anything in its place, the old
antisytemic movements found it extremely difficult to deal with the spontaneous claims that came once more to the fore.

We illustrated these difficulties with the ambiguity with which antisystemic militants confronted three political situations "which may well
serve as prototypes for the forms of struggles of the next 30 years": the
Iranian revolution as the incarnation of the right to total otherness; the
Iraqi invasion of Kuwait as the incarnation of the right of power confrontation; and the massive unauthorized migration from South to North
as the incarnation of the right to instant egalitarianism. In the face of this
ambiguity, we concluded with a rhetorical question and a warning very
similar to that uttered on the eve of 1989: "where is . . . a new *strategy* for
transformation in the direction of a democratic, egalitarian world, the
erstwhile objective of the antisystemic movements? The dilemmas of the
antisystemic movements seem to be even more profound than those of
the dominant forces of the world-system. In any case, without a strategy,
there is no good reason to believe there is any invisible hand that will
guarantee transformation in a good direction, even when and if the
capitalist world-economy falls apart" (Arrighi et al. 1992, 242).

The Great Rehearsal Revisited

Looking back at these utterances and silences ten years later three main
critical considerations come to mind, inspired as much by the observation of trends and events as by the results of new research on the dynamic of the modern world-system (see, especially, Arrighi, Silver, et al.
1999). The first consideration concerns the nature and significance of the
neoliberal counterrevolution that occurred between 1979 and 1982. The
counterrevolution had a financial, a military, and a political aspect. The
financial aspect consisted of the U.S.-driven escalation of interstate competition for mobile capital. The military aspect consisted of a simultaneous escalation of the armament race with the USSR and the replacement
of direct involvement on the ground with wars by proxy through the
instrumental use of Third World conflicts. And the political aspect consisted
of the ideological and practical appropriation by the United States of the
antiauthoritarian and antistatist thrust of 1968. The year 1989 was as much
the result of this counterrevolution as it was the continuation of 1968. In
retrospect, it seems that we underestimated, and in key respects, missed
altogether what all this meant for antisystemic movements.

More specifically, the neoliberal counterrevolution did not just result
in the destruction of the illusions of the older family of antisystemic

movements, as we pointed out. We do not seem to have realized that it also had a profoundly corrupting and divisive impact on the 1968 family of antisystemic movements. In the North in general and in the United States in particular, the corruption of antisystemic forces has primarily taken the form of an uncritical acceptance of the benefits of financial expansion and of the conversion of dominant groups to the antiauthoritarian and antistatist thrust of 1968. In the South, it has taken the form of an equally uncritical acceptance of the neoliberal or some other religious creed as a prop or a substitute for the discredited ideology and practice of national emancipation. In themselves, these trajectories of corruption have divided—and increasingly alienated from one another—antisystemic forces within the South and between North and South. But underlying the division and mutual alienation of antisystemic forces was the success of the neoliberal counterrevolution in shifting competitive pressures from North to South. Corruption and divisions have not prevented antisystemic forces from resisting (with some success) further advances of the counterrevolution—from Seattle, through the formation and consolidation of the Social Forum, to the antiwar movement of 2003. But it remains unclear whether this resistance can produce an agency capable of promoting change in the direction of a more egalitarian and democratic world (see Silver and Arrighi 2001).

The second critical consideration concerns our failure to foresee, as we could have with a different understanding of the long-term dynamic of the modern world-system, the short- and mid-term impact of the counterrevolution and underlying financial expansion, not only on the antisystemic movements of 1968 but on the world capitalist system as instituted under U.S. hegemony. We failed to foresee, first, the inflation of U.S. world power that occurred in the 1990s and, second, the mid-term destabilization and possible systemic breakdown that seem to have begun in the early 2000s. Breakdowns of this kind have been typical of past hegemonic transitions—one may well be on the verge of occurring in the present transition as well (Arrighi and Silver 2001). But whether it does or not, the fact that in the present, as in previous transitions, prosystemic forces have unwittingly played a leading role in creating the conditions of the breakdown makes the very concept of antisystemic forces and movements problematic. It blurs the distinction between pro- and antisystemic forces, because nominally prosystemic forces engage in activities that destabilize the system, while nominally antisystemic forces engage in activities that have the opposite effect. The difficulties we face today in drawing such a distinction are not altogether different from those we still face in interpreting the 1930s and 1940s, when fascism and colonial imperialism were destabilizing forces and communism emerged as a stabilizing force.

Last but not least, looking beyond the *belle époque* of the 1990s and the incipient systemic chaos, we failed to appreciate the world-historical significance of the rise of East Asia as the new epicenter of the global economy. East Asia, most notably Vietnam and China, were the true epicenters of the world revolution of 1968. Whether there is any connection between this fact and the subsequent regional economic renaissance—with Japan, the Four Tigers, and the PRC as its successive protagonists—largely remains an open question. But the more important and equally open question is whether and how the relocation of the epicenter of the global economy from North America to East Asia will be affected economically, politically, and culturally by the incipient systemic chaos. More specifically, will the East Asian economic renaissance be overwhelmed by systemic chaos or will it be transformed into a political and cultural renaissance capable of leading the continuing revolt against the West toward the formation of a more egalitarian and democratic world order?

Gramsci's Piedmontese Function

It is with this connection that Gramsci's notion of a "Piedmontese function" becomes relevant to understanding the past and imagining the future of the "active" and "passive" revolutions of the world capitalist system. Gramsci introduced the concept with reference to the fact that in the Italian Risorgimento a state (Piedmont) exercised the function of a ruling class, that is, that a state replaced social groups in leading a struggle of renewal (1971, 104–6).

> The function of Piedmont in the Italian Risorgimento is that of a "ruling class." In reality, what was involved was not that throughout the peninsula there existed nuclei of a homogeneous ruling class whose irresistible tendency to unite determined the formation of the new Italian national State. These nuclei existed, indubitably, but their tendency to unite was extremely problematic; also, more importantly, they . . . were not "leading". . . . They . . . wanted a new force, independent of every compromise and condition, to become the arbiter of the Nation: this force was Piedmont. . . . Thus Piedmont had a function which can from certain aspects, be compared to that of a party, i.e., of the leading personnel of a social group (and in fact people always spoke of the "Piedmont party"): with the additional feature that it was in fact a State, with an army, a diplomatic service, etc. (Gramsci 1971, 104–5)

As Gramsci underscored, this substitution of a state for a class in leading a struggle for renewal was not, specifically, an Italian phenomenon. Thus, he mentioned Serbia before World War I as the unsuccessful "Piedmont of the Balkans." More importantly for our present purposes, he pointed out that the substitution was not merely a national phenomenon. Thus, in Gramsci's view, France after 1789 up to the *coup d'état* of Louis Napoléon acted as the "Piedmont of Europe" (Gramsci 1971, 105, 115–20). Whether at the national or at the international level, Gramsci saw a close connection between the exercise of a Piedmontese function and the unfolding of what (following Vincenzo Cuoco) he called "passive revolution." As Quintin Hoare points out in an editorial note, Gramsci used the expression "passive revolution" in two distinct and sometimes inconsistent ways. On the one hand, he used it to designate major social and political transformations that occur without mass participation under the impact of outside forces. On the other hand, he used it to designate "molecular" social transformations that occur behind the back and against the declared intentions of conservative/reactionary political regimes (Gramsci 1971, 46–47). These two kinds of transformations may happen (and have happened often, historically) concurrently, strengthening one another. Conceptually, however, they are distinct processes that may occur and, historically, have occurred independently of, or in opposition to, one another.

Bearing this in mind, Gramsci's discussion of nineteenth-century European history as a passive revolution provides us with some insights into the possible uses of his notion of the Piedmontese function in understanding the past and imagining the future of struggles for the renewal of the world social system. In this discussion, Gramsci maintains that the "[h]istorical relationship between the modern French state created by Revolution and the other modern states of continental Europe" created through passive revolutions is one of the most vital aspects of nineteenth-century European history. He goes on to list four elements on which the study of this relationship should be based:

1. revolutionary explosion in France with radical and violent transformation of social and political relations;
2. European opposition to the French Revolution and to any extension of it along class lines;
3. war between France, under the Republic and Napoléon, and the rest of Europe—initially, in order to avoid being stifled at birth, and subsequently, with the aim of establishing a permanent French hegemony tending towards the creation of a universal empire;
4. national revolts against French hegemony, and birth of the modern European states[,] by successive small waves of reform rather than by revolutionary explosions like the original French one. The "successive waves" were made up of a combination of social struggles, interventions from above of the enlightened monarchy type, and national wars—with the two latter phenomena predominating (Gramsci 1971, 114–15).

In proposing these four processes as objects of study, Gramsci insisted on their fundamental unity and took to task Benedetto Croce for starting his narrative of European history in 1815. By so doing, Croce excluded "the moment of struggle; the moment in which the conflicting forces are formed, are assembled and take up their position; . . . the moment in which one system of social relations disintegrates and another arises and asserts itself." As a result, Croce produced only "a fragment of history" that focused exclusively on the "passive" aspects of the longer revolutionary process that "started in France in 1789 and . . . spilled over into the rest of Europe with the republican and Napoleonic armies" (Gramsci 1971, 119).

Gramsci's main interest in reconstructing France's Piedmontese function in the nineteenth-century renewal of European states was to gain some insight into a process that, in his view, was tending to recur in the wake of the Russian Revolution. As he explicitly asked:

> Does the conception of the "passive revolution" have a "present" significance? Are we in a period of "restoration-revolution" to be permanently consolidated, to be organized ideologically, to be exalted lyrically? Does Italy have the same relation *vis-à-vis* the USSR that the Germany (and Europe) of Kant and Hegel had *vis-à-vis* the France of Robespierre and Napoleon? (1971, 118)

Gramsci never answered these questions explicitly, and an analysis of his implicit answers falls beyond the scope of this chapter. All I can do is conclude with a few observations concerning the world-historical significance of Gramsci's twin conceptions of passive revolution and Piedmontese function.

World Hegemonies as Passive Revolutions

As Beverly Silver (2003) has shown, major explosions of social conflicts were crucial components of past hegemonic transitions. They were not merely a factor in the destruction of the old hegemonic world order. In addition, they contributed to defining the social contents of the emerging hegemonic world order by bringing to the fore demands and aspirations of subordinate groups that the new dominant bloc, under the leadership of the rising hegemonic state, selectively repressed and accommodated.

There is a close resemblance between the "repression-accommodation" process through which successive hegemonic powers have increased the social inclusiveness of the world capitalist system and the "restoration-revolution" process that characterizes Gramsci's passive revolutions. Indeed, we may say that each successive hegemony of world capitalism has been characterized by a particular passive revolution, in the course of which the hegemonic state exercised a Piedmontese function vis-à-vis the world capitalist system as a whole. The central question of the twenty-first century is whether the renewal/transformation of the world social system toward greater equality and democracy still requires the exercise of a Piedmontese function and, if it does, which state or coalition of states will have the capabilities and dispositions necessary to exercise it.

A proliferating literature on the crisis of national states and the formation of a transnational capitalist class and world proletariat implicitly or explicitly rules out both the need and the possibility of such a function. Some advocate the formation of a purely class-based "world party" as the most likely agency of the egalitarian and democratic renewal of world society (e.g., Boswell and Chase-Dunn 2000). Others see a rebellious and mobile world proletariat (or "multitude") as already poised to attain instant egalitarianism through massive unauthorized migration from South to North (e.g., Hardt and Negri 2000).

These assessments of both the present and future of antisystemic forces, like some of our own assessments in *Antisystemic Movements*, miss the significance of the U.S.-led neoliberal counterrevolution of the 1980s and 1990s in reflating U.S. world power through an accommodation of the antiauthoritarian and antistatist aspirations of 1968 and a simultaneous repression of its egalitarian aspirations. The result of this new passive revolution has been a general crisis of dictatorships and a sharp increase in between-state and within-state inequality—an increase that belies the idea of increasing equality under the impact of massive migration and makes the idea of a purely class-based "world party" extremely problematic.

From this standpoint, the East Asian economic renaissance has had a major contradictory impact. On the one hand, it has been the single most important force counteracting the tendency toward greater inequality among countries and world regions. On the other hand, it has contributed to growing inequality within countries (Arrighi et al. 2003). As a result of these contrasting tendencies and the growing industrial, commercial, and financial weight of the region in the global economy, East Asia (in general) and China (in particular) have emerged as the arbiters of the egalitarian and nonegalitarian tendencies that confront one another in the ongoing hegemonic transition to a yet unknown destination.

At the present stage of the confrontation, it is impossible to tell which tendency will eventually prevail. The outcome largely depends on the kind of social conflicts that will emerge out of the growing inequality within countries and on the kind of regional order/disorder that will emerge out of these conflicts. Whatever the outcome, however, it is hard to believe that states will not actively intervene in the struggles— not just in support of particular social groups but also as their substitutes, thereby exercising some kind of Piedmontese function. It is unlikely that in exercising this function, any individual East Asian state can become hegemonic globally. However, it is not just possible but likely that, individually or collectively, East Asian states will play a decisive role in shaping the social contents of any future world order.

References

Arrighi, Giovanni, Terence K. Hopkins, and Immanuel Wallerstein. 1989. *Antisystemic Movements*. London: Verso.

Arrighi, Giovanni, Po-keung Hui, Ho-Fung Hung, and Mark Selden. 2003. "Historical Capitalism, East and West." Pp. 256–333 in *The Rise of East Asia: 500, 150, 50 Year Perspectives*, eds. G. Arrighi, T. Hamashita, and M. Selden. London and New York: Routledge.

Arrighi, Giovanni, Beverly Silver, et al. 1999. *Chaos and Governance in the Modern Worldsystem*. Minneapolis, MN: University of Minnesota Press.

Arrighi, Giovanni, and Beverly J. Silver. 2001. "Capitalism and World (Dis)order." *Review of International Studies* 27: 257–79.

———. 1992. "1989: The Continuation of 1968." *Review* 15, no. 2: 221–42.

Boswell, Terry, and Christopher Chase-Dunn. 2000. *The Spiral of Capitalism and Socialism: Toward Global Democracy*. Boulder, CO: Lynne Rienner.

Gramsci, Antonio. 1971. *Selections from the Prison Notebooks*. New York: International Publishers.

Hardt, Michael, and Antonio Negri. 2000. *Empire*. Cambridge, MA: Harvard University Press.

Silver, Beverly. 2003. *Forces of Labor: Workers' Movements and Globalization since 1870*. New York and Cambridge: Cambridge University Press.

Silver, Beverly, and Giovanni Arrighi. 2001. "Workers North and South." *The Socialist Register*. 2001: 51–74.

6

Present Systemic Trends and Antisystemic Movements

Pablo González Casanova

"American people ought to know that it is not them but their government policies that are so hated."
—Arundhati Roy, *The Guardian*, London, September 29, 2001

The 2001 War and Antisystemic Alternatives

The course and discourse of the dialectic of alternatives will have to capture the emerging facets of a persistent system that refuses to die and is not prepared to make any concessions in its increasingly unfair, deregulated, excluding, and aggressive neoliberal policy.

The 2001 alternatives are different from those of the twentieth century. Now, the United States is supposed to be leading a world war against terrorism, without solving either of the two main problems that create terrorism: first, the existence of paramilitary groups, dirty war, unconventional warfare, and low-intensity warfare, at the service of repressive, military-business complexes; and secondly, the growing poverty and exploitation produced by globalizing neoliberal policy.

Instead of destroying the paramilitary apparatuses of low-intensity war and positing the need for a new social pact, the dominant forces declared a world war on arbitrarily defined terrorism, whose principal victims will be the poor. If the Intercontinental Encounter, organized by the Zapatistas in August 1996, called for a fight "[a]gainst neoliberalism and for mankind," G-7, led by the United States, has declared what seems to be a "War for Neoliberalism and against mankind" (First International Encounter for Mankind and against Neoliberalism 2001). This is not an overstatement. As Noam Chomsky said: "This new type of war is an assault against the poor and oppressed people of the World" (Cason and Brooks 2001). It includes the oppressed and poor people of the periphery and the core countries.

The onward great war is certainly not conjunctural and may constitute the end and the beginning of a lengthy historical process. It was triggered by the terrorist attacks against the New York World Trade Center and the Pentagon. Michel Chossudovsky elaborates on the hypothesis that the terrorist attack is a "fabricated blowback" in which proxy terrorists armed and trained by both the United States and England, while accused of betraying their sponsors, continue to obey them (Chossudovsky 2001a).[1] It may be so. New facts, coming from the government of India, seem to confirm what is far from an "idiotic conspiracy hypothesis" (Chossudovsky 2001a). But every serious analysis also includes as significant actors some "desperadoes" full of "cold anger." They do not attack the American symbols of freedom and democracy, "but exactly the opposite things, the U.S. government record of commitment and support to military and economic terrorism, destabilization, insurgency, military dictatorship, religious bigotry and unimaginable genocide outside America" (Roy 2001).

Because of its side effects, the "new war" may be interpreted as a means of dealing with the spiraling economic crisis. It may be interpreted as the continuity of a policy that has lost its legitimacy and that resorts to war against alternative movements and their grassroots supporters at home and abroad (Van Creveld 1991; Navarro 2001). It can be interpreted as part of a strategy for attacking the civil and political organizations that fight for democracy and against neoliberalism. Being at once a defensive and an offensive project, this new war seems to form part of an internal and international project for a world empire in which the United States will increasingly, and overtly, play the role of the sovereign. In any case, the "fourth world war" forces one to reformulate the problem of alternatives to the dominant system and its policies.

Alternatives have changed and will continue to change. In recent history, social movements have expanded both their demands and networks. Their enemy has been redefined and is now in a process of redefining them. It has just declared a worldwide "low-intensity war" whose "side effects" negatively impact civil and political organizations that fight for democracy and against neoliberalism. Both facts, the redefinition of social movements and of the dominant state and its allies, must be considered when examining the strategies put forward for the new antisystemic social movements.

How Emerging Social Movements Have Changed

From the First International Encounter for Mankind and Against Neoliberalism (organized in 1996 by the Zapatistas) to The Other Davos (1999), Seattle (1999), Porto Alegre (2000), and Genoa (2001), the mass protests and organizations against neoliberal policies and globalization have acquired increasing force. Neoliberal governments suffered a growing loss of legitimacy, and it proved impossible for the officials and heads of state of the World Bank, the International Monetary Fund (IMF), World Trade Organization (WTO), and the Group of 7 or 8 (G-7; G-8) to meet. The political systems and the heads of state of the peripheral nations and also those of major powers were involved in corruption or personal scandals and lost their legitimacy both as individuals and leaders. The problem of lack of governance became the order of the day. Conservative forces often expressed their concern over the inability of heads of state to prevent disorder and demonstrations. If alternative movements became radicalized, so did conservative forces.

Not only were demonstrations staged against neoliberalism and its policies, but also a new democratic project, with the power of the world's people and an increasingly widespread anticapitalist position, began to emerge. Many examples include:

- European March from Amsterdam in 1997;
- demonstration of trade union and social organizations in Belo Horizonte in 1997;
- Second Encounter for Mankind in Barcelona in 1997;
- Conference of the People in Geneva in 1998;
- People's Summit in Santiago, Chile (1998);
- activists from thirty countries in Paris in 1998;
- Global Action Day in Geneva in 1998;
- Global Action Conference in Bangalore in 1999;
- Cry of the Excluded in several Latin American countries in 1999;
- Popular Summit against External Debt in Johannesburg in 1999;
- Trade Union Summit in Montevideo in 1999;
- Third Encounter for Mankind in Belem in 1999;

- mass protests in Davos in 2000;
- mobilizations in Bangladesh and the protests of the American people in Washington in 2000;
- "May 1," 2000 throughout the world;
- demonstration of the white monkeys in Bologna in 2000;
- Alternative Summit in Geneva in 2000;
- Japanese mobilizations in Okinawa in 2000;
- Second Meeting of Trade Union Confederations in Brasília in 2000;
- Millennium Encounter in New York in 2000;
- Women's World March against the World Bank in Washington in 2000; and
- mobilizations and protests in Nice, Dakar, and Florianopolis in 2000.

The culmination of these events occurred in Genoa, where the presidents and other heads of state of the most powerful nations on Earth were forced, for security reasons, to dine in their hotel rooms. These are all symptoms of a disillusioned world that is no longer willing to tolerate the current situation ("Cronología internacional del movimento antimundialización" 2001).

The social movements and political organizations that demonstrated peacefully were increasingly disturbed by radical groups and infiltrated by policemen disguised as protesters. Radical groups occupied the scene. Their antiauthoritarianism practice revealed their authoritarianism and the capacity of violence of both the masses and the state. The "metropolitan version of low intensity war" mobilized thousands of *carabinieri* and *polizia montata* (Albertani 2001). Out of 300,000 demonstrators, thirty thousand participated in acts of violence. Genoa's scenario confirmed the inevitable dialectic between "desperadoes" and civic action forces. It also confirmed the way dominant forces behave when they lose their hegemonic power. Well-known *agents provocateurs* served to prevent dialogue and demobilize citizens and people. They also served to justify repression against social movements. The ruling classes proved that they feared social movements more than any terrorist act—more because social movements not only exert pressure on the periphery but also on the center of the world. They not only involve the poorest of the poor but also students, organized workers, employees, and the middle classes who feel deceived and abused, deregulated and impoverished by neoliberal policy and by a democracy that is not a democracy. Many movements took a great step forward; they not only learned from the Marxists that capitalism exists, but from capitalism itself, which is beginning to openly dominate the world scenery.

The Other Davos was a call to change the course of history. It was a call to fight for the economy at the service of the people: It exhorted the people of the world to knock down the wall between North and South, to transform dignity into power, to reject the power of money, to democratize the state, and to raise nations' hopes (Houtart and Polet 2001).

At the Prague Declaration of September 28, 2000, the socialist project was proposed once again without being named as such: "There is a need for a revolution in the economy that will restore power to the people who live off it." It also called to "place the economy at the service of people" and "for the rich and powerful to stop running the economy." The bitter memory of the failure of socialism did not overshadow the fact that the damage caused by capitalism is enormous. In its 2000 report, the World Bank confessed that the "economic transition from the Soviet Union and Eastern Europe resulted in a tenfold increase in poverty in the region." As usual, the World Bank described the evils caused by a policy that it continues to promote ("Documentos del Conflicto" 2001; Chandra 2001).

The criticisms and proposals of social movements continued to focus on the struggle against neoliberalism, but with criticisms that pointed toward a nonsystemic alternative. The international movement ATTAC (Association pour la Taxation des Transactions financières pour l'Aide aux Citoyens), for the control of financial markets and its institutions, not only proposed a tax on financial speculation but also the elimination of "tax havens." At the same time, it proposed extremely attractive measures for victims that constitute the outlines of the antisystemic movement. They include the need for democracy in the financial field itself and in the management of international organizations, the defense of the sovereignty of nation-states in relation to so-called postcolonialism, and the creation of a world democratic sphere.

The farm workers' meeting in Bangalore criticized the "economic model" and the "economic order" and asked to reinforce democratic processes, beginning with the popular organizations themselves.

The sense of ideological change continued at the Women's Summit in Beijing. Women criticized *neoliberal* capitalism using the adjective to moderate their criticism. They also criticized *liberal* democracy with an adjective that specified the type of democracy they were criticizing, and distinguished it from the type of democracy they would like to have. The women also expressed their rejection of present-day capitalism and patriarchy. They did not reduce their commitment to fight the class struggle, but instead, enriched it with the gender struggle.

In Genoa, all the protest flags were waved furiously—many people were incensed by the blindness and deafness of the ruling classes. They caused a scene in order to be heard; they staged riots and insulting, threatening, antiestablishment acts. A forgotten phenomenon wound its way through the crowds and occupied the center of the scene. Agents provocateurs were planted among the genuinely desperate protesters.

Another death was added to the list of those engaged in the fight for a better world.

Shortly afterward, the world witnessed the monstrous acts of terrorism against the World Trade Center in New York and the Pentagon in Washington, D.C. Those involved followed the war cry of the North American wars against the Native Americans when soldiers realized they were in danger of being destroyed: "Kill and be killed." Except this time, the war cry was uttered by a group of terrorists identified with former Central Intelligence Agency (CIA) agents and the fundamentalists of the Islamic world. These acts triggered a no less monstrous response: a permanent world war on terrorism led by the U.S. government. The outbreak substantially changed the struggle for a democratic, socialist alternative. It called for a change in the struggle and a reaffirmation of the pathways that would be more likely to achieve democracy, freedom, and justice under the new conditions.

The Principal Stages of Change

The principal stages of change is a very long story. What happened in 2001 was at least three decades in the making. Neoliberalism has changed since 1970, and, by 2001, G-1 (the political, military, and business complex that dominates the United States) has gone one and half times around the world.

Globalizing neoliberalism had its origins in the 1970s. As Immanuel Wallerstein has shown, by the late 1960s and the beginning of the 1970s, "the profits of production drop considerably" and the downward phase of the Kondratieff cycle has begun (2000). Neoliberalism emerged as an answer to the growing contradictions of real socialism and to powerful attacks led by organized workers in the central countries. The Soviet bloc started supporting liberation struggles and wars in Africa. Left and liberation movements initiated a socialist project in Chile. The sheiks and oil-producing countries seriously affected several members of G-7. If neoliberalism was a response by the ruling classes to declining profits and the economic crisis that broke out in 1973, it was also the policy that the ruling classes organized in the political-military-industrial complex of the United States and G-7. They imposed neoliberalism, with their networks of power and accumulation, on the forces that had achieved a series of social and national concessions during the earlier stage.

Corporate capital and its political, military, and ideological complex took the offensive around 1973. The United States not only had eliminated the gold standard, thereby considerably increasing its financial power at the expense of its associates, but also led the new project of neoliberal globalization.

During this first stage from 1973 to 1980, neoliberalism wore down the resistance of workers and the nation-states (Sader 2001). It ended, or helped to end, strikes, populist, nationalist and communist regimes, social democracies and, above all, the Soviet bloc that had already been eroded by corruption and dogmatic totalitarianism and many of whose leaders were anxious to restore capitalism. Pinochet, supported by the United States and the Chilean oligarchy in 1973, overthrew the socialist government and pioneered the neoliberal structural changes that were subsequently implemented worldwide. The neoliberal policy, first adopted in Chile in the aftermath of a bloody coup d'état, was later applied in the rest of the world using the necessary flexibility. One of the major goals of neoliberalism was to weaken the public sector, particularly in regard to social security and social or welfare policy. Starting in the periphery of the world, neoliberal strategy subsequently organized authoritarian governments, with military and civil bureaucracies, designed to maximize transnational power and business. During that same era, G-3 reinforced the interfaces of dependence of Third World governments, enterprises, and markets. It facilitated governments' internal and external debt in return for providing considerable freedom for creditors to increase interest rates as (and when) they wished. At the same time, a redefined U.S. empire denounced the incompetence and corruption of populist governments while extolling the virtues of free enterprise and the free market in ways that gradually took hold of general beliefs— particularly after the years of corruption and the deterioration of nationalist, social-democratic, labor, and communist governments. Corruption and deterioration were further exacerbated primarily when the subsequent privatization and denationalization took place.

During the second stage, in the 1980s, neoliberalism became the dominant ideology in Latin America and the rest of the world. It was portrayed as a solid, scientific belief, supported by the financial centers and major powers, renowned economists and advertisers, political managers and modern politicians. It raised great hopes for a project of limited democracy to combat the authoritarianism and corruption of communist or populist regimes. At the same time, it continued facilitating the indebtedness of the former Third World and the privatization of the public sector. Privatization, denationalization, and drug trafficking turned corruption into both a form of negotiation and of exercising power. Moreover, neoliberalism endlessly legitimized its decisions by invoking the "unique science" on which it was said to be based, echoing Thatcher's belief: "There is no alternative" (TINA). Thus, the neoliberal globalizing complex imposed its adjustment, deregulation, and flexibility policies, implementing them not only in the periphery but also in the center of the world. The British Conservative Party pioneered the First World strategy. Neoliberalism reached its climax with the fall of the Berlin Wall and the humiliating defeat of "real existing socialism."

The third stage, beginning in approximately 1993, saw the start of social movements that opposed neoliberalism with a "new hegemonic project" and a minimum, rebellious reform program that was the "denial and overcoming of neoliberal frameworks" (Sader 2001). The "new hegemonic project" organized a menacing show in America itself. The collapse of the WTO Round in Seattle was the result of an American and international mass movement. Thousands of ecologists, feminists, students, and human right activists united with political, agricultural, and labor organizations. The movement seemed to be a new American front of radical protest with class and antisystemic global links. Nothing like it had happened in America in previous rallies, not even during the mass demonstrations against the war in Vietnam. The alternative project was gaining force even in the core of the "core countries" (Thomas 2000; Seoane and Taddei 2001).

While the alternative project gained force in the world and in America, the military-industrial complex increased its strength not only in the Middle East and Central Europe but also in the rest of the world. During this stage, the United States assumed all the symbolic roles of the sovereign. It expressed its lack of desire to comply with United Nations law— its right not to meet its international commitments, together with its right to denounce, imprison, judge, and punish, out of its own jurisdiction, those it declared guilty anywhere in the world, regardless of whether they were heads of state. With satellites and the most advanced aircraft, the United States imposed its right to spy on all territories and to bomb nation-states such as Iraq, a country it considered necessary to control, weaken, or punish. It expressed its right to bomb other countries in order to bring criminals to justice, particularly those accused of drug trafficking, beginning with Noriega, the president of Panama, whom it imprisoned after heavily bombing the poor neighborhoods of the capital. Those who thought that the United States was preparing to be a world policeman were underestimating its will. It was getting ready to be the world's sovereign. It was preparing to be the leader and lord of the world in order to enlist the world in its ranks, to regulate and deregulate the world, and to associate it with war or peace, which the world would declare anywhere against any enemy at any time. The U.S. government, practically and symbolically, assumed the part of the world's prosecutor, judge, and policeman. It took on the role of the standard-bearer of freedom and good. But it also sought the support of the largest number of governments, governors, groups of power, and interest groups. It created a sort of International of oligarchies, bourgeoisie, complexes, and elites that would permanently ensure the freedom of markets and the neoliberal credo.

The Principal Alternative

The world war on terrorism, declared in the aftermath of the suicide attacks on the Pentagon and the World Trade Center, had been foreseen by the Pentagon. In 1988, a commission of specialists submitted a "very important report on what the long-term strategy of the United States should be." The commission comprised a former undersecretary of defense, a military analyst who had worked for the Rand Corporation for years, and a former NATO chief. Other prominent members included Henry Kissinger, Zbigniew Brzezinski, Samuel Huntington, and other top-level experts and commanders. Some of the main conclusions reached by this commission were as follows (Gray 1997, 225):

1. The political need to recognize "The growing irrelevance of NATO in the face of the collapse of the Soviet Empire."
2. The need to recognize that U.S. hegemony was declining, and even more so, that of the former USSR. According to the commission, future struggles would take place within "a far more complicated environment than the familiar bipolar competition with the Soviet Union." Over forty countries would be equipped to produce advanced weapons, including atomic, chemical, and biological weapons, as well as missile systems and devices for using them. At the same time, "a broader range of challenges [would emerge] in the Third World that would require highly mobile forces."
3. Since the Cold War with the Soviet Union had ended, "'the wise men'" (quotes in original) "who wrote the report advocated terming Low Intensity Conflicts a form of 'protracted war.' When possible, these threats should be met with U.S. financed, trained and armed 'proxy forces,' supported from afar with long-range precision guided weapons." Chris Hables Gray arrived at the following conclusion: "Basically, the report is a call for the relegitimation of warfare. LICs are to be rehabilitated as 'protracted war'" (1997, 225–26).

The global, cybernetic, information science, and robotic nature of this warfare, planned and carried out with interconnected "war networks," failed to conceal the fact that, although it would be a global war, the main battlefields would be in the Third World. Nor was it able to hide the fact that the "human warriors" deployed in the battlefields would form part of unconventional, paramilitary native forces, supported by the great power and its allies.

What the report neglected to mention was that low-intensity conflict is a new form of colonial and class war. Low-intensity conflict is not cyberwar or old-fashioned class struggle. It is colonial and class war combined with total warfare against the nations and people that defend their sovereignty and autonomy, wealth, fuel, and surplus and who suffer marginalization, exclusion, exploitation, and discrimination. It is also war against the governments and states that refuse to submit to the "global empire" of domination and appropriation of territories and wealth and which fail to cooperate in the repression and exploitation of people and workers. It is an updated colonial war (postcolonial) and a postmodern class war in which the empire of G-8, G-7, G-3, or G-1 subjugates markets, governors, people, and workers at the same time as it participates in dialogue and negotiates with them so that they will contribute to their own subjugation. Their subjugation will not only be the consequence of the violence imposed on them by the empire but also the result of an agreement, of a contract in which free men and free people make a rational decision to negotiate their surrender as citizens, workers, people, firms, or governments.

The global empire supports all the authoritarian regimes that support it through the Bible or the Koran, on the understanding that they will have to bear the consequences if they refuse to do so. The global empire increasingly demonstrates that low-intensity conflict is the form that has been assumed by the struggle for domination and appropriation. It is the class and colonial struggle waged in the twenty-first century by the great military and business complexes and their associates from the oligarchies, elites, and bourgeoisie of both the center and periphery. It is a shared, hierarchical project of domination and accumulation.

The legitimacy of the low-intensity war is no longer based on the vague definition of enemies as Communists or on the doubtful justification of joint actions with Third World military men for pursuing drug traffickers. The new legitimization of war is based on a form of terrorism defined by the sovereign in its capacity as the representative of good against evil. In a memorable lay-religious ceremony at the Congress, President Bush authorized the global empire and its associates to brand all those that sought to "subvert" the established order as terrorists. The only ethical and sacralized violence is that of the hegemonic state, its partners, and its agents. Any terrorist state or individual who follows the United States's lead is not considered a "terrorist" but a "freedom fighter." In regard to the legal struggles for social justice, democracy, and freedom, they are reduced to increasingly narrow fields—not only because of the restrictions on civil rights imposed for "security reasons" to defend "Enduring Freedom" but also because the deregulation and loss of the social rights of people, citizens, and workers will tarry.

Global Trends 2015: A Dialogue about the Future with Nongovernment Experts was published by the National Intelligence Council (2000–2002).

The authors foresee a world in which the United States will be the "key driver of the international system and its main beneficiary." It openly considers that "the top priority of the American private sector, which will be central to maintaining the U.S. economic and technological lead, will be financial profitability, not foreign policy" (National Intelligence Council 2000–2002, 21). A prognosis of financial earnings in the middle of a "chaotic" world does not change avid accumulation policies. Globalization will go on supporting the present model of accumulation with slight changes in investments and "dramatic" changes in governments designed to increase the security and power of the United States and its allies (National Intelligence Council 2000–2002).

The redefinition of the dominant forces calls for a redefinition of the alternatives. The new war waged by Washington and its numerous allies hinders the struggle for democracy, liberation, and socialism. It legitimizes state terrorism and takes up the witch-hunting of the Cold War with all the necessary arbitrariness. It eliminates much of international law and national rights, in both practice and form. It defines as culprits those among the upper classes who refuse to submit to the empire and those from the lower classes who continue fighting for their rights within the law. It reinforces its own positions with highly vertical, disciplined defensive and offensive referents. It militarizes minds and culture, among pragmatic variants and fanciful legitimators who invoke liberty and God.

The war between good and evil compels alternative movements fighting for a freer, more just world to choose between submission and rebellion. They are obliged to use different degrees of violence ranging from civil insubordination to armed defense to rebellion with or without terrorist actions. Within a context of criticisms that are not dealt with, amid social reforms that are rejected, and agreements that are not fulfilled, the system encourages a form of opposition that does not interfere with its neoliberal policies of domination and appropriation. At the same time, the dominant system becomes increasingly willing to use all kinds of coercion against those who oppose the dictates of the World Bank, the IMF, and the political and financial organizations of neoliberal globalization. After demonstrations in Seattle (Nov. 1999), and mainly after September 11, 2001, it counterattacks "the possible emergence of what might be called decentralized progressive struggle on a global scale" and it reinforces "its drive to cement a supra-national trade and investment regime that extends the power of the strongest industrialized nations and transnational corporations" (Marais 2000). The low-intensity war becomes a complex global colonial and class war in which the dominant system is determined to triumph by redefining the world through repression and negotiation.

Once all the original options for an alternative policy to globalizing neoliberalism have been closed, old and new antisystemic alternatives *important point of view!*

are put forward. Over time, the neglect of critical thought, the alignment of political parties with neoliberalism, and the reforms that are both deregulations and counterreforms lead to growing abstention and conformity but also to the reemergence of the classic choice between reform or revolution. Yet another alternative emerges: the creation of new social relations without thinking in reformist or insurrectionary terms. The point is to think in terms of a new revolution that is predominantly political and ethical—the only means of triumphing in a low-intensity world war.

Social movements at the beginning of the twenty-first century have seen the emergence of at least three new theses that redefine the world history of alternatives. All of them have started since 1968, the plaintiff year in which a new revolution was born, "full of hopes as much as discontents" (Arrighi, Hopkins, and Wallerstein 1989, 97–115).

The first thesis consists of proposing the creation of new social relations within civil society and within the units of political society that manage to impose, by law or in fact, a system of autonomies in government, culture, and the economy. It does not envisage islands of well-being, production and consumption cooperatives, or self-managing firms, but rather networks of social networks and autonomous units that will prepare an alternative world by training citizens, workers, and people from now onward to design their plans of government and the management of wealth and surplus. Classic experiences of autonomy and self-management exist not only in communities and organizations but also in sets of articulated communities and organizations.

The second thesis consists of combining the fight for reform with the construction of new social relations and of combining both with the defensive armed actions in which nations are obliged to engage. At the same time, it is necessary to reject any attempt to centralize the various positions. According to experience, alliances must be based on ways of thinking and acting, in which, although one particular pathway is chosen, others are respected. Each collective actor involved in liberation is usually allowed to retain his moral and political responsibility. The fact that combination predominates over disjunction will not prevent the new movements from trying to ensure the hegemony of the peaceful creation of alternatives within the antisystemic process. The struggle for peaceful solutions should also be led by those who are obliged to establish defense systems to protect themselves from the violence caused by low-intensity conflict.

The third thesis consists of fighting for a pluralistic democracy with the power of the people. The participatory and representative nature of this democracy distinguishes it from previous alternatives. The cultivation of ideological pluralism enriches the humanitarian legacy of liberalism, democracy, socialism, communism, national liberation, liberation theology, the New Left of 1968, and critical Marxist and libertarian thought in general. It proposes an alternative that includes the ideological and cultural elements of a universal socialist project in the center of the democratic project.

Social movements that tend to become antisystemic are anticapitalistic yet they give priority to the democratic, pluralistic project as the means of conceiving the transition to socialism and of conceiving socialism. They give priority to the construction of a democracy with the power of the people and pluralism. The objective of a democracy made up of several democracies with the power of the people, workers, and citizens is an objective that combines far more forces than the socialist objective. Moreover, it is the only means of constructing as "side intelligence" a genuine form of socialism, which would go from the local to the global level. Democracy will lead the practice of new values in social relations of production and distribution. Participatory budgets in Brazilian local governments are but one example of this issue. There are many more in the world.

Paradoxically, the road to democracy today links what were superficially regarded as opposites during the long period of the Cold War: democracy and socialism. Successfully combating low-intensity conflict, which includes repression, dialogue, negotiation, and co-optation, requires acknowledging the pedagogical and structural importance of political morality for the construction of power, in order to be able to cope with the double power of the state and the market, of repression and negotiation, on people's consciences.

Coping with a low-intensity world war will also involve giving priority to the struggle for political, social, cultural, and economic rights, from the local to the national to the global level. It will involve a different type of participation by citizens, workers, and the people. In it, a pluralistic democracy with the power of the people will prevail over any project that attempts to construct socialism without practicing democracy. The logic of pluralistic democracy will take precedence over the pathetic logic of socialism without democracy and over the militaristic logic of security. In this respect, the principal antisystemic alternative will continue to be an eminently political, pedagogical, and moral process. However uncertain it may be, it is the only one that will enable nations to win the low-intensity war and construct the power of universal socialism within society, based on a democratic, pluralistic form of world power.

All these issues are subject to increasing pressures. As usual, a climate of war is a serious hindrance to civil liberties, freedom of expression, and peaceful political and social struggles. The issues of the new democratic project may prove to be deceptive in the historical period we are entering. According to Wallerstein, during this period, the "amount of day-by-day violence in the world system will increase." The construction of an antisystemic alternative will suffer the "ongoing processes of the existing world-system" (2000). The National Intelligence Council report, *Global Trends 2015: Dialogue about the Future with Nongovernment Experts*, forecasts a growing gap in the standard of living in the world. It also anticipates "increasingly commercial rather than security calculations in the diffusion of weapons and military related technologies" (National Intelligence Council 2000–2002, 59). Consequently, it says proliferation will tend to spur a reversion to prolonged, low-level conflict by other means: intimidation, subversion, terrorism, proxies, and "guerrilla operatives." In its general scenario, internal conflicts, "exploitation of communal divisions" (National Intelligence Council 2000–2002, 58), as well as "urban fighting" will be typical.

Unconventional warfare will put great pressure on a transitional society trying to build up new social relations in government and the economy. As usual, antisystemic groups will reproduce part of the systemic structures of domination and accumulation. To build democracies with pluralism and power will be more difficult. It will be necessary to overcome adversaries' pressures and authoritarian or greedy partisans' tilts. In an environment of broad warfare policies and technologies, nonmaterial elements of democratic and egalitarian values will increase in importance. The general and efficient practice of values will, in fact, decide the transition.

Note

1. See also http://globalresearch.ca/articles/CHO110A.html.

References

Albertani, Claudio. 2001. "Paint It Black: Provocatori, Blocchi Neri e Tute Bianche nel movimento antiglobalizzazione." Available at: www.sindominio.net/etcetera/CORRESPONDENCIA/albertani.htm.

Arrighi, Giovani, Terence K. Hopkins, and Immanuel Wallerstein. 1989. *Antisystemic Movements*. London: Verso.

Cason, Jim, and David Brooks. 2001. "Entrevista con Noam Chomsky." *La Jornada*. September 15. Available at http://www.jornada.unam.mx/2001/sep01/010915/006n1mun.html.

Chandra, Nirmal Kumar. 2001. "Can Russia Survive the IMF Medicine?" *Working Paper Series* (April). Calcutta: Indian Institute of Management.

Chossudovsky, Michel. 2001a. "Las pistas de Osamagate." *La Jornada* October 14.

———. 2001b. "The Role of Pakistan's Military Intelligence Agency (ISI) in the September 11 Attacks." Available at: http://globalresearch.ca/articles/CHO111A.html.

"Cronología internacional del movimiento antimundialización." 2001. *Observatorio Social de América Latina,* no. 3 (January): 39–44.

"Documentos del Conflicto." 2001. *Revista del Observatorio Social de América Latina,* no. 3 (enero): 45–64.

First Intercontinental Encounter for Mankind and against Neoliberalism. 2001. "Second Declaration at La Realidad, August 3 1996." *Observatorio Social de América Latina,* no. 3 (enero): 45–64.

Gray, Chris Hables. 1997. *Postmodern War: The New Politics of Conflict.* New York: Guilford.

Houtart, François, and François Polet, eds. 2001. *The Other Davos: The Globalization of Resistance to the World Economic System.* London: Zed.

Marais, Hein. 2000. "Sleepless in Seattle." Winter. Available at: www.alternatives-action.org/fma.

National Intelligence Council. 2000–2002. *Global Trends 2015: A Dialogue about the Future with Nongovernment Experts.* Available at: www.cia.gov/cia/reports/global trends2015/globaltrends2015.pdf.

Navarro, Vicenç. 2001. "Las elecciones del año en EEUU." *Sistema,* no. 161 (mayo): 3–19.

Roy, Arundhati. 2001. "The Algebra of Infinite Justice." *The Guardian.* London: September 29. Available at: http://aroy.miena.com

Sader, Emir. 2001. "Antes e depois de Seattle." *Observatorio Social de América Latina,* no. 3 (January): 5–8.

Seoane, José, and Emilio Taddei, eds. 2001. *Resistencias mundiales (De Seattle a Porto Alegre).* Buenos Aires: CLACSO.

Thomas, Janet. 2000. *The Battle in Seattle: The Stories Behind and Beyond the WTO Demonstrations.* Golden, CO: Fulcrum Publishing.

Van Creveld, Martin. 1991. *The Transformation of War.* New York: The Free Press.

Wallerstein, Immanuel. 2000. "Globalization or the Age of Transition? A Long-Term View of the Trajectory of the World-System." *International Sociology* XV, no. 2 (June): 249–65.

7

Proletarian Internationalism: A Long View and Some Speculations

Marcel van der Linden

The words *proletarian* and *internationalism* do not appear to have been used in combination until World War I (Friedemann and Hölscher 1982). Since then, the term *proletarian internationalism* has often been misused as justification for oppression and military intervention. If we are to apply it again in its proper sense in this new century, we should restrict it to activities "from below," thus excluding the activities of states, but covering autonomous working-class activities in full.

Proletarian internationalism calls forth associations with socialism and communism, with efforts to abolish world capitalism. Consistent with these connotations, those who use the concept in referring to workers' activities generally mean the collective actions of a group of workers in one country who set aside their short-term interests as a national group on behalf of a group of workers in another country in order to promote their long-term interests as members of a transnational class.[1] In this sense, proletarian internationalism was indeed witnessed regularly in the past. The question, however, is whether this narrow interpretation does justice to the concept. First, it fails to encompass the most numerous forms of cross-border workers' solidarity. In addition to "strategic internationalism," there are four reasons why groups of workers in different countries may undertake the joint promotion of their shared interests.

1. *Identity of group interests in the short term*: The living and working conditions of workers in two or more countries change in such a way that their resultant interests become more or less identical, raising the possibility of joint promotion of interests. In such instances, trade unions need do no more than "tot up," as it were, the individual interests involved.

2. *Identity of group interests in the longer term*: Workers in one country support the interests of workers in a worse situation elsewhere, and forgo the prospect of achieving short-term successes of their own with the expectation that they could or would eventually find themselves in the same situation. Thus, they are concerned to effect improvement in the situation of others which, in time, could benefit them.

3. *Indirect identity of group interests*: Workers in one country support improvement in the position of workers in another country that is inferior to theirs because such an improvement constitutes a precondition for the successful promotion of their own interests.

4. *Normative involvement*: Workers support fellow workers elsewhere whose treatment by the state or by employers conflicts with the standards of justice and decency they themselves uphold. No personal material interests are involved. Humanitarian or political considerations may play a part, while cultural and religious influences (e.g., Islam or Christianity) may likewise be unifying factors. In all such instances, there is a tendency to forge a transnational group identity separate from other sections of the world working class.

Normative involvement also creates a link to a further widening of the more limited concept of internationalism. Workers may feel solidarity with groups that are not primarily concerned with workers' interests but seek to achieve other emancipatory goals. Solidarity of this kind can take many forms. Examples include the support given by the International Working Men's Association (IWMA, later known as the First International) to Poland's struggle for freedom after the insurrection of 1863, and similarly, that of the Australian longshoremen for Indonesia's fight for independence in the 1940s. Moreover, normative involvement encompasses "long-distance nationalism" on an ethnic basis, as exemplified by the emotional ties with Ireland existing among Irish workers in North America (Anderson 1992). Another variant is the Pan-African solidarity that many African Americans have felt for the people of sub-Saharan Africa since World War II, a solidarity in which the workers' struggle has occasionally played an important part (Von Eschen 1997).

Proletarian internationalism is a more multiform and less consistent phenomenon than is often supposed. The aim of this chapter is to describe long-term trends in the efforts of workers to develop cross-border solidarity, focusing on trade union activities. I begin with the motives behind such activities, progressing to the different phases in the development of that solidarity from the early nineteenth century up to the present, and concluding with a few speculative remarks about the century ahead. Much of what I posit is based on partial evidence. Research into the history of working-class internationalism is still in its infancy, notwithstanding important advances made in recent years.[2]

A Grammar of Motives

Cross-border solidarity may seem logical, but in fact is not so at all. Attempts at internationalism are uncertain because of the counterforces involved. There can be many reasons for international cooperation. New motives have appeared over the years and others have faded away. At least seven economic motives can be distinguished.

Motive 1: Combating the Import of Foreign Competitors

Employers refusing local workers' demands for higher wages or better working conditions may seek to attract cheaper labor from other countries, preferably neighboring countries. Conflicts about this issue have often crystallized during strikes. Gérard Brey, for example, describes how building contractors in Spanish Galicia brought workers from northern Portugal to break strikes in 1895 (Brey 1988). Fighting back, in 1901, trade unions in the two countries set up the Unión Galaico-Portuguese, which organized solidarity so effectively that the building contractors stopped recruiting unorganized Portuguese labor after 1904 and the union was eventually dissolved.

Motive 2: Creating Institutional Arrangements for Transnational Labor Circulation

This motive relates to both skilled and highly skilled workers seeking work in other countries. In the nineteenth century, glovers, for example, plied their trade in an international labor market concentrated in cities like Grenoble, Prague, Brussels, and Naples. Some glovers were itinerant, traveling from place to place in search of work. As these highly skilled workers numbered no more than a few thousand across Europe, they were able to set up trade unions at an early date and gain influence among glovers arriving from other countries. As early as 1871, the Vienna glovers' union established contact with the German organization, and somewhat later, with similar organizations in Prague and Scandinavia (Deinhardt 1907, 837; Logue 1983).

Motive 3: Control of Cross-Border Labor Processes

Some groups of transport workers (e.g., seamen) travel continually from one country to another, and hence are organized on a multinational basis. Therefore, it follows that collective activities relating to working conditions are transnational. It is in this section of the working class that cross-border solidarity has long been highly developed. The International Transport Workers' Federation has frequently played a leading part in transnational collective action (Simon 1993; Reinalda 1997; Koch-Baumgarten 1999).

Motive 4: Reducing Competition between Workers in the Same Industries in Different Countries

In the early 1990s, a trade union in the United States, the United Electrical Workers (UE), began to work with the Mexican-based Authentic Workers Front. A UE representative explained the move in an interview:

> We lost something like 15,000 members in the last few years; this is a large amount for a union of our size. We had to increasingly face companies comparing our wages to those in Mexico during negotiations. Then it became clear to us we just do not want Mexicans to earn more, or that we feel sorry for them. We realized that if Mexican wages did not come up, ours were going down fast. It was in our union's self-interest to try to raise standards of living in Mexico. (Armbruster 1995, 84)

The same reasoning prompted the 1950s decision of the United Steel Workers of America to support the Jamaican bauxite miners in their organizational efforts (Harrod 1972, 329–30).

Motive 5: Lobbying International Organizations

Since 1919, when Western countries responded to the Bolshevik threat by establishing the International Labor Organization, a substantial part of the international trade-union movement has sought to influence this tripartite organization's formulation of international labor standards (Linden 2000). When European unification began to take shape in the 1960s, European trade unions intensified their cooperation to enable them to influence the new policy at the highest levels (Elsner 1974; Platzer 1991; Portelli 1990; Windmuller 1992).

Motive 6: The Promotion of Interests within Multinational Corporations

During the twentieth century, an increasing number of companies established themselves in more than one nation-state. This meant that workers in a number of countries were under the same management, which called for cross-border cooperation. The result, especially from the 1960s onward, was the emergence of multinational collective bargaining and world corporation councils (Barnett and Muller 1974, 312–19; Bendiner 1987; Cox 1971).

Motive 7: The Exchange of Information

Trade union officials long recognized the need for insight into the development of wages and prices, labor legislation, and other factors in other countries. With the growth of multinationals, the need for data on corporate policies arose.

> The (IMF) [International Monetary Fund] Economic and Social Department, for instance, maintains files on more than 500 multinational companies. Such information has proven particularly valuable to IMF affiliates seeking to implement campaigns (increasingly global in extent) against corporations. (Herod 1997, 183)

In addition to economic motives, international cooperation may have a political motive as well. As a rule, this takes the form of collective action aimed at promoting or opposing a particular political model. Political action of this kind may be unconnected with states, as was often the case between 1917 and 1921, a period that witnessed a worldwide upsurge of actions stemming not so much from short-term self-interest as from the desire to bring about a new and just social order (Thorpe 1989; Wörner 1979). Similar examples are the solidarity with the Republican forces in the Spanish Civil War and with opponents of apartheid in South Africa. At the same time, trade unions sometimes identified with a particular state, so, in a certain sense, their international activities were incorporated into the foreign policy pursued by that state and served primarily to further its interests, as exemplified by the Red

International of Labor Unions (1921–1937), which quickly became an instrument of Soviet foreign policy (Tostorff 1999). Conversely, for a large part of the twentieth century, the American Federation of Labor (and later, the AFL-CIO) was a loyal partner of the U.S. government, bent on proselytizing anticommunism throughout the world (Carew 1998; Radosh 1969).

All in all, the reasons why workers succeed in organizing international solidarity cover a wide spectrum. They tend to be economic in nature, and hence relate to short-term interests. However, there are also situations in which long-term interests are the dominant factor, as at times with an intensified class struggle. In practice, the various motives can overlap, often blurring the dividing lines between different expressions of internationalism.

There are also numbers of reasons why workers in specific situations may wish to form international ties with other workers. Those reasons may be economic, political, or cultural. In the economic sphere, commodity chains are a case in point. When a group of workers processes or distributes a product that has been processed or distributed by another group at a previous stage, the "later" group will stand to benefit if the "earlier" group is paid a low wage. The less the latter earns, the lower will be the price of the product and the greater the chance that it will find a ready market. The political orientation of trade unions can both further and impede certain forms of cross-border cooperation. For decades, the ideology of free-trade unionism espoused by the AFL-CIO and the International Confederation of Free Trade Unions ruled out all possibility of cooperation with communist trade unions. Cooperation between trade unions can also be hampered by cultural influences such as racism, nationalism, or religion.

In many instances, internationalism is ambivalent. Anticommunism, for example, is conducive to some forms of international cooperation but stands in the way of others. Moreover, international cooperation is often resorted to only when the means available at the national level are inadequate. A typical example is that of the U.S. window-glass workers in the 1880s, as described at the time by T. V. Powderly, the leader of the Knights of Labor:

> In 1883 manufacturers of window glass entered into an agreement to import foreign workmen to take the places of American glass-blowers. Local Assembly No. 300 [LA 300] of the Knights of Labor had reached a stage in organization which approached nearer to perfection than any other association of workingmen in America. . . . [The] manufacturers became desirous of overthrowing the power of Local Assembly No. 300, so that they might secure the assistance of cheaper workmen

from abroad, and through the presence in this country of more glass-blowers than could find employment, they hoped to render the reduction of wages a task which would be easy of accomplishment. (1889, 442)

LA 300 fought back with a dual strategy: They set about blocking the import of skilled glaziers by political means, bringing pressure to bear on the Senate and the House of Representatives, and, at the same time, directed their efforts to the source, sending emissaries to Europe to persuade their fellow workers there of the impropriety of their actions. The first part of their strategy was rewarded with success in 1885, when the U.S. Senate passed the Foran Act prohibiting the import of "contract labor." This rendered the second part superfluous and the organization soon recalled its representatives from Europe.

In attempting to reconstruct the historical development of proletarian internationalism, we must bear in mind that we are dealing with complicated, ever-changing causal configurations. In each new historical situation, different combinations of factors are significant, as I shall illustrate in the following pages.

Five Stages of Development

First Stage: The Labor Movement Defines Itself (pre-1848)

In the first half of the nineteenth century, highly skilled workers gradually became aware that they comprised a separate class with a historic "mission": They personified technological and social progress while the greater part of the lower classes was reactionary and destined for ultimate collapse. To appreciate this dawning awareness, it is necessary to understand that the concepts of "proletariat" and "working class" were, at first, by no means identical. The proletariat was originally the estate of people without property, beyond honor (Conze 1984, 41). The workers were only a part of this amorphous mass. According to the French nobleman Adolphe Granier de Cassagnac, writing in the 1830s, the proletariat formed "the lowest rank, the deepest stratum of society," which consisted of four groups: "the workers, the beggars, the thieves and public women":

> The worker is a proletarian, because he works in order to live and earns a wage; the beggar is a proletarian, who does not want to work or cannot work, and begs in order to live; the thief is a proletarian, who does not want to work or beg, and, in order to make a living,

steals; the prostitute is a proletarian, who neither wants to work, nor beg, nor steal, and, in order to live, sells her body. (1838, 30)

Some years later, Heinrich Wilhelm Bensen distinguished seven categories of proletarians. Apart from three groups of workers, he also noted "the poor, who are bereft of support from the public purse . . . the common soldiers . . . gypsies, prostitutes, bandits etc." and "the small servants of religious and secular origin" (Bensen 1847, 344).

As capitalist relations crystallized more and more, the desire arose among the "respectable" workers to distinguish themselves from the rest of the proletariat. The Communist League clearly articulated this in its *Manifesto,* placing "the modern working class—the proletarians" (Marx 1973, 73) between two social strata that it considered to be doomed in the capitalist process of social polarization: the petty bourgeoisie and the lumpen proletariat.

> Of all the classes that stand face to face with the bourgeoisie today, the proletariat alone is a really revolutionary class. The other classes decay and finally disappear in the face of modern industry. . . . The lower middle class, the small manufacturer, the shopkeeper, the artisan, the peasant, all these fight against the bourgeoisie, to save from extinction their existence as fractions of the middle class. They are therefore not revolutionary, but conservative. . . . If by chance they are revolutionary, they are so only in view of their impending transfer into the proletariat . . . they desert their own standpoint to place themselves at that of the proletariat. The "dangerous class", the social scum, that passively rotting mass thrown off by the lowest layers of old society, may, here and there, be swept into the movement by a proletarian revolution; its conditions of life, however, prepare it far more for the part of a bribed tool of reactionary intrigue. (Marx 1973, 77)

The concept of "working class" was historically marked off in three ways: from the petty bourgeoisie, from the lumpenproletariat, and from the unfree workers. All three boundaries were moreover gendered, the working class being, in principle, conceived as comprising male breadwinners. The subsequent stereotype thereafter dominated the representation of the workers' movement for well over a century. It was clear to the perceptive observer at an early stage that the workers' movements of the day consisted no more than partly, if at all, of "pure workers" in the sense of the *Communist Manifesto,* but it was a long time before this led to any conclusions. The emerging labor movements in Western Europe had evolved a self-image that was indeed conducive to internal cohesion but at the same time excluded large sections of the proletariat. It was to remain dominant until far into the twentieth century.

Second Stage: Subnational Internationalism (1848–1870s)

The first significant expressions of organized internationalism stemmed from London, then the center of the hegemony of world capitalism, during the lengthy period of economic growth between the late 1840s and the early 1870s. Shortly before, in the 1830s, a few groups of highly skilled English workers had already shown an interest in developments abroad. One of the first written expressions of workers' internationalism was a document endorsed by William Lovett's Working Men's Association (WMA), on November 1, 1836. In this document, *Address to the Belgian Working Classes*, the WMA stated its conviction "that our interests—nay, the interests of working men in all countries of the world—are identified." The Belgian "brethren" were advised "to form, if possible, a union with countries around you," because "a federation of the working classes of Belgium, Holland and the Provinces of the Rhine would form an admirable democracy" (Lehning 1970, 210–14).

This interest intensified after the revolutions of 1848, producing a number of small organizations with a multinational membership, such as the Fraternal Democrats and the Communistische Arbeiter-Bildungs-Verein (Communist Association for the Education of Working Men), the latter which counted many non-Germans among its members (Lattek 1988). A parallel development was the provision of international aid in strikes, notably between England and the European continent. It generally took two forms.

- First, financial aid for strikes in other countries, either intraoccupational in the sense of support for workers in the same occupation or wider in scope. The first variant seems to have been the more frequent. In 1852, and again in 1862, the London Society of Compositors sent funds to a sister organization in Paris; and Paris construction workers aided their London counterparts in 1860. Shortly before the establishment of the IWMA, Limoges potters appealed to potters in Staffordshire for help (Merriman 1985, 112–14). In the 1850s there were even attempts to publish bilingual trade journals, such as the printers' *Gutenberg* and the shoemakers' *Innovator.*
- Second, opposition to the use of strikebreakers. During several strikes, British employers tried to import strikebreakers from the continent, as occurred "in the strikes by tin-plate workers in Wolverhampton in 1851 and Birmingham in 1853, and gas-stokers, bakers, cigar-makers, tailors and pianoforte-makers in London." In some cases, their efforts were foiled. "The London type-founders on strike in 1850 appealed to Paris society, who agreed to stop

men being recruited, and circularized all type-foundries in France, Germany, Belgium, the Netherlands, and Switzerland to this effect." (Prothero 1997, 116)

The establishment of the First International (International Working Men's Association) was, to some extent, a product of this development. In 1863, a number of English trade unionists drew up an address, "To the Workmen of France from the Working Men of England," which contained the following:

> A fraternity of peoples is highly necessary for the cause of labour, for we find that whenever we attempt to better our social conditions by reducing the hours of toil, or by raising the price of labour, our employers threaten us with bringing over Frenchmen, Germans, Belgians, and others to do our work at a reduced rate of wages; and we are sorry to say that this has been done, though not from any desire on the part of our continental brethren to injure us, but through a want of regular and systematic communications between the industrious classes of all countries, which we hope to see speedily effected, as our principle is to bring up the wages of the ill-paid to as near a level as possible with that of those who are better remunerated, and not to allow our employers to play us off one against the other, and so drag us down to the lowest possible condition, suitable to their avaricious bargaining. (*Beehive*, December 5, 1863)

Eight months later, the existence of the IWMA was a fact. Its first active involvement concerned an attempt at strikebreaking in 1866. In April of that year, the London tailors had become organized and demanded a wage increase of a penny an hour. The employers responded with a lockout, and tried to recruit strikebreakers in Germany, as they had done on other occasions. The IWMA helped to block their efforts in Hamburg and Berlin, thus contributing to the successful outcome of the tailors' action (Prothero 1997, 116).

Note that all cross-border solidarity on these occasions was at a subnational level. As no national trade unions yet existed, international contacts were always between local organizations. It was, in fact, subnational internationalism.

Third Stage: Transition (1870s–1890s)

In the early 1870s, this form of collective action was faced with a growing number of difficulties. First, trade unions were gradually managing to consolidate at the national level. Beginning with the foundation of the Amalgamated Society of Engineers in 1851, amalgamated unionism

Table 7.1. Founding Years of National Trade-Union Confederations

1868	Great Britain	1898	Sweden
1880	Switzerland		Denmark
1883	Canada		Hungary
1886	United States		Belgium
1888	Spain	1903	Serbia
1890	Germany	1904	Bulgaria
1893	Austria	1906	The Netherlands (social-democratic)
	The Netherlands		Italy
	(syndicalist)		Romania
1895	France	1907	Finland
1897	Czech Lands	1911	Greece

pressed forward. In the leading industrial cities of Glasgow, Sheffield, Liverpool, Edinburgh, and London, permanent trade councils were established between 1858 and 1867, which led to the foundation of the Trades' Union Council (TUC) in 1868. At about the same time, and in the framework of the societal incorporation of the working class, the labor movement gained some form of state recognition. The franchise was extended by the Reform Act of 1867; and the Trade Union Act, improving the legal status of the unions, came into force in 1871, followed by an Amending Act in 1876. The result proved to be detrimental to an active British interest in the International, which by about 1870 was lukewarm anyway.[3] In other North Atlantic countries, the process of national consolidation continued, albeit with some delay. After Switzerland and Canada, most other countries in the region followed within a few decades (see table 7.1).

Another difficulty arose in the early 1870s, when the upward trend of capitalism was reversed in a slowdown of economic growth. The years up to about 1895 may be described as a period of retarded economic growth, stagnation, and recession in a complex relationship. A gap appeared in the development of the British economy; the German and American economies were in a severe crisis, and the French economy of the 1880s was in serious trouble. In addition, after the Franco-Prussian War of 1870–1871, the working classes entered into a closer relationship with the nation-states. As Hobsbawm, among others, has pointed out, the intrusion of a nationalist and chauvinist attitude into ever-expanding social strata was, to a large extent, the result of a conscious policy—expressed in primary education, military service, public ceremonies, mass production of public monuments, and so on—which, of course, corresponded to certain desires of the working classes (Linden 1988).

This combination of factors resulted in the undermining of subnational internationalism, as was apparent from the decline of the First International after 1872. What followed was a transitional period in which the old form of internationalism crumbled away while a new form was still in its embryonic stage.

Fourth Stage: National Internationalism (1890s–1960s)

Around the turn of the century, when the national consolidation of trade unions in the North Atlantic region was far advanced, a new stage—that of national internationalism—entered the picture. There seem to have been at least three areas in which international cooperation grew out of practical activities.

First, there was the area of highly skilled (artisan) occupational groups with international mobility. Among printers, for example, there were long-standing cross-national relationships, especially in certain linguistic regions (e.g., the French region comprising France, parts of Belgium, and Switzerland); they had attended the conferences of fraternal trade organizations in other countries as early as the 1860s. Issues like the *viaticum* (travel money) loomed large in those years (Chauvet 1956, 632–34; 1971, 245; Musson 1954, 305–8).

Second, there was the area of international migration. Countries with fast-growing economies attracted hundreds of thousands of immigrants from less developed parts of the world. Chinese and Japanese migrated to California, Poles and Italians to Germany, and so on. The trade unions in the immigration countries tried either to organize the new arrivals or to exclude them from the national labor market. The German federation of construction workers sought to organize Italian immigrants, sometimes successfully (Schäfer 1982, 208–10; Herbert 1986, 68–70; Del Fabbro 1996).

Third, there was the area of international transport. Here, the labor market and the labor process were inherently international, which enhanced collaboration. The tendency toward internationalism was particularly marked in this section of the working class, as evidenced by the large-scale international transport strike of 1911 and by the fact that branches of the British seamen's union (NAS&FU) existed for a short time in the early 1890s in Norway, Sweden, Denmark, Germany, and the Netherlands (Marsh and Ryan 1989, 51–52).

The first organizations to be set up were the international trade secretariats, federations of national trade unions representing different occupational groups. A substantial impetus had come from the institution of the Second International in 1889 as a cooperative mechanism for socialists (and anarchists until 1896). The congresses held by the International were meeting points for trade unionists (see table 7.2).

Table 7.2. Founding Years of International Trade Secretariats

1889	Typographers and printers	1898	Foundry workers
	Hatters	1900	Carpenters
	Cigar makers and tobacco workers	1902	Stone workers
	Shoemakers	1903	Construction workers
1890	Miners	1904	Wood workers
1892	Glass workers	1905	Porcelain and china workers
1893	Tailors	1906	Public service workers
	Metal workers	1907	Book binders
	Railway workers		Hairdressers
1894	Textile workers	1908	Factory workers
	Furriers		Hotel workers
1896	Lithographers	1910	Post-office workers
	Brewery workers	1911	Painters
1897	Transport workers		

Source: Dreyfus 2000, 36–39.

Notwithstanding publications on the history of some of these trade secretariats, little is still known of most of them.[4] Many existed largely on paper or confined their activities to correspondence with member organizations. The trade unions affiliated to the secretariats were initially almost exclusively European and, to a lesser extent, North American.

With the establishment of the international trade secretariats well under way, cooperation between national trade-union confederations gathered pace as well. In 1903, the International Secretariat of National Trade Union Confederations (ISNTUC) came into being. Following preparatory meetings of trade unionists from various countries in Copenhagen (1901) and Stuttgart (1902), the international center was set up in Dublin in 1903 under the aegis of Carl Legien, the leader of the German trade-union movement. At the urging of the AFL, it became the International Federation of Trade Unions (IFTU) in 1913. Until far into the twentieth century, the ISNTUC and the IFTU were also primarily focused on the North Atlantic region.

Thus, the period between 1889 and 1903 was very important for the subsequent rise of the international trade-union movement. The structures devised during those years remained largely unchanged throughout the twentieth century. Labor economist James Scoville has rightly observed: "[T]he initial structure of the labor movement exercises an impact on the future course of its evolution." He attributes this to the persistence of ideology formed at the beginning, the survival imperative of institutions, and the labor movement's influence on the surrounding society, which subsequently reverberates on the movement (1973, 74).

The course of events a century ago has endowed the international trade-union movement with the dual structure of international trade secretariats on the one hand, and international confederations (with changing names) on the other. It is not the most logical structure. The international trade secretariats could have formed an international federation of their own. Had they done so, only one international umbrella organization would exist today: an arrangement that probably would have been more effective. Reorganizing the movement along these lines was suggested by a few individuals, such as Edo Fimmen in the 1920s, but to no avail. The forces of institutional inertia prevailed. Why did the international trade secretariats not form their own federation at the outset? One possible explanation is that they were focused on direct economic aspects (the worldwide problems of certain industries), whereas the International Confederation of Free Trade Unions (ICFTU) and its precursors were more politically oriented. Nonetheless, the activities of the secretariats and the confederations often overlapped, causing tensions between them.

While the structure consolidated at the beginning of the twentieth century remained unchanged for many decades, several significant shifts within the structure did take place over the years. Prior to World War I, Germany occupied the dominant position. In 1913, the headquarters of at least seventeen of the twenty-eight trade secretariats were in that country. The major exceptions to the rule were the miners and textile workers, whose headquarters were in Manchester (Dreyfus 2000, 36–39). After 1918, Great Britain and the United States assumed the leading roles. Whereas the German trade-union movement had stood more or less "outside" its own state, in the postwar years the TUC and AFL (-CIO) entered into close collaboration with their respective states. For a while, collaboration between the labor federation and the U.S. government and big business was so close that it was likened by some to a corporative structure, a *blocco storico* à la Antonio Gramsci (Cox 1980). During World War II, the British TUC moved toward "a close relationship with the government in developing labour policy in the colonies," often emulating the enlightened extension of a colonial power in Africa, Asia, and the Caribbean (Davies 1964, 24). As Peter Weiler has noted:

> TUC activities . . . helped to perpetuate the British empire. In part, this effect was unintentional. The TUC urged colonial trade unions to follow the same moderate reformist path that it did at home, although reformism produced different results in the colonies than it did in Britain. British workers had at least the political possibility to change their society while colonial workers did not. Thus although reformism was not endorsed as part of a calculated strategy to preserve British rule, it inevitably had that effect. On another level, however, this

effect was intended because British labor leaders accepted the idea of Britain's imperial mission and rejected any violent attempts to end it. (1984, 384)

In the course of the "national" phase of internationalism, the number of international trade secretariats both swelled through the advent of additional umbrella organizations and dwindled as the result of amalgamation. The social-reformist mainstream of the IFTU and its successor after 1949, the ICFTU, was eventually confronted with a number of rivals. They included not only the syndicalist international calling itself like the First International and the IWMA (since 1922), but also the communist Red International of Labor Unions (RILU, 1921–1937) and the International Federation of Christian Trade Unions (IFCTU, since 1920) (Thorpe 1989, 1990; Tostorff 1999; Pasture 1999).[5] In 1945, the IFTU joined forces with the communist trade unions in the WFTU, but their alliance came to an end with the Cold War. The ICFTU was founded in 1949, while the WFTU fell under communist domination (Carew 2000a, b).

In the interwar years, interest in trade unionism increased in the peripheral and semiperipheral countries. The RILU sought to put down roots in those regions almost from the moment of its inception in 1921, followed a few years later, in about 1928, by the IFTU, partly to counter the rival communist organization, which was intent upon gaining greater influence in the colonial and semicolonial countries (Post 1997, 49). Another factor was the concurrent growth of the labor movement in the Third World, making the question of which course it would pursue all the more urgent. The IFCTU followed the same path somewhat later. Up to World War II, it was solely oriented toward Europe, but this changed out of necessity after 1945, in part because several of its former member organizations had disbanded or amalgamated with trade unions encompassing all ideologies (e.g., in Germany and Austria). The IFCTU set up a reasonably successful regional organization in Latin America (1954) and recruited support in Vietnam and Africa as well (Wahlers 1990; Pasture 1999).

The IFTU and ICFTU were both dominated by the British TUC and the American AFL(-CIO), investing them in the Third World with the reputation of allies of colonialism and neocolonialism. Nor were those suspicions entirely unfounded. The ICFTU tried for years to propagate a certain model of proper unionism. One of the aims formulated at the time of its founding in 1949 was "to provide assistance in the establishment, maintenance and development of trade union organizations, particularly in economically and socially under-developed countries" (*Official Report* 1949, 226). It was assumed that "proper" trade unions would: (1) remain fully independent of political parties and states; (2) concentrate on collective bargaining and lobbying for social security legislation; and (3) defend and promote parliamentary democracy. These principles often proved difficult to apply in the so-called Third World.[6] Much later, Adolf Sturmthal observed that especially in the Anglo-American countries (whose trade unions dominated the ICFTU) there had been "a naïve belief in the universal applicability of some form of collective bargaining" (1973, 5). He listed a series of conditions for "a genuine collective bargaining system," including "a legal and political system permitting the existence and functioning of reasonably *free* labor organizations" (a condition that was fully compatible with the early ICFTU views) and the requirement that "unions be more or less stable, reasonably well organized, and fairly evenly matched with the employers in bargaining strength" (Sturmthal 1973, 9).

Effective unions have rarely, if ever, been organized by noncommitted workers, that is, casual workers who change jobs frequently, return periodically to their native village, and have no specific industrial skill, even of a very simple kind. Yet even fully committed industrial workers with little or no skill are capable of engaging in effective collective bargaining only under certain conditions, which are rarely found. In most (though by no means all) newly industrializing countries, large excess supplies of common labor are available for nonagricultural work. Not only are unskilled workers rarely capable of forming unions of their own under such conditions; if they succeed in doing so, their unions have little or no bargaining power (Sturmthal 1973, 10).

Fifth Stage: A New Transition (since the 1960s)

Since the 1960s the international trade-union movement has been confronted with a substantial number of new challenges that together have progressively undermined the old model of national internationalism. Significant changes include the decolonization process; the new transnational division of labor; the emergence of regionalism and trading blocs, such as the European Union, North American Free Trade Association (NAFTA), Association of Southeast Asian Nations (ASEAN), and Mercado Común del Sur (MERCOSUR, the Common Market of South America); the collapse of so-called socialism in the Soviet Union and Eastern Europe; the rise of feminist movements; proletarianization processes in the periphery and semiperiphery, expanding the so-called informal sector with breathtaking speed; and the increasing influence of women.

The following major challenges currently facing international trade unionism are worthy of note:

- The impressive growth of foreign direct investment in the core and semiperiphery, and of transnational corporations (TNCs). In response to this development, world corporation councils were set up in the mid-1960s, notably in the chemical and automobile industries. Although many trade-union militants had high expectations of these new bodies, their effectiveness has been less than anticipated due to the conflicting interests of employees in different countries (Bendiner 1987; Olle and Schoeller 1987; Tudyka 1986).

- The formation of trading blocs. They led to a certain equalization of legal and political parameters, so that the building of transnational trade-union structures within each bloc was an obvious step. In NAFTA, this collaboration is not evolving primarily at the top level of national trade-union confederations, but at the subnational or branch level. In many cases institutions other than trade unions, such as religious and human rights organizations, are also partners in projects of this kind. Examples include the 1980s Coalition for Justice in the Maquiladores, the Comité Fronterizo de Obreras, and La Mujer Obrera (Armbruster 1995, 77–78, 80–82; Borgers 1996, 81–85; Carr 1999). Equally worthy of note, in this context, is the Council of Ford Workers instituted by the United Auto Workers (Bina and Davis 1993, 165–66).
- The formation of new supranational institutions to regulate the dynamics of the "new" capitalism. A foremost example is the World Trade Organization, established in 1995.
- The social and economic changes in the periphery and semiperiphery, facilitating the emergence of new, often militant, workers' movements (social movement unions) in countries such as Brazil, South Africa, the Philippines, Taiwan, and South Korea.
- New forms of rank-and-file trade unionism outside the established channels appearing since the 1970s, with international connections at the shop-floor level "bypassing altogether the secretariats, which they see as too often beholden to the bureaucracies of their various national affiliates" (Herod 1997, 184). A well-known example is the Transnationals Information Exchange (TIE), a center in which a substantial number of research and activist labor groups exchange information on TNCs. Another example is the "counter foreign policy" existing since the early 1980s in the AFL-CIO (Spalding 1992).
- The joint actions against TNCs conducted over the past decade by trade unions representing particular occupations in different countries (e.g., coal miners and electrical workers) (Herod 1995, 342; Armbruster 1998). When the French car maker Renault announced the closure of its Belgian factory in February 1997, solidarity strikes and demonstrations were organized in France, Spain, Portugal, and Slovenia, giving birth to the term *Eurostrike.*

- Spurred on by the uneven development of trade unions in core and periphery countries, a growing tendency on the part of international trade secretariats to engage in the *direct* recruitment of members in the latter countries. (See the activities of the secretariat for the service sector Union Network International relating to IT specialists in India: SZ 2001.)
- The increasing number of activities carried out by nongovernmental organizations (NGOs) that should be the responsibility of the international trade-union movement, such as the struggle to regulate and abolish child labor.

These challenges compel the international trade-union movement to review its aims and activities. The need for such a review is further underscored by the fact that the changing composition of the world working class highlights the weakness of the movement. In 2001, the membership of the ICFTU and World Confederation of Labor (WCL) combined is some 150 million, or between 5 and 10 percent of the world working classes. In other words, the vast majority of wage-earners are not reached by the traditional trade union movement. That does not necessarily mean they are entirely without representative organizations— alternative organizational models exist here and there—but it certainly illustrates the shortcomings of the present situation.

Speculations about the Future

The periodization suggested here can be roughly related to long waves of capitalist development, as illustrated in table 7.3.

International trade unionism does not follow exactly the same rhythm as world capital. For instance, hegemonic influence within the international labor movement is not congruent with hegemonic influence within the world-system; and national internationalism was dominant during only one-and-a-half long waves.[7]

In the light of the developments over the past 150 years, I believe that the current prolonged transitional phase must be regarded as leading into an entirely new stage, that of *transnational internationalism.* The contours of this new form of trade-union internationalism have yet to emerge, but several minimum requirements are already apparent.

- The target group should be demarcated anew. The first-phase demarcation of the working classes is extremely narrow and Eurocentric, and needs to be revised and expanded (see also Antunes 1999, 101–17). A considerable number of trade unions in both the

Table 7.3. Long Waves and Types of Trade-Union Internationalism

1825–1848	Down	Demarcation of "Working Class"		Geographical Focus on North-Atlantic Region
1848–1873	Up	Subnational Internationalism	British Hegemony	
1873–1894	Down	First Transition		
1894–1917	Up	National Internationalism	German Hegemony	
1917–1940	Down		British-American (+ Temporary Russian) Hegemony	
1940–1968	Up			Geographical Expansion in Asia, Africa, Latin America
1968–	Down	Second Transition		

periphery and semiperiphery have now abandoned the old de-marcation and recruit all kinds of "half-proletarian" groups.

- There can be no doubt that the newly defined target group will no longer be dominated by white male workers in the North Atlantic region, but by women and people of color; many in forms of self-employment, precarious jobs, or debt bondage. Trade unions will need to effect a drastic change in their operational systems in order to assist these new workers to further their interests effectively. This also implies terminating the centrality of collective bargaining strategies (cf. Hensman 2001a, b).
- The dual structure of the international trade-union movement—collaboration of national confederations plus international trade secretariats—is a problematic relic of the past that should be discarded. Probably the best option would be a new unitary structure facilitating the inclusion of new target groups in the international trade secretariats.
- The somewhat autocratic approach prevailing in the present-day international trade-union movement should be replaced by a dem-ocratic approach and greater participation of the rank-and-file workers. The possibilities offered by the Internet would be a positive contribution to a renewed structure of this kind (Lee 1997).

- While lobbying governments and transnational organizations, to date, has been the principal activity of the international trade-union movement (with the notable exception of the antiapartheid campaign of the 1980s), and efforts are made to cultivate the good will of states, much greater effort must henceforth be put into active measures in the form of boycotts, strikes, and so on, which in turn demand a substantial strengthening of the internal structures (Greenfield 1998). As Dimitris Stevis has rightly observed, international labor organizations are "not simply sleeping giants, but fundamentally weak intersocietal federations" (1998, 66).

The question now is whether the existing international trade-union movement can meet these challenges. During the first transitional phase of the late nineteenth century, the difficulties were so overwhelming that the old organizations collapsed. Only after a quarter of a century did it become possible to build new international organizations. Remember that the unions of the "subnational" phase were often still extremely fragile and lacking in experience. In the current transitional phase, there seems to be a greater chance that the existing organizational forms will manage to adapt. Nonetheless, it remains very likely that the coming of transnational internationalism will be a difficult process interspersed with failed experiments and moments of deep crisis. Organizational structures and patterns of behavior that have existed for a century are not easily changed. Moreover, it is highly unlikely that new structures and patterns will be shaped through reforms from above, through the central leadership. If there is one thing that history has taught us, it is that trade-union structures almost never develop smoothly by means of piece-meal engineering. They are generally the outcome of conflicts and risky experiments. Pressure from below (through competitive networks, alternative action models, etc.) will be highly important in deciding the outcome. What precisely those pressures will be, and whether they will be sufficient to bring about major changes, no one can say.

Notes

1. I am aware that in North America *internationalism* may also refer to interethnic solidarity in one country. This form of solidarity is, however, not discussed here.

2. Since the historiography of trade-union internationalism is far more advanced than the historiography of the world working class, I use the development of labor organizations as my point of departure. In the long run, however, the approach will have to be reversed, and the development of the world working class will have to become the analytical background against which trade-union internationalism is analyzed.

3. "The membership of affiliated British trade unions never reached more than about 50,000, possibly less, out of a total trade-union membership at the time of perhaps 800,000. The unions which joined, such as the bricklayers, tailors, shoemakers, cabinetmakers etc., were mostly in declining or vulnerable handicraft trades, mainly in London . . . nor were these very assiduous in attendance or payment of subscriptions. Interest soon dwindled and affiliations ceased" (Musson 1972, 58).

4. See for example, Herrmann (1994); Koch-Baumgarten (1999); Carl and Köbele (1993); Kulemann (1898); Nyström and Rütters (1989); Rebérioux (1990); Reinalda (1997); Rütters (1989, 1990, 1995); Schneider (1982); Schnorbach (1989); Simon (1993).

5. The IFCTU became the World Confederation of Labor in 1968.

6. Sometimes they also seemed insincere. Regarding the emphasis placed by the British TUC in the 1950s on the nonpolitical nature of "proper" trade unionism, Davies has correctly observed: "Some of these sentiments sound odd in the context of the history of the British trade union movement, which had supported a general strike, maintained a close association with the Labour Party, and in its annual congresses regularly debated resolutions on a large number of issues outside the field of industrial relations" (Davies 1964, 26).

7. My periodization does not imply that subnational and national internationalism are mutually exclusive, as of course they are not. Cross-border solidarity can take various forms. For instance, the international solidarity with the strike staged by the Liverpool dockers in the 1990s was, to a large extent, subnational (Castree 2000).

References

Anderson, Benedict. 1992. *Long Distance Nationalism: World Capitalism and the Rise of Identity Politics.* Amsterdam: CASA.

Antunes, Ricardo. 1999. *Os sentidos do trabalho: ensaio sobre a afirmação e a negoção do trabalho.* São Paulo: Boitempo.

Armbruster, Ralph. 1995. "Cross-National Labor Organizing Strategies," *Critical Sociology* XXI, no. 2: 75–89.

———. 1998. "Cross Border Labor Organizing in the Garment and Automobile Industries," *Journal of World-Systems Research* IV, no. 1: (Winter). Available at http://jwsr.ucr.edu.

Barnett, R., and R. E. Muller. 1974. *Global Reach: The Power of the Multinational Corporations.* New York: Simon and Schuster.

Bendiner, Burton. 1987. *International Labour Affairs: The World Trade Unions and the Multinational Companies.* Oxford: Clarendon Press.

Bensen, Heinrich Wilhelm. 1847. *Die Proletarier: Eine historische Denkschrift.* Stuttgart: n.p.

Bina, Cyrus, and Chuck Davis. 1993. "Transnational Capital, the Global Labor Process, and the International Labor Movement." Pp. 152–70 in *The Labor Process and Control of Labor: The Changing Nature of Work Relations in the Late Twentieth Century,* ed. B. Berberoglu Westport, CT: Praeger.

Borgers, Frank. 1996. "The Challenges of Economic Globalization for U.S. Labor." *Critical Sociology* XXII, no. 2: 67–88.

Brey, Gérard. 1988. "Une tentative d'internationalisme concret: L'Union Galaïco-Portugaise (1901–1904)." Pp. 392–409 in *Internationalism in the Labour Movement 1830–1940,* Vol. II., ed. F. L. van Holthoon and M. van der Linden. Leiden: E. J. Brill.

Carew, Anthony. 1998. "The American Labor Movement in Fizzland: The Free Trade Union Movement and the CIA." *Labor History* XXXIX, no. 1 (Feb.): 25–42.

———. 2000a. "A False Dawn: The World Federation of Trade Unions, 1945–1949." Pp. 165–84 in *The International Confederation of Free Trade Unions*, ed. M. van der Linden. Berne: Peter Lang Academic.

———. 2000b. "Towards a Free Trade Union Centre: The International Confederation of Free Trade Unions, 1949–1972." Pp. 187–339 in *The International Confederation of Free Trade Unions*, ed. M. van der Linden. Berne: Peter Lang Academic.

Carl, Konrad, and Bruno Köbele, eds. 1993. *Auf der Suche nach Solidarität: Eine Geschichte der Internationalen Bau- und Holzarbeiterbewegung.* Colgone: Bund Verlag.

Carr, Barry. 1999. "Globalization from Below: Labour Internationalism under NAFTA." *International Social Science Journal* LI, no. 159 (Mar.): 49–59.

Castree, Noel. 2000. "Geographic Scale and Grass-Roots Internationalism: The Liverpool Dock Dispute, 1995–1998." *Economic Geography* LXXVI, no. 3 (July): 272–92.

Chauvet, Paul. 1956. *Les ouvriers du livre en France de 1789 à la constitution de la Fédération du Livre.* Paris: Rivière.

———. 1971. *Les ouvriers du livre et du journal: La Fédération Française des Travailleurs du Livre.* Paris: Editions Ouvrières.

Conze, Werner. 1984. "Proletariat, Pöbel, Pauperismus." Pp. 27–68 in *Geschichtliche Grundbegriffe* Vol. V. Stuttgart: Klett-Cotta.

Cox, Robert W. 1971. "Labor and Transnational Relations." *International Organization* XXV, no. 2 (Spring): 554–84.

———. 1980. "Labor and Hegemony: A Reply." *International Organization* XXXIV, no. 1: 159–76.

Davies, D. I. 1964. "The Politics of the TUC's Colonial Policy." *The Political Quarterly* XXXV, no. 1 (Jan.–Mar.): 23–34.

Deinhardt, Ernst. 1907. "Die internationalen Beziehungen der Gewerkschaften." *Sozialistische Monatshefte* II: 835–46.

Del Fabbro, René. 1996. *Transalpini: Italienische Arbeitswanderung nach Süddeutschland im Kaiserreich 1870–1918.* Osnabrück: Universitätsverlag Rasch.

Dreyfus, Michel. 2000. "The Emergence of an International Trade Union Organization (1902–1919)." Pp. 25–71 in *The International Confederation of Free Trade Unions*, ed. M. van der Linden. Berne: Peter Lang Academic.

Elsner, Wolfram. 1974. *Die EWG: Herausforderung und Antwort der Gewerkschaften.* Cologne: Bund Verlag.

Friedemann, Peter, and Lucian Hölscher. 1982. "Internationale, International, Internationalismus." Pp. 367–97 in *Geschichtliche Grundbegriffe* Vol. 3., ed. O. Brunner, W. Conze, and R. Koselleck. Stuttgart: Klett-Cotta.

Granier de Cassagnac, Adolphe. 1838. *Histoire des classes ouvrières et des classes bourgeoises.* Paris: Desrez.

Greenfield, Gerard. 1998. "The ICFTU and the Politics of Compromise." Pp. 180–89 in *Rising from the Ashes? Labor in the Age of "Global" Capitalism*, ed. E. Meiksins Wood, P. Meiksins, and M. Yates. New York: Monthly Review Press.

Gumbrell-McCormick, Rebecca. 2000. "Facing New Challenges: The International Confederation of Free Trade Unions, 1972–1990s." Pp. 341–517 in *The International Confederation of Free Trade Unions*, ed. M. van der Linden. Berne: Peter Lang Academic.

Harrod, Jeffrey. 1972. *Trade Union Foreign Policy: A Study of British and American Union Activities in Jamaica.* Garden City, NY: Doubleday.

Hensman, Rohini. 2001a. "The Impact of Globalisation on Employment in India and Responses from the Formal and Informal Sectors," Working Paper of the Changing Labour Relations in Asia (CLARA) Research Programme, International Institute of Social History, Amsterdam. Available at www.iisg.nl/asia.

Hensman, Rohini. 2001b. "Organizing Against the Odds: Women in India's Informal Sector." *Socialist Register* XXXVIII: 249–57.

Herbert, Ulrich. 1986. *Geschichte der Ausländerbeschäftigung in Deutschland 1880 bis 1980.* Berlin and Bonn: Dietz.

Herod, Andrew. 1995. "The Practice of International Labor Solidarity and the Geography of the Global Economy." *Economic Geography* LXXI, no. 4 (Oct.): 341–63.

———. 1997. "Labor as an Agent of Globalization and as a Global Agent." Pp. 167–200 in *Spaces of Globalization: Reasserting the Power of the Local,* ed. K. R. Cox. New York: The Guilford Press.

Herrmann, Karl Georg. 1994. *Die Geschichte des Internationalen Bergarbeiterverbandes, 1890–1939.* Frankfurt am Main and New York: Campus Verlag.

International Working Men's Association. 1863. "To the Workmen of France from the Working Men of England." *Beehive,* December 5.

Koch-Baumgarten, Sigrid. 1999. *Gewerkschaftsinternationalismus und die Herausforderung der Globalisierung: Das Beispiel der Internationalen Transportarbeiterföderation.* Frankfurt am Main and New York: Campus Verlag.

Kulemann, Wilhelm. 1898. "Die internationale Organisation der Buchdrucker." *Jahrbuch für Gesetzgebung, Verwaltung und Volkswirtschaft im Deutschen Reich* XXII: 374–409.

Lattek, Christine. 1988. "The Beginnings of Socialist Internationalism in the 1840s: The 'Democratic Friends of All Nations' in London." Pp. 259–82 in *Internationalism in the Labour Movement 1830–1940,* Vol. I., ed. F. L. Van Holthoon and M. van der Linden. Leiden: E. J. Brill.

Lee, Eric. 1997. *The Labour Movement and the Internet: The New Internationalism.* London and Chicago: Pluto Press.

Lehning, Arthur. 1970. *From Buonarroti to Bakunin: Studies in International Socialism.* Leiden: E. J. Brill.

Linden, Marcel van der. 1988. "The National Integration of European Working Classes, 1870–1914: Exploring the Causal Configuration." *International Review of Social History* XXXIII, no. 3: 285–311.

———, ed. 2000. *The International Confederation of Free Trade Unions.* Berne: Peter Lang Academic.

Logue, John. 1983. "'Da blev jeg svend og så tog jeg på valsen.' Svendevandringer og internationalisme i fagbevægelsen barndom," *Meddelelser om Forskning i Arbejderbevaegelsens Historie,* no. 20 (Apr.): 3–24.

Marsh, Arthur, and Victoria Ryan. 1989. *The Seamen: A History of the National Union of Seamen, 1887–1987.* Oxford: Malthouse Press.

Marx, Karl. 1973. "Manifesto of the Communist Party." In K. Marx, *The Revolutions of 1848. Political Writings,* Vol. I, D. Fernbach, trans. Harmondsworth: Penguin.

Merriman, John. 1985. *The Red City: Limoges and the French Nineteenth Century.* Oxford: Oxford University Press.

Musson, A. E. 1954. *The Typographical Association.* London: Oxford University Press.

———. 1972. *British Trade Unions, 1800–1875.* London and Basingstoke: Macmillan.

Nyström, Sigvard, and Peter Rütters. 1989. *History of the IUF.* Bonn: Friedrich-Ebert-Stiftung.

Official Report of the Free World Labour Conference and of the First Congress of the International Confederation of Free Trade Unions. 1949. London, Nov.-Dec.

Olle, Werner, and Wolfgang Schoeller. 1987. "World Market Competition and Restrictions upon International Trade Union Policies." Pp. 26–47 in *International Labour and the Third World,* ed. R. E. Boyd, R. Cohen, and P.C.W. Gutkind. Aldershot: Avebury.

Pasture, Patrick. 1999. *Histoire du syndicalisme chrétien international: La difficile recherche d'une troisième voie.* Paris: L'Harmattan.

Platzer, Hans-Wolfgang. 1991. *Gewerkschaftspolitik ohne Grenzen? Die transnationale Zusammenarbeit der Gewerkschaften im Europa der 90er Jahre.* Bonn: J.H.W. Dietz Nachf.

Portelli, Hugues. 1990. "La Confédération Européenne des Syndicats (CES)." Pp. 143–56 in *Syndicalisme: Dimensions Internationales,* ed. G. Devin. La Garenne-Colombes: Erasme.

Post, Ken. 1997. *Revolution's Other World: Communism and the Periphery, 1917–1939.* Houndmills, UK: Macmillan.

Powderly, T. V. 1889. *Thirty Years of Labor: 1859 to 1889.* Columbus, OH: Excelsior.

Prothero, Iorwerth. 1997. *Radical Artisans in England and France, 1830–1870.* Cambridge, UK: Cambridge University Press.

Radosh, Ronald. 1969. *American Labor and United States Foreign Policy: The Cold War and the Unions from Gompers to Lovestone.* New York: Random House.

Rebérioux, Madeleine. 1990. "Naissance du Secrétariat typographique international." Pp. 37–52 in *Syndicalisme: Dimensions Internationales,* ed. G. Devin. La Garenne-Colombes: Erasme.

Reinalda, Bob, ed. 1997. *The International Transportworkers Federation 1914–1945: The Edo Fimmen Era.* Amsterdam: Stichting beheer IISG.

Roberts, Clayton. 1996. *The Logic of Historical Explanation.* University Park, PA: Pennsylvania State University Press.

Rütters, Peter. 1989. *Chancen internationaler Gewerkschaftspolitik: Struktur und Einfluß der internationalen Union der Lebens- und Genußmittelarbeiter-Gewerkschaften (1945–1985).* Cologne: Bund Verlag.

———. 1990. "Histoire et développement des secrétariats professionels internationaux (SPI)." Pp. 251–67 in *Syndicalisme: Dimensions Internationales,* ed. G. Devin. La Garenne-Colombes: Erasme.

———. 1995. *Der Internationale Bergarbeiterverband 1890 bis 1993: Entwicklung und Politik.* Cologne: Bund Verlag.

Schäfer, Hermann. 1982. "Italienische 'Gastarbeiter' im deutschen Kaiserreich, 1890–1914." *Zeitschrift für Unternehmensgeschichte* XXVII, no. 3: 192–214.

Schneider, Dieter, ed. 1982. *Anfänge: Die Internationale der Arbeiter öffentlicher Betriebe.* Stuttgart: Courier.

Schnorbach, Hermann. 1989. *Lehrer im internationalen Gewerkschaftsbund: Entstehung und Entwicklung des Internationalen Berufssekretariats der Lehrer von 1918 bis 1945.* Weinheim and Munich: Juventa.

Scoville, James G. 1973. "Some Determinants of the Structure of Labor Movements." Pp. 58–78 in *The International Labor Movement in Transition,* ed. A. Sturmthal and J. G. Scoville. Urbana, IL: University of Illinois Press.

Simon, Hartmut. 1993. *Die Internationale Transportarbeiter-Föderation: Möglichkeiten und Grenzen internationaler Gewerkschaftsarbeit vor dem ersten Weltkrieg.* Essen: Klartext.

Sombart, Werner. 1924. *Der proletarische Sozialismus,* II: *Die Bewegung.* Jena: Gustav Fischer.

Spalding, Hobart A. 1992. "The Two Latin American Foreign Policies of the U.S. Labor Movement: The AFL-CIO Top Brass vs. Rank-and-File." *Science and Society 76*, no. 4 (Win.): 421–39.

Stevis, Dimitris. 1998. "International Labor Organizations, 1864–1997: The Weight of History and the Challenges of the Present." *Journal of World-Systems Research IV*, no. 1 (Win.): 52–75. Available at http:// jwsr.ucr.edu.

Sturmthal, Adolf. 1973. "Industrial Relations Strategies." Pp. 1–33 in *The International Labor Movement in Transition*, ed. A. Sturmthal and J. G. Scoville. Urbana, IL: University of Illinois Press, 1–33.

SZ. 2001. "Solidarität als Gegengewicht zur Globalisierung: Erster Weltkongress der Dienstleistungsgewerkschaft UNI in Berlin sucht Wege zur Wahrung der Arbeitnehmerinteressen." *Süddeutsche Zeitung*, 8–9 Sept.

Thorpe, Wayne. 1989. *"The Workers Themselves": Revolutionary Syndicalism and International Labour, 1913–1923*. Dordrecht: Kluwer.

———. 1990. "Syndicalist Internationalism before World War II." Pp. 237–60 in *Revolutionary Syndicalism: An International Perspective*, ed. M. van der Linden and W. Thorpe. Aldershot: Scolar Press.

Tostorff, Reiner. 1999. "'Moskau oder Amsterdam': Die Rote Gewerkschafts-Internationale 1921–1937." Habilitationsschrift, Johannes-Gutenberg-Universität, Mainz.

Tudyka, Kurt P. 1986. "Die Weltkonzernräte in der Krise." *WSI-Mitteilungen XXXIX*: 324–29.

Von Eschen, Penny M. 1997. *Race Against Empire: Black Americans and Anticolonialism, 1937–1957*. Ithaca, NY: Cornell University Press.

Wahlers, Gerhard. 1990. *CLAT: Geschichte einer lateinamerikanischen Gewerkschaftsinternationale*. Witterschlick/Bonn: Verlag M. Wehle.

Weiler, Peter. 1984. "Forming Responsible Trade Unions: The Colonial Office, Colonial Labor, and the Trades Union Congress." *Radical History Review*, nos. 28–30: 367–92.

Windmuller, John P. 1992. "European Regional Organizations." Pp. 527–44 in *European Labor Unions*, ed. J. Campbell. Westport, CT: Greenwood Press.

Wörner, Axel. 1979. "Die Rolle des IGB während der Solidaritätsbewegung 'Hände weg von Sowjetrussland' in den Jahren 1919/1920." *Beiträge zur Geschichte der Arbeiterbewegung XXI*, no. 4: 573–82.

*

PART II

Structures of Knowledge and Constructed Knowledge in the Modern World

＊

8

Commonality and Divergence of World Intellectual Structures in the Second Millennium CE

Randall Collins

Let us begin with a snapshot of the world intellectual situation at the turn of the first millennium, roughly in the centuries between 1000 and 1200 CE: In the Sung Dynasty, China is in its great period of intellectual efflorescence. Philosophy is led by the neo-Confucian movement and the most sophisticated of the Chinese metaphysicians, including Ch'eng-I, Ch'eng-Hao, and Chu Hsi—names that ought to be better known in the Western world, since they are as important as Aquinas, Leibniz, and Spinoza (whom they somewhat resemble). These are comprehensive, all-around thinkers, coordinating cosmology with moral imperatives and doctrines of government and naturalistic observation. Sung thinkers are the high points of what we would call natural science. There is also a movement of mathematicians, separate from the neo-Confucians, which creates a higher algebra using methods parallel to (but technically different from) those developed four centuries later by European mathematicians. These innovations are promoted by a shift in the institutional base for intellectual life. The examination system for selecting government officials is now being institutionalized on a large scale. This fosters debate over the content of the curriculum, opens up new careers for teachers preparing students for the exams, and, due to an overflow of intellectual contention, even promotes dissident schools that oppose the exams entirely. Institutional struggle fosters creative factions of opposing intellectual programs while getting maximal exposure by holding them together around a collective focus of attention.

The Chinese case illustrates my method, which I describe more fully in *The Sociology of Philosophies* (Collins 1998). I examine the networks of leading intellectuals (several hundred, in the case of China), looking for ways in which they constitute one another as factional chains across the generations. The famous individual names always appear in clusters, and, indeed, the intellectual productivity of each is a focal point constituted by the alliances and oppositions of collective movements, sharpened and glorified to epitomize a larger field of ongoing debate. Networks are useful, too, in charting long-distance transmission of intellectual action: In China, during the Sung dynasty, Japanese sojourners picked up the network connections that they transmitted back to Japan, which was the beginning of the major lineages of Japanese philosophy. In this case, these were largely Buddhist networks, the faction which had become displaced in China by the neo-Confucian upheaval, but which found continuation in a new institutional niche as monasteries became viable economic bases in Japan. Such patterns of sojourning enable us to map cultural dependence quite precisely. For this period, Japan was an importer of Chinese intellectual life. These links were broken in following centuries, and Japan became intellectually creative in its own right.

The method—charting the outstanding names and the lesser names that surround them, examining their network patterns, rivalries, and their material bases—gives us a sociological snapshot of intellectual communities and of their transformative conditions. For India, from roughly 1000–1200 CE, there were a series of philosophers, the high point of sophistication in metaphysical systems: Ramanuja, Shri Harsha, Madhva, Chitsukha, Gangesha, and others. Again, one is struck by the lack of global appreciation of regional intellectual history; with tiny exceptions, the intellectual accomplishments of each major world civilization are little-known elsewhere. The vigor of Indian intellectual life at that time was shaped by struggles among rival religious sects. The once-dominant Advaita monks (whose aconceptual cosmology was patterned on the Buddhist thinkers they displaced around the eighth and ninth centuries) were challenged by theistic Hindu sects; each made a statement of intellectual independence in the form of a new metaphysics, and thus pro-

moted another leading name among philosophers. Splits between fol-
lowers of the chief popular gods, Vishnu and Shiva, and rival religious
successions undergirded further creativity of rival philosophies. High
levels of epistemological acuteness emerged as opposing thinkers sought
new weapons for undercutting one another's constructions. Hindu religious life was far from being a mystical faith renouncing arguments, but
pushed instead to critical standards in theory of knowledge adumbrating those of Berkeley, Hume, and Kant. The specialized logic school
(Nyaya), and teachers of debate techniques, moved on to highly technical logic rivaling in its intricacies the formal logic of Europe in the twentieth century.

The institutional bases for this vigorous intellectual life were the
conflicts of expanding religious movements; the older monastic elite
of Advaita monks (founded by the famous Shankara in the eighth
century) was challenged by religious movements proselytizing among
the populace, with temples supported by mass donations. At these
bases, sectarian private schools emerged; "maths" supported specialists and kept up lineages of transmission. In one respect, India had
declined from its glory days several centuries earlier. During the period around 400–700 CE, Chinese monks traveled to India to visit the
great Buddhist monastery-universities, carrying back wave after wave
of new philosophies into China. Intellectually, India was no longer a
culture exporter (except, to some extent, to the newly consolidating
kingdoms of Southeast Asia) and China was no longer a culture importer.

In the House of Islam—Dar al-Islam, the regions where Islam holds
sway—the centuries around the millennium were also a high point of intellectual life. Here lived the great philosophers known even in the West: Ibn
Sina (Avicenna), al-Ghazali, Ibn Rushd (Averroës), and the Jewish philosopher Maimonides, along with scientists and mathematicians such as Ibn al-
Haitham, al-Biruni, and the heliocentric astronomer al-Tusi. Here again, we
find the pattern of new institutional bases and rival movements promoting
a field of creative action. The older bases of Islamic intellectual life—the
networks of jurists/theologians arguing at the mosques and the cosmopolitan translators under court patronage importing and elaborating ancient
Greek philosophy and science—were then upstaged by the proliferation of
"madrasas," endowed colleges with full-time professorships. The struggle
to work out the content of the curriculum, to define Islamic orthodoxy and
demarcate it from the heterodox, and to relate Sufi mysticism to textual
religion and accumulated tools of logical argument promoted many lines of
sophisticated argument and counterargument.

European Christendom of this period occupied a politically weak and
economically undeveloped corner of the world-system, but its intellectual

institutions were crystallizing and underpinning a first efflorescence of philosophical creativity. Networks of traveling teachers moved among the cathedral towns and leading monasteries in the eleventh century; by the twelfth and thirteenth centuries, guilds of teachers had formed universities, acquiring both feudal and ecclesiastical endowments, and were becoming a key component of the administrative and judicial system of the centralizing papacy as well as recruiting grounds for incipient royal bureaucracies. Fragmentation of authority promoted competition in founding universities and gave scholars autonomy and rights of collective self-government. The proliferation of universities and the boom in student enrollments generated credential inflation and, along with it, an elaborate set of examinations and degrees and an outpouring of intellectual productivity. This scholasticism, as it came to be known, was later derided by the Humanist movement, which rejected university education in favor of direct court patronage. But in its day, the university scholars of the high middle ages generated philosophies at levels of abstraction and of reflexive critique matching those contemporarily produced in India and the Islamic world. The very abstractness that its critics were to complain about later is a mark of the distance traveled by a specialized intellectual community—both from the naive reifications of everyday discourse and from received religious tradition. Better said, repeated generations of scholars controlling their autonomous careers within degree-granting institutions created their own topics and standards, and successively refined them to the point where they had become a self-conscious community of intellectuals over and above their identities as priests and defenders of the faith. Philosophy broke free from theology, even as it tried to maintain harmonious relations with it. This autonomous intellectual base fostered an ideology of intellectual independence that would be strengthened by later generations even as institutional bases shifted.

Through the twelfth century, European Christendom was in the position of culture importer, above all through contact with the Islamic world in Spain. The success of the Reconquista in 1248, which left only a sliver of Muslim Spain around Granada, and the hardening of religious lines on both sides at that time, broke off most of this transmission. It should be kept in mind, however, that the institutional base for autonomous intellectuals was already becoming active by the late twelfth century—above all in France, England, and Italy. The universities were generating their own dynamism, and networks of Christian scholars actively sought out cultural transmission from the Islamic world (later these networks would do the same thing from Byzantium) and brought this material into a matrix of indigenous developments.

My argument, so far, does not make intellectual productivity rest simply upon hegemonic position, either in world trade or in geopolitical power. Such conditions play into material and organizational structures that are more local: the institutional bases that allowed intellectuals to devote themselves to shaping chains of ideas into new levels of argument. The government examination system in China and its surrounding network of preparatory schools; the various monastic and popular movements in India, again with their schools; the Islamic madrasas and their relations with older networks of mosque jurists and court translators; the Christian university corporations of self-governing teaching bodies—these were the local bases that sustained and elaborated philosophies. Vigorously active networks of intellectuals could exist only where there were local bases. Given such bases, it was possible for sojourners to come, or for intellectual missionaries to go out and spread intellectual action to another region. Thus, sometimes there was interstimulation between distinct regional bases, and sometimes there was intellectual colonization that might or might not give rise to an independent intellectual scene (as happened in the case of Japan, after building its networks by connection with China).

Fast forward now through the following centuries, keeping an eye on these institutional bases. What is striking is that intellectual creativity generally becomes routine in most world regions, except in Japan and Europe. Usually, there are active communities of scholars but no further golden ages. The common denominator appears to be that the instructional base for intellectuals established around the turn of the millennium stays in place, but it reproduces the same intellectual lineages and the same style of ideas. In China, neo-Confucianism, which started out as a quasi-oppositional ideology contesting the examination system, became the standard position. The Chinese texts became the canonical requirements for examinations; the teachers dominated both government and private schools. From time to time, there are movements attacking neo-Confucian orthodoxy (such as the Wang Yang-Ming idealism in the early 1500s; and movements of naturalistic scholarship in the 1600s and 1700s), but these remain largely within the framework of scholarly routine. This state of affairs was satirized in a famous eighteenth-century novel, *The Scholars,* depicting their rather leisured lives during decades spent in preparing for examinations (Wu 1972).

Comparison with Japan shows that the contents of Chinese intellectual life are not to blame for this relative stagnation. The Japanese imported Chinese culture in several waves; following the imports of Buddhist philosophy in the twelfth and thirteenth centuries, a distinctively Japanese elaboration of aristocratic Buddhism appeared, especially Zen-inspired aestheticism, which has shaped the image of Japanese culture ever since. With the unification of Japan under the Tokugawas (ca. 1600–1850), the politically powerful Buddhist monasteries were deprived of their property and influence, and a concerted effort was made to replace their cultural dominance by neo-Confucian philosophy. But a half-dozen rival Confucian schools quickly developed in Japan, whose interlinked networks and competitive splits gave rise to innovative programs of thought. Some took neo-Confucianism into a naturalistic empiricism, promoting indigenous forms of economics and political philosophy comparable to those of the contemporary European enlightenment. Others revolted in a nationalist and neoconservative direction, with emphasis on textual scholarship and self-consciously historicist contextualization to combat the universalistic claims of the Confucians. Conservative thought in Japan was reflexive and sophisticated, comparable to European romanticism and neoorthodox defenses of theology. It is not surprising that after the Meiji revolution opened Japan to the world, the Japanese intellectual community responded quickly to contacts with European networks with creative innovations of their own. Japanese philosophers of the early twentieth century met, and trumped, phenomenologists and existentialists, as well as produced their own nationalist amalgams with evolutionist and Marxist ideas. The mixture is hard to fit into unilineal conceptions of what might be considered progressive, but it indicates that Japanese intellectual institutions acted on a level of considerable sophistication, meeting European culture not passively, but on its own trajectory. Within a generation after the Meiji opening, Japan quickly became a culture exporter, acquiring European proselytes to Japanese (mainly Zen) philosophy. Japanese cultural independence is matched by its economic and political independence in responding to the West: It met outside culture and the capitalist world-system on its own terms.

Routinization in India prevailed. By the seventeenth century, major new developments in Indian philosophy had come to an end. Initially, this was not because scholarship ceased, but rather because it grew increasingly technical (as in the case of the neo-Nyaya logicians, whose work was so refined that it was incomprehensible to most, except to a small community of initiates). Lineages and traditions did not cross and combat one another into innovation, but winnowed into a narrowing set of routines that attracted less and less attention, even around the Indian subcontinent. Later, under the European colonial regime, indigenous Indian traditions amalgamated into a defensive coalition, losing most of their sharp epistemological and logical edges and becoming a defensive ideology of "timeless Indian spiritual wisdom," a lowest common denominator suitable for contrasting with European outsiders. Looking at this process more closely, we see that the defensive amalgamation of Indian philosophies into a crude idealist religiosity had begun earlier, under the Mogul conquest. The overriding pattern is not defensive reaction to European thought per se, but a defensive huddling together of once-independent intellectual lineages into a coalition against dominant outsiders of whatever stripe. Intellectual decline began with routinization of Indian intellectual institutions, followed by several centuries of defensiveness against both Islamic and European Christian dominance, in both cases promoting a united front among Hindu thinkers that stifled innovation.

In the House of Islam, we see routinization setting in by the twelfth century (although held off longer in the unsettled conditions of Spain). The madrasas had settled into a fixed curriculum and become increasingly impervious to heterodox religious and intellectual elements. Islamic thought became promoted in a mode that extolled tradition. We must see the source of this conservatism in the institutional base rather than in the content of Islamic ideas, since those ideas were the ingredients of numerous creative combinations from the era of the great mixture and clash of positions in the Abbasid caliphate (eighth and ninth centuries) and through the eleventh century. Again, we can find highly technical work (in logic, mathematics, astronomy, and other areas of scholarship) in the era of the madrasas, but it did not travel well, and set up no atmosphere of intellectual action, no sense of excitement in intellectual careers. Unlike earlier centuries, when wave and counterwave brought new oppositions and syntheses, intellectual life after the twelfth century made little splash and attracted little attention.

Europe began to diverge as it built on the dynamism of its own millennial centuries. Rather than listing a few names emblematic of these movements, let me concentrate on the institutional shifts, singling out two of wide-ranging consequence. The first is the so-called scientific revolution of the sixteenth and seventeenth centuries. In one respect, this is a misnomer since study of the natural world, as well as exercise of mathematical techniques, existed widely before this period of European intellectual life. Medieval Christian philosophers like Grosseteste, Aquinas, Buridan, and Oresme engaged in natural science and mathematics as part of their comprehensive philosophies. The occupation of philosopher was a relatively undifferentiated, all-purpose scholarly role. This was true also in the Islamic world, where the "falasifa" typically covered scientific topics, sometimes with a high degree of creativity. In India, China, and Japan there are long-standing traditions of scientific and mathematical work. (One difference in the organization of intellectual communities in China and Japan was that the scientists or mathematicians and the philosophers were usually in distinct networks with very different institutional bases. In Islam and Christendom, the networks were generally identical; thus science and mathematics had far greater cultural resonance in Islam and Christendom and were doomed to obscurity in China and Japan.) What we call the "scientific revolution" ought to be called the rise of "rapid-discovery science": a movement consciously aware of its rapid and cumulative development of naturalistic knowledge. The chief ideologists of the movement, Bacon and Descartes, trumpeted the theme that it had discovered the means of discovery.

Rapid-discovery science became a split in the European network of all-purpose intellectuals. Explaining this new organization of intellectual networks is more complicated than I can explain here (see Collins 1998, ch. 10). Suffice it to mention that rapid-discovery science was, so to speak, a cyborg network combining human intellectuals with lineages of research equipment elaborated through generations of modification and cross-breeding, which guaranteed a stream of new empirical phenomena for which intellectuals could produce new explanations. These equipment genealogies were tied to capitalist competition, but their interpretation was generalized and intellectualized by symbiosis with philosophical networks. The scientific movement, for all its ideological aspirations, did not eliminate the older network of philosophers, the scholars whose work lacked this character of rapid discovery and its rush for consensus on a trail of past results in order to move forward to the next discovery. Philosophy remained, and, indeed, was goaded toward yet further metaphysical abstraction and epistemological reflexivity, precisely by having to take account of its boundaries with rapid-discovery science. Rapid-discovery science has propelled Western intellectual life ever since the seventeenth century: to some extent by emulation (not often successful when extended to the topics of humanistic culture or the social world); more deeply by reflections on demarcation and difference among regions of intellectual action; and often profoundly by antagonism and deeper exploration of what is nonscientific, nonrapid-discovery science. All these movements and countermovements meant that in the wake of the rapid-discovery science revolution, Western intellectual life would be repeatedly cloven by well-focused conflict and thus pushed onto new levels of innovation.

The second major institutional innovation was the research university. The breakthrough was the German university revolution, the movement at the time of Kant, Fichte, Hegel, and Humboldt (and indeed, led by just these people) to free the university from dominance by the church, and to make professors' careers dependent upon their innovative publications. This structure set off repeated rounds of innovation: first in humanistic scholarship; then by linking scientific laboratories to the "publish or perish" of scholarly careers; still later, with differentiation of the empirical social sciences. The institutional structure of the research university was emulated, with lags of a generation or more, throughout

Europe, America, and Japan by the end of the nineteenth century; in each instance, proving its creative power by setting off scholarly innovation wherever it was first adopted.

The domination of European intellectual culture throughout the world during the twentieth century came about in part through direct imposition, the prestige of Western military power and economic superiority, and, above all, through the spread of the university model. This was the same process of emulation by which the German research university had been adopted throughout the Western orbit. Paradoxically, the natural sciences and their technological applications could spread with the least violence to local intellectual traditions. Humanistic scholarship based on Western contents, and, above all, the social sciences with their additional layer of reflexivity, made the sharpest challenges to indigenous thought, especially when still packaged in religious form.

In conclusion, let me ask: What accounts for the uneven pattern of intellectual change among world regions, since their rough parity in innovation at the turn of the first millennium? It is important to note that intellectual stagnation is not necessarily a matter of a low level of material and social support for intellectual production. This can, of course, happen, as in the deep decline in the material bases for cultural production (and other kinds of production) in Europe after the fall of the Roman Empire. But what we see in the second millennium around the world is generally a continued, if essentially flat and unchanging, level of support. My argument, put in terms of configurations of the material bases of intellectual production, emphatically does not locate the cause of stagnation in "conservative" values. When organizational conditions are such that rival networks of intellectuals can compete over recognition, they generate creative departures from older traditions by recombining and working through those traditional texts at a new level of reflexivity. This has happened repeatedly, in all the world civilizations, even where the dominant ideology holds that all truth has already been revealed. Intellectual creativity often occurs in a conservative guise. For instance, the neo-Confucians, who innovated by claiming to be going back to original meanings and reviving long-neglected classic texts, or similar movements in India and Japan.

It is change in the material bases of intellectual life that generates creativity rather than the static level of material support, even if that level is adequate to keep many intellectuals at work. It is the upheavals in the bases of intellectual production that rearrange the competitive networks, displacing some and leaving niches in attention space for new lineages to fill. At these times, old stocks of cultural capital become recombined in new ways, new arguments are picked along new axes of opposition, and the level of reflexive sophistication is raised. In this light, from the middle of the millennium onward, China, India, and the Islamic world suffered not from lack of support for intellectual production but from stability in those bases. In this sense, to extend Gunder Frank's argument for the long-term superiority of China in the world economy, it is possible to say that the disadvantages of comparative abundance are even more severe in the realm of intellectual production.

It was chiefly in Japan where there were a series of changes from one intellectual base to another, and above all in Europe, where a series of such shocks and transitions in these intellectual bases came one on the heels of another. The crisis and decline of the medieval religious universities and their challenge by court-based Humanists; the great religious schism of the Reformation and its rearrangement of cultural alliances; the movement of rapid-discovery science, initially in cosmopolitan networks tied to religious parties, political factions, and commercial interests in complicated ways that gave plenty of scope for creative rivalries; the rise and spread of the research university; internal structural differentiation within the modern university, the reorganization of subdisciplines and the clash and negotiation of disciplinary boundaries and alliances; even the tug of war with new bases of intellectual production outside the university such as industrial and government laboratories for the rapid-discovery sciences; and journalistic and mass culture institutions tugging on the mind-sets and career chances of humanists and social scientists—each of these transitions, each of these struggles among rival bases of intellectual production, has generated rearrangements of intellectual fields. It is this repeated pattern of conflict that has kept Western intellectual networks, for the most part, from settling into routine, and has provoked them into repeated rounds of innovation. This is not to say that pockets of routine do not exist. Long-standing institutions of cultural production tend toward canonicity and scholasticism rather than innovation, and this is found in the most sheltered and stable parts of Western intellectual institutions as much as in the privileged Chinese mandarin class of the later dynasties spending their lives studying for endless rounds of examinations. It has been the higher level of conflict within and among bases of intellectual production, from the previous millennium to the most recent one, that has kept Western intellectual innovation high.

The prestige of Western intellectual production has led to its emulation around the world, under the protective umbrella of colonialism and after that umbrella has folded. Even rebellions against Western cultural dominance have been mobilized primarily through the use of Western modes of cultural production, most notably, the structure of the university. Universities retain their collective organization and their ethos of autonomy, even where they are put under constraint; thus the spread of universities around the world has provided the mobilizing bases for movements of nationalism, communism, and even religious fundamentalism. Intellectual contents vary, but the mobilizing package is much the same. University structures are doubly mobilizing, insofar as they are linked in networks back to their origins in the West and to the centers of world scholarship. This is especially true in the rapid-discovery sciences, where both prestige and technological payoff depend upon the speed with which one follows up the previous forefront of laboratory instrumentation. Thus, there is an endless succession of sojourners to the core universities of the West, siphoning off some of the most ambitious noncore intellectuals and sending others home with a combination of cosmopolitan reflexivity and localistic resentment.

The university operates as a bastion of autonomy for intellectuals, even where it is under siege. Indeed, siege conditions tend to provoke further rebellion from intellectuals in this base that makes them rich in mobilizing conditions, if poor in other respects. Efforts for the extension of democracy and technocratic ideologies about economic development make mass universities increasingly ubiquitous. In this ongoing expansion of education, there have been some alternatives to Western-style education, such as the movement to revive traditional madrasas in the Islamic world—the very structures that provided the original mobilizing base for the Taliban in Afghanistan (*Taliban* means students of a madrasa teacher, bound to him by ties of patrimonial and religious obligation). But the expansion of these alternative forms has occurred within the matrix of educational expansion, provoked by competitive emulation of Western-style educational democracy. Again, there is revolt over specifics within participation in a universal and seemingly inescapable process.

Can we expect future revival of distinct intellectual traditions in world regions, which would reduce Western intellectual culture back to its status at the previous millennium, as just one enclave among others? On the whole, I would say we cannot—not because Western intellectual culture is universally valid, but because the organization of intellectual production that undergirds it has become a world network. In the underlying competition among modes of intellectual production, Western-style institutions retain the advantage for the foreseeable future. This is because they are intellectually more innovative and thus attract more attention than their rivals, and because their structure (combining mass participation and collectively supported autonomy) makes them superior sites for mobilizing movements of all stripes. In the realm of cultural production, antisystemic movements are fated to use the organizational weapons of the very system that they rebel against.

References

Collins, Randall. 1998. *The Sociology of Philosophies*. Cambridge, MA: Harvard University Press.

Wu Ching-Tzu. 1972. *The Scholars*. New York: Grosset & Dunlap (orig. ca. 1750).

9

Africa and African Studies

Mahmood Mamdani

The critique of area studies comes from two sources: the *disciplines* of which it was a historical offshoot, and the *areas* it came to embrace as objects of knowledge. The discipline-based critique revolves around the observation that area studies are so turf-based that they know little else. The tendency to fetishize the area means that this knowledge is seldom available for comparative studies or for theorization. The regime of area studies is both very conscious and deeply sensitive about this critique. The response of area specialists has been to enumerate claims regarding the theoretical contributions of area studies (Bates, Mudimbe, and O'Barr 1993).

In contrast, the critique from the areas being studied is hardly audible. This is particularly the case with Africa, an area marked by an institutionally weak intelligentsia. I argue that the real source of weakness in African studies is the relative absence of an African voice—why more often than not, African studies seems like a settler representation of the native, its practitioners eager to patronize the native but fearful of the native intelligentsia. The corollary is that the stronger the intelligentsia in Africa, the more effectively it would hold accountable the area specialist outside Africa. One only needs to recall Jomo Kenyatta's observation when he wrote *Facing Mount Kenya* that he felt like a "rabbit turned poacher" (1978, xviii). Lest I be misunderstood, I hasten to add that this is not an argument that only Africans should study Africa. It is, however, an argument that African studies will continue to lack an even keel without an institutionally strong intelligentsia inside Africa.

The focus of this chapter is not the first critique, that from the disciplines, but the second: The critique from the native that is hardly audible but needs to be heard. In addition, I also argue that, for the critique of area studies to be adequate, it needs to be joined to that of the disciplines. Here, in a nutshell, is my argument: African studies was developed outside of Africa, but not within it. It was a study of Africa, but not by Africans. In this construct, the African was presented as a racial being, and Africa was geographically demarcated as equatorial Africa.

This racialized ontology—and geography—became the basis of an associated epistemology that treated political boundaries as boundaries of knowledge production and evolved a disciplinary specialization between the study of the "savage" and that of the "civilized." In contrast, the study of Africa in the African university has never been an area study. Fiercely modernist, it tends to treat the racialized legacy of the disciplines administratively rather than intellectually. If these statements sound like an exaggeration, it is because they are meant to problematize the body of knowledge known as African studies.

The Problem

Five years ago, I moved from Kampala to take up a job at the University of Cape Town. I soon tired of being asked, "So, you are from Africa?" My initial response was an equally rhetorical question: "Where do you think you are from?" My second response, however, was to stop and think—to remember that I had been asked the same question in Cairo, in Khartoum, even in Addis Ababa. These responses are anchored in a particular history, immediately the history of the past five or so centuries. Perhaps an even earlier history of Arab notions of "Bilad-al-Sudan," meaning the land of the Black people, to the south—one that came to differentiate tropical Africa from its northern and southern neighbors. It is a history that turned tropical Africa into a site for the large-scale plunder of human populations while leaving behind others in the hold of an ongoing process of political and social fragmentation and crisis. From this encounter developed the notion of "real" Africa, one with a double reference: spatially, to tropical Africa, and socially, to Bantu or Negro Africa. This doubly referenced terrain was the true domain of African studies.

It is in the tropical African colonies—those conquered in the aftermath of the Berlin Conference in the 1880s—that colonial knowledge was consciously joined to colonial power. The linkage took place under the regime of indirect rule. To appreciate it, we need to underline a key respect in which indirect rule was different from direct rule (Mamdani 1996). Direct-rule colonialism saw itself as a civilizational mission; it shunned custom as backward and sought to nurture a native intelligentsia in modern-style educational institutions. Macaulay made it clear in the *Minute on Education* that India could truly be reshaped in England's image by education alone (Metcalf 1995, 39–41). In contrast, Lord Frederick Lugard thought of a native intelligentsia not as an agent of progress (as earlier British colonizers had) but as an Indian disease, a carrier of unrest that must be avoided like the plague in the African indirect-rule colonies (Lugard 1965a, ch. 10). The point of indirect rule was not to "civilize" through the imposition of Western education and Western rule of law. Rather, it was to stabilize—with the accent more on order than law—through a mode of rule that legitimated a patriarchal version of "custom" that tapped the agency of a no longer stable patriarchal power.

Unlike direct rule, which dogmatically ignored the history and agency of the colonized, instead treating them as some kind of tabula rasa, the bent of indirect rule was far more analytic: Its practitioners were determined to understand the history of the colonized so as to better tap native agency. Lugard, in *The Dual Mandate in British Tropical Africa*, wrote:

> I have throughout these pages continually emphasized the necessity of recognizing, as a cardinal principle of British policy in dealing with native races, that institutions and methods, in order to command success and promote the happiness and welfare of the people, must be deep-rooted in their traditions and prejudices. (1965b, 211)

He then spelled out the practical significance of this shift in perspective:

> The history, the traditions, the idiosyncrasies, and the prejudices of each must be studied by the Resident and his staff, in order that the form adopted shall accord with natural evolution, and shall ensure the ready co-operation of the chiefs and the people. (1965b, 211)

As a form of power, indirect rule sought to reproduce two different kinds of political identities: a *racial* identity among its beneficiaries and an *ethnic* identity among its subjects (the former through a racialized citizenship and the latter through the imposition of ethnically defined Native Authorities given powers to enforce an ethnicized version of custom on their subjects). Knowledge—in this case, anthropology—

focused exclusively on the subject, as an ethnic being. If Orientalism, particularly in the version that flowered after the 1857 Indian mutiny, cast the Asian subject as essentially religious, Africanism defined the African subject as essentially ethnic. In each case, knowledge cast identity as primordial and essential, the very identity that power sought to reproduce as political. One begins to understand why the postcolonial power in independent Africa, militantly anticolonial, banned anthropology as a discipline.

Higher Education in Tropical Africa: A Nationalist Bequest

One central claim of indirect-rule colonialism was that subjects lacked the ability to think for themselves and needed intelligent tutelage: Good government could not come out of self-government. By proceeding on this assumption, education policies in the colonies gave life to the assumption as the end product of these policies. The number of universities in the whole of British colonial Africa—and the British were no exception among colonial powers—could be counted on the fingers of a single hand. No wonder university education had to be an achievement of the nationalist movement. Most tropical African countries received a university with independence. It came with the flag and the national anthem. It was a symbol no less important.

The one country/one university phenomenon meant that, more often than not, the national university functioned as an extension of the state apparatus. The only country with the number of universities and academics that could constitute a critical minimum in an internal struggle for academic freedom—whether that struggle was successful or not—was Nigeria. It is important to remember that Nigeria had one university with 1,000 students at independence in the early 1960s and forty-one universities with 131,000 students three decades later, in the early 1990s (Bako 1994). Everywhere else, those who sought space in creative work in the academy, sooner or later, turned to regional or continental initiatives to build the institutions from which to do so.

The most important such initiative was the Dakar-based Council for the Development of Social Research in Africa (CODESRIA), established in the early 1970s. Alongside new national universities, it provided an institutional framework for aggressive anticolonial thought. Most national universities, as I have already stated, banned anthropology as an academic discipline. The vice chancellor of the University of Ife dissolved the Center for African Studies, saying that there was no need for such a center in an African country. After all, the whole university was a center for African studies. Typified by CODESRIA and the University of Dar es Salaam, the postindependence academy in Africa was aggressively modern. In the postcolonial academy, political economy replaced anthropology as the mother of all disciplines. If the colonial state in Africa reified difference, nationalism reified unity. Shaped by a militant anti-imperialist perspective, political economy became the nationalist discipline par excellence. It upheld a singular sense of the self as the nation.

This reified sense of the self in the singular was shattered by two developments in the 1970s—one spectacular and external to the academy, the other internal and little noticed at the time. The former was the Ethiopian Revolution of 1975. In giving birth to a state power that spoke the language of Marxism, but at the same time brutally suppressed the student and the urban movements that also wore Marxist mantles, this revolution cracked open the singular self (Donham 1999). Its counterpart within the academy was the development of feminism, typified by the formation of the African Association of Women Researchers in Development (AAWORD). Not surprisingly, AAWORD was led by an Ethiopian executive secretary.

Critiquing Area Studies

If the postcolonial African academy was aggressively modernist and was discipline-based as any other university, the study of Africa in the Western academy continued to flourish as a preoccupation of an area-specific expertise. The area studies enterprise came to be underpinned by two core methodological claims. The first sees state boundaries as boundaries of knowledge, thereby turning political into epistemological boundaries. From this point of view, every expert must cultivate his or her own local patch, where geography is forever fixed by contemporary political boundaries. Even when radical area studies linked developments in the colony to those in imperial centers, it did not cross boundaries between colonies, especially not colonies occupied by different colonial powers. Rather than break free of the intellectual claustrophobia characteristic of the enterprise called area studies, the radical impulse in area studies linked local outcomes to colonialism historically, but not to broader developments regionally. As a result, the radical variant of area studies also tended to treat colonial political boundaries as if they were transhistorical; it too failed to historicize geography (Mamdani 2001).

The second methodological claim characteristic of area studies is born of a preoccupation with the production of facts. It translates into a stubborn resistance to theory in the name of valorizing fact. The claim is that theory is deadening: Instead of illuminating, it manipulates fact.

The assumption is that facts speak for themselves. But facts need to be put in context and interpreted; neither is possible without a theoretical illumination. This profoundly antitheoretical thrust links expertise to an incessant search for new facts. The area is mined over and over again in search of new facts. Every new book is read for evidence as to what new fact, if any, it contributes. In the process, the empirical is detached and set up in opposition to the theoretical.

To the extent that the area studies enterprise was driven by a search for the latest empirical fact, it needed native informants—not native intellectuals—as partners in the pursuit of knowledge. In the best of circumstances, the outcome was a polite coexistence whereby local intellectuals and area-study experts acknowledged one another through what, in a different context, has been called benign neglect. This was not simply because local intellectuals would appear as competitors to an outside expert seeking empirical expertise about an area. It reflected a fundamental difference in both perspective and methods, in how locals and area experts understood the process of the production of knowledge. It never dawned on me until I left East Africa that, whether at Makerere or Dar es Salaam, we were never really practitioners of area studies. In the pursuit of knowledge, we knew no boundaries. Our searches were inevitably thematic. However selective, the limits of our reach were global, from China to Nicaragua, and the former Soviet Union to South Africa. Yet, we never lost sight of our own location: We looked at the world from within Africa (Tandon 1982; Shivji 1986).

Problematizing Disciplines

If the thrust of colonialism—and I include apartheid as part of the colonial experience in Africa—was to reproduce a racial identity among its beneficiaries and an ethnic identity among its victims, to what extent were these identities grounded in the knowledge produced by the academy? If identities are institutionally reproduced, and institutionally transformed or erased, then is the institutional locus of identity formation simply political, or is it also cultural and academic? To what extent was the reproduction of particular identities, of Whites as racial and Blacks as ethnic beings, grounded in disciplinary divisions (or in a division of labor inside disciplines) that took these "facts" for granted? To what extent do epistemological boundaries reflect and legitimize certain identities and deflect and erode others? What, in other words, is the relation between the epistemological question (the boundaries of African studies) and the ontological question (the African identity) (Makgoba 1999)?

Rather than unrelated adversaries, disciplines and areas need to be seen as close cousins. To see them as related outcomes of both a shared imperial project and perspective is to problematize not just area studies but also the history of disciplines. The question is clearest if one focuses on the institutional boundaries of knowledge production in apartheid South Africa, which had the longest history of disciplines and area study within a single country (the disciplines focusing on the settler experience and area studies on the Bantu experience). Was not the division of labor between the study of White society on the one hand, and Black society on the other, anchored from the outset in a division between the sciences for the study of the civilized and those for the study of the savage? The former is strongly historical, while the latter is largely non-historical. The former is imbued with notions of progress, but the latter is marked by assumptions of premordiality and instinct (Cloete et al. 1997).

By banning the teaching of anthropology as an academic discipline, the postcolonial academy in Africa treated this heritage administratively. In contrast, the revolt of the postcolonial intelligentsia in the Western academy was possibly more creative, particularly in anthropology (the home discipline for the study of the savage.) Yet, the question needs to be asked: To what extent is this same division currently legitimized as specialization, as reflected by the binaries nationalism/tribalism, civic/ethnic, civil/customary, modernity/tradition, and rights/custom—binaries now reproduced inside disciplines originally meant for the study of the civilized, such as political science, sociology, and law?

A query guided by these questions is likely to bring to light the process by which power has shaped knowledge, by defining the boundaries between one type of knowledge and another, and, indeed, between knowledge and the lack of it. By historicizing the relationship between power and knowledge, we are likely to yield a bountiful harvest. African studies is a fruitful vantage point from which to interrogate the disciplines, not as much for the rationale for any disciplinary boundary, but the historical and political logic of the actual boundaries that do exist among and within the disciplines.

Beyond Imperialism and Nationalism

Of the two modes of producing knowledge of Africa I have discussed above, knowledge produced through the enterprise of area studies came to be known as African studies. The knowledge produced in the African academy had little to do with African studies. The African academy, I have emphasized, was discipline-based, not area-based. We did not think of ourselves as "doing" area studies. Debates were thematically driven. From our vantage point, African studies was a foreign preoccupation, propelled initially by colonial conquest, then by Cold War rivalry. At most, it was found in northern and southern parts of the continent, where the African was understood as the "other," either distant as tropical or intimate as Bantu.

If colonialism constructed the African as a racial being, then to come to terms with the legacy of colonialism requires transcending this racial identity, so as to fully humanize the construct of "African." If this is not to turn into a mere posture—say, one that moves from defining the African as a racial being to a multiplicity of "races"—one needs to grasp African as a historical identity, the result of an ongoing process. To study Africa today is to be profoundly subversive of the tradition of African studies. It is to redefine the study of Africa as the study of selves—in the plural and not the singular—in a postcolonial world. To do so without reifying the notion of self, without giving it a singular identity, is to embark on a journey that is likely to be marked by a double encounter with nationalism, whether it reifies unity or difference, a particular history, or a particular geography. On the one hand, we need comparative statements to locate particular histories in larger contexts. On the other hand, we need historical depth to identify the shift in regional (and not simply local and global) dynamics, allowing us to understand how the same locality may belong to different geographies at different times, allowing us to historicize geography.

If the study of Africa is to have the potential of triggering the process of self-examination that can unleash the energies necessary for this emancipatory process, it will have to be the institutional home for the study of selves. I suggest that this endeavor be defined by a double epistemological focus: The first, a query that problematizes knowledge specialization through a historical understanding of the study of Africa; the second, an endeavor that casts the study of Africa within broad intellectual terms. The first has a bearing on the disciplines, the second on area studies. If to participate in African studies today is to historicize and problematize the boundaries that frame it, and the binaries that divide this world and its inhabitants into those "civilized" and "civilizable," and the rest savage and irredeemable, then a reflection on the disciplinary location of knowledge about Africa should provide fruitful raw material for a wider reflection on the broad division of labor inside and among the disciplines.

The single most important failing of area studies is that it has failed to frame the study of the Third World in broad intellectual terms. If the "area" in area studies was perceived through narrow colonial and Cold War lenses, then the end of apartheid regionally and the Cold War globally offer us an opportunity to liberate the study of Africa from the shackles of area studies. To do so, one would need to recognize that decolonization in one sphere of life does not necessarily and automatically lead to decolonization in other spheres. If dependency theory taught us that political decolonization did not automatically lead to decolonization of the economy, postcolonial studies brings home the fact that intellectual decolonization will require no less than an intellectual movement to achieve this objective. To decolonize the study of Africa is to recognize that the study of Africa is not and cannot be only about Africa; it must also teach us something of late modern life.

References

Bako, Sabo. 1994. "Education and Adjustment in Nigeria: Conditionality and Resistance." Pp. 150–75 in *Academic Freedom in Africa*, ed. M. Diouf and M. Mamdani. Dakar: Codesria.

Bates, Robert H., V. Y. Mudimbe, and Jean O'Barr, eds. 1993. *Africa and the Disciplines.* Chicago: University of Chicago Press.

Cloete, Nico, Johan Muller, Malegapuru W. Makgoba, and Donald Ekong, eds. 1997. *Knowledge, Identity and Curriculum Transformation in Africa.* Cape Town: Maskew Miller Longman

Donham, Donald L. 1999. *Marxist Modern: An Ethnographic History of the Ethiopian Revolution.* Berkeley: University of California.

Kenyatta, Jomo. 1978. *Facing Mount Kenya: The Traditional Life of the Gikuya.* Nairobi: Heinemann Educational Books.

Lugard, Lord Frederick J. D. 1965a. *The Dual Mandate in British Tropical Africa*, 5th ed. London: Frank Cass.

———. 1965b. "Methods of Ruling Native Races." Pp. 193–229 in *The Dual Mandate in British Tropical Africa.* London: Frank Cass.

Makgoba, Malegapuru William, ed. 1999. *African Renaissance.* Cape Town: Tafelberg Publishers.

Mamdani, Mahmood. 1996. *Citizen and Subject: Contemporary Africa and the Legacy of Late Colonialism.* Princeton: Princeton University Press.

———. 2001. *When Victims Become Killers: Colonialism, Nativism, and Genocide in Rwanda.* Princeton: Princeton University Press.

Metcalf, Thomas R. 1995. *Ideologies of the Raj.* Cambridge: Cambridge University Press.

Shivji, Issa. 1986. *Limits of Legal Radicalism.* Dar es Salaam: University of Dar es Salaam.

Tandon, Yash, ed. 1982. *University of Dar es Salaam Debate on Class, State and Imperialism.* Dar es Salaam: Tanzania Publishing House.

10

A Critique of Lazy Reason: Against the Waste of Experience

Boaventura de Sousa Santos

This chapter builds upon my recent research project, entitled "Reinventing Social Emancipation."[1] The central topic of this project was the study of the alternatives to neoliberal globalization and global capitalism produced by social movements and NGOs, both local and global, struggling against exclusion and discrimination in various social domains and countries. The project's principal objective was to determine how alternative globalization is being generated from below, and what its possibilities and limits may be. I chose six countries, five of them semiperipheral, on different continents. My working hypothesis was that the conflicts between hegemonic, neoliberal globalization and counterhegemonic globalization are more intense in these countries. To confirm my hypothesis, I added one of the poorest countries in the world: Mozambique. The six countries selected were, including Mozambique as a peripheral country, South Africa, Brazil, Colombia, India, and Portugal. In these countries, initiatives, movements, and experiments were identified in five thematic areas: participatory democracy; alternative production systems; multiculturalism, collective rights, and cultural citizenship; alternatives to intellectual property rights and capitalist biodiversity; and new labor internationalism. As part of the project, and with the aim of identifying other discourses or narratives about the world, I conducted extended interviews with activists or leaders of the social movements or initiatives analyzed. This project elicited profound and interesting responses.

Here are the factors and circumstances of the project that most contributed to my epistemological reflection. First, it was a project conducted outside the hegemonic centers of social science production. Its aim was to create an international scientific community that was not linked to any hegemonic center of social science production. Second, the project included crossings not only of different theoretical and methodological traditions of social science but also of different cultures and forms of interaction between culture and knowledge—crossings, as well, between scientific and nonscientific knowledge. Third, this project dealt with struggles, initiatives, and alternative movements, many of them local and often in remote parts of the world, and thus easily discredited as irrelevant or too fragile or localized to offer a credible alternative to capitalism.

The factors and circumstances described above led me to three conclusions. First, social experience in the world is much wider and more varied than what Western scientific or philosophical tradition knows and considers important. Second, this social wealth is being wasted. On this waste feed the ideas that proclaim that there is no alternative, that history has come to an end, and so forth. Third, to fight against the waste of experience, to render visible the initiatives and the alternative movements and to give them credibility, resorting to social science as we know it is of very little use. After all, social science has been responsible for concealing or discrediting alternatives. There is no point in proposing another kind of social science to fight against the waste of social experience. Rather, a different model of rationality must be proposed. Without undertaking a critique of the model of Western rationality that has dominated for at least 200 years or all the proposals presented by the new social analysis, no alternative, however it may conceive of itself, will tend to reproduce the same effect of concealment and discrediting.

In this chapter, I engage in a critique of this model of rationality which, after Gottfried Willhelm Leibniz, I call *lazy reason,* and propose the prolegomena to another model that I designate as *cosmopolitan reason.* I try to ground three sociological procedures on this cosmopolitan reason: the sociology of absences, the sociology of emergences, and the work of translation.

There are three starting points. First, the understanding of the world exceeds (considerably) the Western understanding of the world. Second, the understanding of the world and the way it creates and legitimates social power has a lot to do with conceptions of time and temporality.

Third, the most fundamental characteristic of the Western conception of rationality is that, on the one hand, it contracts the present and, on the other, it expands the future. The contraction of the present, brought about by a peculiar conception of totality, turned the present into a fleeting instant, entrenched between the past and the future. By the same token, the linear conception of time and the planning of history allowed the future to expand infinitely. The larger the future, the more exhilarating the expectations vis-à-vis the experiences of today. In the 1940s, Ernst Bloch wondered in perplexity: "If we only live in the present, why is it so transient?" (1995, 313). The same perplexity lies at the core of this chapter.

I propose a cosmopolitan rationality that, in this phase of transition, must trace the inverse trajectory: to expand the present and contract the future. Only then will it be possible to create the time-space needed to know and valorize the inexhaustible social experience under way in our world today. In other words, only then will it be possible to avoid the massive waste of experience we suffer today. To expand the present, I propose a sociology of absences; to contract the future, a sociology of emergences.

Because we live, as Ilya Prigogine (1997) and Immanuel Wallerstein (1999) show, in a situation of bifurcation, the immense variety of social experiences these procedures can reveal is not adequately accounted for by a general theory. Instead of a general theory, I propose a theory or procedure of translation capable of creating mutual intelligibility among possible and available experiences.

In the preface to his *Theodicy* (1985 [1710]), Leibniz mentions the perplexity the sophism the ancients called "indolent" or "lazy reason" had always caused: If the future is necessary, and what must happen happens regardless of what we do, it is preferable to do nothing, to care for nothing, and merely to enjoy the pleasure of the present. This form of reason is lazy because it gives up thinking in the face of necessity and fatalism, of which Leibniz distinguishes three types: *Fatum Mahometanum, Fatum Stoicum,* and *Fatum Christianum.*

The laziness of this reason occurs in four different ways:

- *impotent reason* does not exert itself because it thinks it cannot do anything against necessity conceived of as external to itself;
- *arrogant reason* feels no need to exert itself because it imagines itself as unconditionally free and, therefore, free from the need to prove its own freedom;
- *metonymic reason* claims to be the only form of rationality and, therefore, does not exert itself to discover other kinds of rationality; or, if it does, it only does so to turn them into raw material;[2] and

- *proleptic reason* does not exert itself by thinking of the future because it believes the future is already known—it conceives of the future as linear, automatic, and infinitely overcoming the present.[3]

Under its various forms, lazy reason underlies the hegemonic knowledge, whether philosophical or scientific, produced in the West in the past 200 years. The consolidation of the liberal state in Europe and North America, the industrial revolutions and capitalist development, colonialism, and imperialism constituted the social and political context in which lazy reason evolved. Partial exceptions, like Romanticism and Marxism, were neither strong enough nor different enough to become an alternative to lazy reason. Thus, lazy reason created the framework of the large philosophical and epistemological debates of the last two centuries and, indeed, presided over them. For example, impotent and arrogant reason shaped the debate between determinism and free will, and, later, the debate between structuralism and existentialism. No wonder these debates were intellectually lazy. Metonymic reason, in turn, took over old debates (such as the debate between holism and atomism) and originated others, such as the *methodenstreit* between nomothetic and ideographic sciences and explanation and understanding. In the 1960s, metonymic reason led the debate on the two cultures launched by C. P. Snow (1959, 1964). In this debate, metonymic reason still considered itself as a totality, although a less monolithic one. The debate deepened in the 1980s and 1990s under feminist epistemology, cultural studies, and the social studies of science. By analyzing the heterogeneity of the practices and narratives of science, the new epistemologies further pulverized that totality and turned the two cultures into an unstable plurality. Metonymic reason, however, continued to lead the debates, even when the topic of multiculturalism was introduced, and science started to see itself as multicultural. Other knowledges, neither scientific nor philosophical, particularly non-Western knowledges, have remained largely outside the debate until now.

Regarding proleptic reason, the way it conceived of history planning dominated the debates on dialectical idealism, materialism, historicism, and pragmatism. From the 1980s onward, proleptic reason was contested mainly by the complexity and chaos theories. Based on the linear idea of progress, it was confronted with the ideas of entropy and disaster, although no alternative has yet emerged from such confrontation.

The debate generated by the two cultures and the various third cultures thereby emerging—the social sciences (Lepenies 1988) or the popularization of science (Brockman 1995)—did not affect the domination of lazy reason under any of its four forms.[4] There was, therefore, no restructuring of knowledge. Nor could there be, because the indolence of reason manifests itself particularly in the way it resists changes of routine and transforms hegemonic interests into true knowledge. As I see it, in order for deep changes to occur in the structure of knowledge, it is necessary to change the form of reason that presides over knowledge and its structure. In a word, lazy reason must be confronted.

In this chapter, I confront lazy reason in two of its forms: as metonymic and proleptic reason.[5] The two other forms have elicited more debate (on determinism or free will, realism or constructivism).

The Critique of Metonymic Reason

Metonymic reason is obsessed with the idea of totality in the form of order. There is no understanding or action without reference to the whole, the whole having absolute primacy over each one of its parts. Therefore, there is only one logic ruling both the behavior of the whole and each of its parts. There is homogeneity between the whole and its parts, the parts having no independent existence outside of their relation to the whole. Possible variations in the movement of the parts do not affect the whole and are viewed as particularities. The most complete form of totality according to metonymic reason is dichotomy, because it combines symmetry and hierarchy most elegantly. The symmetry of parts is always a horizontal relation that conceals a vertical relation. It is so because, contrary to what is proclaimed by metonymic reason, the whole is less, not more, than the sum of its parts. The whole is a part turned into a term of reference for the others. This is why all dichotomies sanctioned by metonymic reason contain a hierarchy: scientific culture/literary culture; scientific knowledge/traditional knowledge; man/woman; culture/nature; civilized/primitive; capital/labor; white/black; North/South; West/East, and so on.

All this is too well known today and needs no further elaboration. I will instead focus on its consequences.[6] The two main ones are the following. First, because nothing exists outside the totality that is, or deserves to be, intelligible, metonymic reason claims to be exclusive, complete, and universal, even though it is merely one of the logics of rationality that exists in the world and prevails only in the strata of the world comprised by Western modernity. Metonymic reason cannot accept that the understanding of the world is much larger than the Western conception. Metonymic reason cannot accept that the understanding of the world is much larger than the Western conception. Second, none of the parts can be conceived outside its relation with the totality. The North is not intelligible outside its relation with the South just as traditional knowledge is not intelligible outside its relation with scientific knowledge, or woman outside her relation with man. It is inconceivable that each of the parts may have its own life beyond the dichotomous relation, let alone be a different totality. The understanding of the world promoted by metonymic reason is, therefore, not only partial but also very selective. Western modernity, controlled by metonymic reason, has a limited understanding of the world and also a limited understanding of itself.

Before I address the processes that sustain understanding and police its limits, I must explain how such a limited rationality ended up having such primacy in the last 200 years. Metonymic reason is, with proleptic reason, the response of the West, which is intent on the capitalist transformation of the world, to its own cultural and philosophical marginality vis-à-vis the East. As Karl Jaspers and others have shown, the West constituted itself as a deserter part of a founding matrix—the East (Jaspers 1951, 1976; Marramao 1995, 160).[7] This founding matrix is truly totalizing because it encompasses a multiplicity of worlds (both earthly and nonearthly) and a multiplicity of times (past, present, future, cyclical, linear, and simultaneous). As such, it has no need to claim totality or to subordinate its parts to itself. It is an antidichotomic matrix because it does not have to control or police limits. On the contrary, the West, aware of its own eccentricity vis-à-vis this matrix, takes from it only what can encourage the expansion of capitalism. Thus, the multiplicity of worlds is reduced to the earthly world and the multiplicity of times is reduced to linear time.

Two processes preside over such a reduction. The reduction of the multiplicity of worlds to the earthly world comes about by means of secularization and laicization as analyzed by Max Weber (1958, 1963, 1968), Reinhart Koselleck (1985), and Giacomo Marramao (1995), among many others. The reduction of the multiplicity of times to linear time is achieved by means of the concepts replacing the soteriological idea that used to link the multiplicity of worlds, namely, the concepts of progress and revolution upon which proleptic reason came to be based. This crippled conception of Eastern wholeness, precisely because it is crippled, must affirm itself as a totality and impose homogeneity on its parts. It was with it that the West took possession of the world in a productive way and turned the East into a stagnated, unproductive center. With it, too, Weber countered the unproductive seduction of the East with the disenchantment of the Western world.

As Marramao notes, the supremacy of the West, created from the margins, never turned culturally into an alternative centrality vis-à-vis the East (1995, 160). For this reason, the power of Western metonymic reason always exceeded the power of its foundation. This power is, however, undermined by a weakness that paradoxically grounds the very reason for its power in the world. This dialectic between power and weakness ended up translating itself into the parallel development of two opposite urges, the *Wille zur Macht* from Hobbes to Nietzsche, Carl Schmitt, and Nazism/fascism, and the *Wille zur Ohnmacht* from Rousseau to Kelsen, democracy, and the primacy of the law. In each of these urges, totality is nonetheless present. Because it is crippled, totality must ignore what it cannot contain and impose its primacy on its parts; and the parts, to be maintained under its control, must be homogenized as parts. Because it is unsure of its foundations, metonymic reason does not insert itself in the world through argumentation and rhetoric. It does not explain itself; rather it imposes itself by the efficacy of its imposition. Such efficacy manifests itself twofold: by productive and legislative thought. Instead of the reasonableness of argumentation, it resorts to productivity and legitimate coercion.

Grounded on metonymic reason, the transformation of the world cannot be based on or accompanied by an adequate understanding of the world. In this case, inadequacy means violence, destruction, and silencing for all those who, outside the West, were subjected to metonymic reason. In the West, it means alienation, malaise, and uneasiness. Walter Benjamin was witness to this uneasiness when he showed the paradox that has dominated life in the West ever since: the fact that the wealth of events translates itself into the poverty, rather than wealth, of our experience (Benjamin 1972, II, pt. 1, 213–19).[8] This paradox came to coexist with another: the fact that the vertigo of change frequently turns itself into a feeling of stagnation.

Today, it begins to be obvious that metonymic reason has contracted the world in the very process of expanding the world according to its own rules. Herein lies the crisis of the idea of progress and hence the crisis of the idea of totality that grounds it. The abbreviated version of the world became possible because of a conception of the present time that reduces it to the fleeting instant between what no longer is and what not yet is. The brevity of the gaze conceals the abbreviation of the gazed upon. As such, what is considered contemporaneous is an extremely reduced part of the simultaneous. The gaze that sees a person plowing the land only sees the premodern peasant. This much acknowledges Koselleck when he speaks of the noncontemporaneity of the contemporaneous (1985). But he does not problematize that in such asymmetry a hierarchy is hidden, namely, the superiority of those who establish the time that determines contemporaneity. The contraction of the present conceals most of the inexhaustible richness of the social experiences in the world. Benjamin identified the problem, but not its causes. The poverty of experience is not the expression of what is lacking, but rather, the expression of an arrogance: the arrogance to refuse to see, let alone valorize, the experience around us, only because it is outside the reason that allows us to do so.

The critique of metonymic reason is, therefore, a necessary condition to recuperate the wasted experience. Is what is at stake the expansion of the world through the expansion of the present? Only by means of a new time-space will it be possible to identify and valorize the inexhaustible richness of the world and the present. But this new time-space presupposes another kind of reason. Up until now, the aspiration of the expansion of the present was formulated by literary creators alone. An example, among many, is Franz Kafka's parable about the precariousness of modern man stuck between two formidable adversaries: the past and the future.[9]

The expansion of the present lies in two procedures that question metonymic reason's foundations. The first consists of the proliferation of totalities. The question is not to amplify the totality propounded by metonymic reason, but rather, to make it coexist with other totalities. The second consists of showing that any totality is made of heterogeneity and that the parts that comprise it have a life outside of it. This is to say, their being part of a certain totality is always precarious, whether because the parts always hold, at least in latency, the status of totality, or because parts migrate from one totality to another. What I propose is a procedure denied by metonymic reason: to think of the terms of the dichotomies, regardless of the power articulations and relations that bring them together, as a first step to free them of such relations. Also to reveal other alternative relations that have been obscured by hegemonic dichotomies—to conceive of the South as if there were no North, to conceive of woman as if there were no man, to conceive of the slave as if there were no master. The assumption underlying this procedure is that metonymic reason was not entirely successful when it dragged these entities into the dichotomies, because components or fragments not socialized by the order of totality were left out. These components or fragments have been wandering outside the totality like meteorites hovering in the space of order, not susceptible to being perceived and controlled by order.

In this transition phase in which metonymic reason, although much discredited, is still dominant, the enlargement of the world and the expansion of the present must begin with a procedure that I designate as *sociology of absences*. It consists of an inquiry that aims to explain that what does not exist is in fact actively produced as nonexistent, that is, as a noncredible alternative to what exists. Its empirical object is deemed impossible in the light of conventional social science, and, for this reason, its formulation already represents a break with it. The objective of the sociology of absences is to transform impossible objects into possible objects and absent objects into present objects. It does so by focusing on the fragments of social experience that have not been fully socialized by metonymic reason. What exists in the South that escapes the North/South dichotomy? What exists in traditional medicine that escapes the modern/traditional medicine dichotomy? What exists in woman apart from her relation with man? Is it possible to see the subaltern regardless of the relation of subalternity?

There is no single, univocal way of not existing. The logics and processes, through which metonymic reason produces the nonexistence of what does not fit its totality and linear time, are various. Nonexistence is produced whenever a certain entity is disqualified and rendered invisible, unintelligible, or irreversibly discardable. What unites the different logics of production of nonexistence is that they are all manifestations of the same rational monoculture. I distinguish five logics or modes of production of nonexistence.

The first derives from the monoculture of *knowledge and rigor of knowledge.* It is the most powerful mode of production of nonexistence. It consists in turning modern science and high culture into the sole criteria of truth and aesthetic quality, respectively. The complicity that unites the two cultures resides in the fact that both claim, each in its own field, to be the exclusive canons of production of knowledge or artistic creation. All that is not recognized or legitimated by the canon is declared nonexistent. In this case, nonexistence appears in the form of ignorance or lack of culture.

The second logic resides in the monoculture of *linear time,* the idea that history has unique and well-known meaning and direction. This meaning and direction have been formulated in different ways in the last 200 years: progress, revolution, modernization, development, and globalization. Common to all these formulations is the idea that time is linear and that ahead of time proceed the core countries of the world-system and, along with them, the dominant knowledges, institutions, and forms of sociability. This logic produces nonexistence by describing as backward whatever is asymmetrical vis-à-vis whatever is declared forward. It is according to this logic that Western modernity produces the noncontemporaneity of the contemporaneous and that the idea of simultaneity conceals the asymmetries of the historical times that converge into it. An encounter between an African peasant and an officer of the World Bank on his field trip illustrates this condition. In this case, nonexistence assumes the form of residuum, which, in turn, has assumed many designations for the past 200 years, the first being the primitive, closely followed by the traditional, the premodern, the simple, the obsolete, and the underdeveloped.

The third logic is the logic of social classification, which is based on the monoculture of *naturalization of differences.* It consists of distributing populations according to categories that naturalize hierarchies. Racial and sexual classifications are the most salient manifestations of this logic. Contrary to what happens in the relation between capital and labor, social classification is based on attributes that negate the intentionality of social hierarchy. The relation of domination is the consequence, rather than the cause, of this hierarchy, and it may even be considered as an obligation of whoever is classified as superior (for example, the White man's burden in his civilizing mission). Although the two forms of classification (race and sex) are decisive for the relation between capital and labor to stabilize and spread globally, racial classification was the one most deeply reconstructed by capitalism, as Immanuel Wallerstein and Etienne Balibar (1991) and Aníbal Quijano (2000), among others, have shown.[10] According to this logic, nonexistence is produced as a form of inferiority, insuperable inferiority because it is natural. The inferior ones, because they are insuperably inferior, cannot be a credible alternative to those that are superior.

The fourth logic of the production of nonexistence is the *logic of the dominant scale.* According to this logic, the scale adopted as primordial determines the irrelevance of all other possible scales. In Western modernity, the dominant scale appears under two different forms: the universal and the global. Universalism is the scale of the entities or realities that prevail regardless of specific contexts. For that reason, they take precedence over all other realities that depend on contexts and are, therefore, considered particular or vernacular. Globalization is the scale that, in the last twenty years, has acquired unprecedented relevance in various social fields. It is the scale that privileges entities or realities that widen their scope to the whole globe, thus earning the prerogative to designate rival entities as local. According to this logic, nonexistence is produced under the form of the particular and the local. The entities or realities defined as such are captured in scales that render them incapable of being credible alternatives to what exists globally and universally.

Finally, the fifth logic of nonexistence is the *logic of productivity.* It resides in the monoculture of the criteria of capitalist productivity. According to this logic, economic growth is an unquestionable rational objective. As such, the criterion of productivity that best serves this objective is unquestionable as well. This criterion applies both to nature and human labor. Productive nature is nature at its maximum fertility in a given production cycle, whereas productive labor is labor that maximizes profit generation, likewise, in a given production cycle. According to this logic, nonexistence is produced in the form of nonproductivity. Applied to nature, nonproductivity is sterility; applied to labor, it becomes sloth or professional disqualification.

There are five principal social forms of nonexistence produced by metonymic reason: the ignorant, residual, inferior, local, and nonproductive. They are social forms of nonexistence because the realities to which they give shape are present only as obstacles vis-à-vis the realities deemed relevant, be they scientific, advanced, superior, global, or productive. They are, therefore, disqualified parts of homogeneous totalities that merely confirm what exists and precisely as it exists. They are what exist under irretrievably disqualified forms of existing.

The social production of these absences results in the subtraction of the world and the contraction of the present, and hence in the waste of experience. The sociology of absences aims to identify the scope of this subtraction and contraction so that the experiences produced as absent may be liberated from those relations of production and thereby made present. To be made present means to be considered alternatives to hegemonic experience, to have their credibility discussed and argued for, and their relations taken as an object of political dispute. The sociology of absences aims to create a want and to turn the lack of social experience into the waste of social experience. It thereby creates the conditions to enlarge the field of credible experiences in this world and time, thus contributing to enlarging the world and expanding the present. The enlargement of the world occurs not only because the field of credible experiences is widened but also because the possibilities of social experimentation in the future are increased. The expansion of the present occurs as what is considered contemporaneous is augmented, as present time is flattened out so that all experiences and practices occurring simultaneously may eventually be considered contemporaneous.

How does the sociology of absences work? The sociology of absences starts from two inquiries. The first one inquires about the reasons why such a strange and exclusive conception of totality could have acquired such primacy in the past 200 years. The second inquiry aims to identify the ways to confront and overcome such a conception of totality as well as the metonymic reason that sustains it. The first, more conventional inquiry has been tackled by various aspects of critical sociology—from the social and cultural studies of science to feminist criticism, deconstruction, postcolonial studies, and so on. In this chapter, I focus on the second inquiry, which has been less addressed until now.

Homogeneous and exclusive totalities and the metonymic reason that sustains them can be superseded by confronting each one of the modes of production of absence mentioned previously. Because metonymic reason shaped conventional social science, the sociology of absences cannot be anything but transgressive, and as such, is bound to be discredited. Nonconformity with such discredit and struggle for credibility, however, make it possible for the sociology of absences not to remain an absent sociology.

The Ecology of Knowledges

The first logic, the logic of the monoculture of scientific knowledge and rigor, must be confronted with the identification of other knowledges and criteria of rigor that operate credibly in social practices pronounced nonexistent by metonymic reason. Such contextual credibility must be deemed a sufficient condition for the knowledge in question to have enough legitimacy to participate in epistemological debates with other knowledges, namely, with scientific knowledge. The central idea of the sociology of absences is that there is no ignorance or knowledge in general. All ignorance is ignorant of a certain knowledge, and all knowledge is the overcoming of a particular ignorance (Santos 1995, 25). This principle of incompleteness of all knowledges is the condition of the possibility of epistemological dialogue and debate among the different knowledges. What each knowledge contributes to such a dialogue is the way in which it leads a certain practice to overcome a certain ignorance. Confrontation and dialogue among knowledges is confrontation and dialogue among the different processes through which practices that are ignorant in different ways turn into practices that are knowledgeable in different ways.

In this domain, the sociology of absences aims to substitute an ecology of knowledges for the monoculture of scientific knowledge. Such an ecology of knowledges overcomes the monoculture of scientific knowledge and permits the idea that the nonscientific knowledges are alternatives to scientific knowledge. The idea of alternatives presupposes the idea of normalcy, and the latter the idea of norm, and so, nothing being further specified, the designation of something as an alternative carries a latent connotation of subalternity. Let us take biomedicine and African traditional medicine as examples. It makes no sense to consider the latter, by far the predominant form of medicine in Africa, as an alternative to the former. The important thing is to identify the contexts and the practices in which each operates, and the way they conceive of health and sickness and overcome ignorance (as undiagnosed illness) in applied knowledge (as cure).

The Ecology of Temporalities

The second logic, the logic of the monoculture of linear time, must be confronted with the idea that linear time is only one among many conceptions of time and that, if we take the world as our unit of analysis, it is not even the most commonly adopted. The predominance of linear time is not the result of its primacy as a temporal conception, but the result of the primacy of Western modernity that embraced linear time as its own. Linear time was adopted by Western modernity through the secularization of Judeo-Christian eschatology, but it never erased—not even in the West—other conceptions of time such as circular time, the doctrine of the eternal return, and others that are not adequately grasped by the images of the arrow or circle.

The need to take into account these different conceptions of time derives from the fact, pointed out by Koselleck (1985) and Marramao (1995), that societies understand power according to the conceptions of temporality they hold. The most resistant relations of domination are those based on hierarchies among temporalities. Such hierarchies are constitutive of the world-system. They reduce much of social experience to the condition of residuum. Experiences become residual because they are contemporary in ways that are not recognizable by the dominant temporality: linear time.

In this domain, the sociology of absences aims to free social practices from their status as residuum, devolving to them their own temporality and thus the possibility of autonomous development. Once liberated from linear time and devolved to its own temporality, the activity of the African or Asian peasant stops being residual and becomes contemporaneous of the activity of the hi-tech farmer in the United States or the activity of the World Bank executive. By the same token, the presence or relevance of the ancestors in one's life in different cultures ceases to be an anachronistic manifestation of primitive religion or magic to become another way of experiencing contemporaneity.

By freeing alternative realities from their status as residuum, the sociology of absences replaces the monoculture of linear time with the ecology of temporalities. Societies are constituted of various temporalities. Many practices are disqualified, suppressed, or rendered unintelligible because they are ruled by temporalities that are not contained in the temporal canon of Western capitalist modernity. Once these temporalities are recuperated and become known, the practices and sociabilities ruled by them become intelligible and credible objects of argumentation and political debate. The expansion of the present occurs, in this case, by the relativization of linear time and the valorization of other temporalities that may articulate or conflict with it.

The Ecology of Recognition

The third logic of the production of absences is the logic of social classification. Although in all logics of production of absence the disqualification of practices goes hand in hand with the disqualification of agents, it is here that the disqualification affects mainly the agents (and only secondly, the social experience of which they are the protagonists). The coloniality of Western modern capitalist power mentioned by Quijano (2000) consists in collapsing difference and inequality, while claiming the privilege to ascertain who is equal or different. The sociology of absences confronts coloniality by looking for a new articulation between the principles of equality and difference, thus allowing for the possibility of equal differences—an ecology of differences comprised of mutual recognition. It does so by submitting hierarchy to critical ethnography (Santos 2001b). This consists of deconstructing both difference (To what extent is difference a product of hierarchy?) and hierarchy (To what extent is hierarchy a product of difference?). The differences that remain when hierarchy vanishes become a powerful denunciation of the differences that hierarchy reclaims in order not to vanish.

The Ecology of Trans-Scale

The sociology of absences confronts the fourth logic, the logic of the dominant scale, by recuperating what, in the local, is not the result of hegemonic globalization. The local that has been integrated in hegemonic globalization is what I designate as localized globalism, that is, the specific impact of hegemonic globalization on the local (Santos 1998b, 2000). As it deglobalizes the local vis-à-vis hegemonic globalization, the sociology of absences also explores the possibility of counterhegemonic globalization. In sum, the deglobalization of the local and its eventual counterhegemonic reglobalization broaden the diversity of social practices by offering alternatives to localized globalism. The sociology of absences requires, in this domain, the use of cartographic imagination, whether to see in each scale of representation not only what it reveals but also what it conceals, or to deal with cognitive maps that operate simultaneously with different scales, namely, to identify local/global articulations (Santos 1995, 456–73; 2001a).

The Ecology of Productivity

Finally, in the domain of the fifth logic, the logic of productivity, the sociology of absences consists of recuperating and valorizing alternative systems of production, popular economic organizations, workers' cooperatives, self-managed enterprises, solidarity economy, and so on, which have been hidden or discredited by the capitalist orthodoxy of productivity. This is perhaps the most controversial domain of the sociology of absences, for it confronts both the paradigm of development and infinite economic growth and the logic of the primacy of the objectives of accumulation over the objectives of distribution that sustain global capitalism.

In each of the five domains, the objective of the sociology of absences is to disclose the diversity and multiplicity of social practices and confer credit to them in opposition to the exclusive credibility of hegemonic practices. The idea of multiplicity and nondestructive relations is suggested by the concept of ecology: of knowledges, temporalities, recognition, and of social production and distribution. The idea that reality cannot be reduced to what exists is common to all of these ecologies. It amounts to an ample version of realism that includes the realities rendered absent by silence, suppression, and marginalization—realities that are actively produced as nonexistent.

In conclusion, the exercise of the sociology of absences is counterfactual and takes place by confronting conventional scientific commonsense. To be carried out, it demands sociological imagination, both epistemological and democratic imagination. Epistemological imagination allows for the recognition of different knowledges, perspectives, scales of identification and analysis, and evaluation of practices. Democratic imagination allows for the recognition of different practices and social agents. Both the epistemological and the democratic imaginations have deconstructive and reconstructive dimensions. Deconstruction assumes five forms, corresponding to the critique of the five logics of metonymic reason, namely, unthinking, deresidualizing, deracializing, delocalizing, and deproducing. Reconstruction is comprised of the five ecologies mentioned previously.

The Critique of Proleptic Reason

Proleptic reason is the face of lazy reason when the future is conceived from the vantage point of the monoculture of linear time. The monoculture of linear time expanded the future enormously at the same time that it contracted the present, as we saw when metonymic reason was analyzed. Because the meaning and direction of history reside in progress, and progress is unbounded, the future is infinite. Because it is projected according to an irreversible direction, however, the future is, as Benjamin clearly saw, an empty and homogeneous time.[11] The future is as abundant as empty, a future that only exists, as Marramao says, "to become past" (1995, 126). A future thus conceived need not be the object of thought; this consists of the laziness of proleptic reason.

Whereas the objective of the critique of metonymic reason is to expand the present, the objective of the critique of proleptic reason is to contract the future. To contract the future means to make it scarce and hence the object of care. The future has no other meaning or direction but what results from such care. To contract the future consists of eliminating, or at least diminishing, the discrepancy between the conception of the future of society and the conception of the future of individuals. Unlike the future of society, the future of individuals is limited by the duration of their lives—or reincarnated lives, in cultures where metempsychosis is a matter of faith. In either case, the limited character of the future, and the fact that it depends on the management and care of individuals, makes it possible for the future to be reckoned with as an intrinsic component of the present. In other words, the contraction of the future contributes to the expansion of the present.

Whereas the expansion of the present is obtained through the sociology of absences, the contraction of the future is obtained through the *sociology of emergences.* The sociology of emergences consists of replacing the emptiness of the future according to linear time (an emptiness that may be all or nothing) with a future of plural and concrete possibilities, utopian and realist at one time, and constructed in the present by means of activities of care.

The concept that rules the sociology of emergences is the concept of Not Yet (*Noch Nicht*) advanced by Ernst Bloch (1995). Bloch takes issue with the fact that Western philosophy was dominated by the concepts of All (*Alles*) and Nothing (*Nichts*), in which everything seems to be contained in latency and from which nothing new can emerge. Western philosophy is, therefore, a static philosophy. For Bloch, the possible is the most uncertain and the most ignored concept in Western philosophy (1995, 241). Yet, only the possible reveals the inexhaustible wealth of the world. Besides All and Nothing, Bloch introduces two new concepts: Not (*Nicht*) and Not Yet. The Not is the lack of something and the expression of the will to surmount that lack. The Not is thus distinguished from the Nothing (1995, 306). To say no is to say yes to something different. The Not Yet is the more complex category because it expresses what exists as mere tendency, a movement that is latent in the very process of manifesting itself. The Not Yet is the way in which the future is inscribed in the present. It is not an indeterminate or infinite future, but rather a concrete possibility and a capacity neither of which exists in a vacuum that is not completely predetermined. Indeed, these terms actively redetermine all they touch, thus questioning the determinations that exist at a given moment. Subjectively, the Not Yet is anticipatory consciousness; a form of consciousness that, although extremely important in people's lives, was completely neglected by Freud (Bloch 1995, 286–315). Objectively, the Not Yet is, on the one hand, capacity (potency) and, on the other, possibility (potentiality). Possibility has a dimension of darkness as it originates in the lived moment (which is never fully visible to itself), as well as a component of uncertainty that derives from a double want: (1) the fact that the conditions that render possibility concrete are only partially known; and (2) the fact that the conditions exist only partially. For Bloch, it is crucial to distinguish between these two wants. It is possible to know, relatively well, conditions that exist only partially, and vice versa.

The Not Yet inscribes in the present a possibility that is uncertain, but never neutral; it could be the possibility of utopia or salvation (*Heil*) or the possibility of catastrophe or damnation (*Unheil*). Such uncertainty brings an element of chance, or danger, to every change. This uncertainty is what, in my opinion, expands the present, while at the same time contracting the future and rendering it the object of care. At every moment, there is a limited horizon of possibilities, and that is why it is important not to waste the unique opportunity of a specific change offered by the present: *carpe diem* (seize the day). In accord with Marxism, which he interpreted in a very creative way, Bloch thinks that the succession of horizons leads or tends toward a final state. Not agreeing with Bloch, in this regard, is not relevant. Bloch's emphasis stresses the critique of the mechanical conception of matter, on the one hand, and the affirmation of our capacity to think and act productively upon the world, on the other. Considering the three modal categories of existence—reality, necessity, and possibility—lazy reason focused on the first two and neglected the third one entirely (Bloch 1995, 244–45). According to Bloch, Hegel is mainly responsible for the fact that the possible has been neglected by philosophy. For Hegel, because the possible is contained in the real, either it does not exist or is not different from what exists; in any case, it need not be thought of. Reality and necessity have no need of possibility to account for the present or future. Modern science was the privileged vehicle of this conception. For this reason, Bloch invites us to focus on the modal category that has been the most neglected by modern science: possibility. To be human is to have a lot ahead of you (1995, 246). Possibility is the world's engine. Its moments are: want (the manifestation of something lacking), tendency (process and meaning), and latency (what goes ahead in the process). Want is the realm of the Not; tendency the realm of the Not Yet; and latency the realm of the Nothing and the All, for latency can end up in either frustration or hope.

The sociology of emergences is the inquiry into the alternatives that are contained in the horizon of concrete possibilities. Whereas the sociology of absences amplifies the present by adding to the existing reality what was subtracted from it by metonymic reason, the sociology of emergences enlarges the present by adding to the existing reality the possibilities and future expectations it contains. In the latter case, the enlargement of the present implies the contraction of the future inasmuch as the Not Yet, far from being an empty and infinite future, is a concrete future, forever uncertain and in danger. As Bloch says, "[B]y every hope there is always a coffin" (1995, 311). Caring for the future is imperative because it is impossible to arm hope against frustration, advent against nihilism, or redemption against disaster. It is impossible to have hope without the coffin.

The sociology of emergences consists of undertaking a symbolic enlargement of knowledges, practices, and agents in order to identify the tendencies of the future (the Not Yet) upon which it is possible to intervene so as to maximize the probability of hope vis-à-vis the probability of frustration. Such symbolic enlargement is actually a form of sociological imagination with two aims: (1) to know better the conditions of the possibility of hope; and (2) to define principles of action to promote the fulfillment of those conditions.

The sociology of emergences acts both on possibilities (potentiality) and on capacities (potency). The Not Yet has meaning (as possibility) but no direction, for it can end either in hope or disaster. Therefore, the sociology of emergences replaces the idea of determination with the idea of care. The axiology of progress is thus replaced by the axiology of care. Whereas in the sociology of absences the axiology of care is exerted vis-à-vis available alternatives, in the sociology of emergences the axiology of care is exerted vis-à-vis possible alternatives. Because of this ethical dimension, neither is a conventional sociology. But they are not conventional for another reason: Their objectivity depends upon the quality of their subjective dimension. The subjective element of the sociology of absences is cosmopolitan consciousness and nonconformism before the waste of experience. The subjective element of the sociology of emergences is anticipatory consciousness and nonconformism before a want whose fulfillment is within the horizon of possibilities. As Bloch says, "[T]he fundamental concepts are not reachable without a theory of the emotions" (1995, 306). The Not, the Nothing, and the All shed light on such basic emotions as hunger or want, despair or annihilation, trust or redemption. One way or another, these emotions are present in the nonconformism that moves both the sociology of absences and the sociology of emergences.

Whereas the sociology of absences acts in the field of social experiences, the sociology of emergences acts in the field of social expectations. The discrepancy between experiences and expectations is constitutive of Western modernity. Through the concept of progress, proleptic reason polarized this discrepancy so much so that any effective linkage between experiences and expectations disappeared. No matter how wretched current experiences may be, they do not preclude the illusion of exhilarating expectations. The sociology of emergences conceives of the discrepancy between experiences and expectations without resorting to the idea of progress, instead seeing it as concrete and measured. Whereas proleptic reason largely expanded the expectations, thus reducing the field of experiences and contracting the present, the sociology of emergences aims at a more balanced relation between experience and expectation, which, under the present circumstances, implies dilating the present and shrinking the future. The question is not to minimize expectations, but rather to radicalize the expectations based on real possibilities and capacities, here and now. These are the real utopias, the study of which Wallerstein designates as utopistics (1998).

Modernist expectations were grandiose in the abstract, falsely infinite, and universal. As such, they have justified death, destruction, and disaster in the name of a redemption never to come. With the crisis of the concept of progress, the future stopped being automatically prospective and axiological. The concepts of modernization and development diluted those characteristics almost completely. Today what is known as globalization consummates the replacement of the prospective and axiological by the accelerated and entropic. Thus, direction turns into rhythm without meaning, and if there is a final stage, it cannot be but disaster. Against this nihilism, which is as empty as the triumphalism of hegemonic forces, the sociology of emergences offers a new semantics of expectations. The expectations legitimated by the sociology of emergences are both contextual, because they are gauged by concrete possibilities, and radical, because, in the ambit of those possibilities and capacities, they claim a strong fulfillment that protects them (though never completely) from frustration. In such expectations resides the reinvention of social emancipation, or rather, emancipations.

By enlarging the present and contracting the future, the sociology of absences and the sociology of emergences, each one in its own way, contribute to decelerate the present, giving it a denser, more substantive content than the fleeting instant between the past and the future to which proleptic reason condemned it. Instead of a final stage, they propose a constant ethical vigilance over the unfolding of possibilities, aided by such basic emotions as negative wonder that provokes anxiety, and positive wonder that feeds hope.

The symbolic enlargement brought about by the sociology of emergences aims to analyze in a given practice, experience, or form of knowledge what in them exists as tendency or possibility. It acts upon both possibilities and capacities. It identifies signals, clues, or traces of future possibilities in whatever exists. Proleptic reason has totally dismissed this kind of inquiry, because it assumes that the future is predetermined or can only be identified by precise indicators—clues are too vague, subjective, and chaotic to be credible predictors. By focusing intensely on the clue side of reality, the sociology of emergences aims to enlarge, symbolically, the possibilities of the future that lie, in latent form, in concrete social experiences.

The notion of *clue,* something that announces what is to come next, is essential in various practices, both human and animal. For example, it is well known that animals announce when they are ready for reproductive activity by means of visual, auditory, and olfactory clues. The preciseness and detail of such clues are remarkable. In medicine, criminal investigation, and drama, clues are crucial to decide on future action, be it diagnosis and prescription, identification of suspects, or development of plot. In the social sciences, however, clues have no credibility. On the contrary, the sociology of absences valorizes clues as pathways toward discussing and arguing for concrete alternative futures. Whereas animal clues carry highly codified information, societal clues are more open and can be fields of argumentation and negotiation about the future. The care of the future exerts itself in such argumentation and negotiation.

The Field of the Sociology of Absences and of the Sociology of Emergences

While the sociology of absences expands the realm of social experiences already available, the sociology of emergences expands the realm of possible social experiences. The two sociologies are deeply interrelated because the more experiences that are available in the world, the more experiences will be possible in the future. The ampler the credible reality, the wider the field of credible clues and possible, concrete futures. The greater the multiplicity and diversity of the available and possible experiences (knowledges and agents), the wider the expansion of the present and the contraction of the future. The sociology of absences reveals multiplicity and diversity through the ecologies of knowledges, temporalities, differences, scales, and production, whereas the sociology of emergences reveals them through the symbolic amplification of clues. The most important social fields in which multiplicity and diversity are likely to be revealed are explained below.

Experiences of Knowledges

These are conflicts and possible dialogues among different forms of knowledge. The richest experiences in this domain are likely to occur in biodiversity (between biotechnology and indigenous or traditional knowledges); in medicine (between modern and traditional medicine); in justice (between indigenous jurisdiction or traditional authorities and modern, national jurisdictions); in agriculture (between industrial and peasant or sustainable agriculture); and in studies of environmental impact (between technical and lay knowledge, between experts and common citizens).[12]

Experiences of Development, Labor, and Production

These are conflicts and possible dialogues among different forms and modes of production. On the margins or underneath the dominant forms and modes (the capitalist mode of production and pattern of development as infinite growth), forms and modes of solidarity-based economy—from alternative development to alternatives to development—are available or possible. They include ecofeminist production or Gandhian *swadeshi*; popular economic organizations (workers' cooperatives, mutualities, self-managed firms, and microcredit associations);[13] forms of social redistribution based on citizenship rather than productivity;[14] initiatives of fair trade as alternatives to free trade;[15] struggles for labor standards;[16] antisweatshop movements;[17] and the new international labor movement.[18]

Experiences of Recognition

These are conflicts and possible dialogues among systems of social classification. On the margins or underneath the dominant systems—capitalist nature, racism, sexism, and xenophobia—experiences of anticapitalist nature, equal differentiation, multicultural constitutionalism, and postnational and cultural citizenship are available or possible (see note 12).

Experiences of Democracy

These are conflicts and possible dialogues between the hegemonic model of democracy (liberal representative democracy) and participatory democracy.[19] As salient illustrations, I mention the participatory budgeting in the city of Porto Alegre, also in force, under different forms, in many other Brazilian and Latin American cities;[20] the decentralized participatory planning in Kerala, India (based on district, block, and *grama panchayats*);[21] forms of communitarian deliberation in indigenous or rural communities, mainly in Latin America and Africa;[22] and citizen participation in decisions concerning scientific or technological impacts.[23]

Experiences of Communication and Information

These are conflicts and possible dialogues arising from the revolution of communication and information technologies, between global capitalist flows of information and global media, on the one hand and, on the other, transnational advocacy networks of information and alternative independent media.[24]

From Absences and Emergences to Translation Theory

The multiplicity and variety of the available and possible experiences raise two complex problems: The extreme fragmentation or atomization of social reality, and, derived from this fragmentation, the impossibility of conferring meaning to social transformation. As we saw, these prob-lems have been solved by metonymic and proleptic reason through the concept of totality and the conception of history as having both meaning and direction. We also saw that these solutions led to an excessive waste of experience and, for that reason, they are discredited today. Since dis-crediting solutions does not imply discrediting problems, the latter must be addressed. For certain currents that I designate as celebratory post-modernism, the problems themselves are discredited (Santos 1998b). For such currents, social fragmentation and atomization are not a problem. Rather, they are a solution, and the very concept of society that would provide the cement to give coherence to fragmentation is of little use. On the other hand, according to the same currents, social transformation has no meaning or direction, whether because it occurs chaotically or because what changes is our discourse on society and not society itself.

I believe that these stances are closer to metonymic and proleptic reason than they are ready to admit, for they share the idea that they provide universal answers to universal questions. From the point of view of cosmopolitan reason, the task before us is not so much to iden-tify new totalities or to adopt other meanings for social transformation, but to propose new ways to think about such totalities and meanings. This task includes two autonomous, but intrinsically linked, tasks. The first consists of answering the question below. If the world is an inexhaustible totality, as Bloch maintains, it holds many totalities, all of them necessarily partial, which means that all totalities can be seen as parts, and all parts can be seen as totalities. This means that the terms of any dichotomy have (at least) one life beyond dichotomous life. Accord-ing to this conception of the world, there is no sense in attempting to grasp the world by any single grand theory, because any general theory always presupposes the monoculture of a given totality and the homo-geneity of its parts. Hence the question: What is the alternative to the grand theory?

The second task consists of answering the following question. If meaning, let alone direction, is not predefined—if we do not know for sure if a better world is possible, what legitimates and motivates us to act as if we do? And if we are, indeed, legitimated and motivated, how could we define that better world and fight for it? In other words, what is the meaning of the struggles for social emancipation?

In this chapter, I try to answer the first question. In my opinion, the alternative to a general theory is the work of translation. Translation is the procedure that allows for mutual intelligibility among the experiences of the world, both the available and the possible ones, as revealed by the sociology of absences and the sociology of emergences. This procedure does not ascribe the status of exclusive totality or homogenous part to any set of experiences. The experiences of the world are viewed at different moments of the work of translation as totalities or parts and as realities that are not exhausted in either totalities or parts. For example, to see the subaltern both within and without the relation of subalternity.

As Banuri asserts, what most negatively affected the South since the beginning of colonialism was to have to concentrate its energies in adapting and resisting the impositions of the North.[25] Likewise concerned, Serequeberhan identifies the two challenges that confront African philosophy today (1991, 22). The first is a deconstructive challenge and consists of identifying the Eurocentric residua inherited from colonialism and present in various sectors of collective life, from education to politics, from law to culture. The second is a reconstructive challenge and consists of giving new life to the cultural and historical possibilities of the African legacy interrupted by colonialism and neocolonialism. The work of translation tries to catch these two moments: the hegemonic relations among experiences and what lies beyond such relations. In this double movement, the social experiences disclosed by the sociology of absences and the sociology of emergences are reconstructed in such a way as to offer themselves to relations of mutual intelligibility.

The work of translation concerns both knowledges and practices (and their agents). Translation of knowledges takes the form of diatopical hermeneutics. It consists of interpretation work between two or more cultures to identify isomorphic concerns among them and the different responses they provide. I have been proposing a diatopical hermeneutics on the isomorphic concern of human dignity between the Western concept of human rights, the Islamic concept of *umma,* and the Hindu concept of *dharma* (Santos 1995, 340).[26] Two other exercises of diatopical hermeneutics strike me as important in our time. The first focuses on the concern for productive life in capitalist conceptions of development and in the *swadeshi* conception proposed by Gandhi.[27] The conceptions of capitalist development have been reproduced by conventional economics and the metonymic and proleptic reasons underlying it. They are based on the idea of infinite growth reached through the increasing subjection of the practices and knowledges to mercantile logic. The swadeshi, in turn, is based on the idea of sustainability and reciprocity that Mahatma Gandhi defined in 1916 in the following way:

> [S]wadeshi is that spirit in us which restricts us to the use and service of our immediate surroundings to the exclusion of the more remote. Thus as for religion, in order to satisfy the requirements of the definition I must restrict myself to my ancestral religion. . . . If I find it defective I should serve it by purging it of its defects. In the domain of politics I should make use of the indigenous institutions and serve them by curing them of their proven defects. In that of economics, I should use only things that are produced by my immediate neighbors and serve those industries by making them efficient and complete where they might be found wanting. (Quoted in Gandhi 1941, 4–5)

The other exercise of diatopical hermeneutics that I consider important focuses on concern for wisdom and enabling worldviews. It takes place between Western philosophy and the African concept of philosophical sagacity. The latter is an innovative contribution of African philosophy propounded by H. Odera Oruka and others (1990, 1998).[28] It resides in a critical reflection on the world that has as its protagonists what Oruka calls *sages*, be they poets, traditional healers, storytellers, musicians, or traditional authorities. According to Oruka, sage philosophy

> consists of the expressed thoughts of wise men and women in any given community and is a way of thinking and explaining the world that fluctuates between *popular wisdom* (well known communal maxims, aphorisms and general commonsense truths) and *didactic wisdom*, an expounded wisdom and a rational thought of some given individuals within a community. While popular wisdom is often conformist, didactic wisdom is at times critical of the communal set-up and the popular wisdom. Thoughts can be expressed in writing or as unwritten sayings and argumentations associated with some individual(s). In traditional Africa, most of what would pass as sage-philosophy remains unwritten for reasons which must now be obvious to everyone. Some of these persons might have been partly influenced by the inevitable moral and technological culture from the West. Nevertheless, their own outlook and cultural well being remain basically that of traditional rural Africa. Except for a handful of them, the majority of them are "illiterate" or semi-illiterate. (Oruka 1990, 28)

Diatopical hermeneutics starts from the idea that all cultures are incomplete and can, therefore, be enriched by dialogue and confrontation with other cultures. To acknowledge the relativity of cultures does not imply.

the adoption of relativism as philosophical stance. However, it does imply to conceive of universalism as a Western peculiarity, whose idea of supremacy does not reside in itself, but rather in the supremacy of the interests that sustain it. The critique of universalism derives from the critique of the possibility of a general theory. Diatopical hermeneutics presupposes, rather, what I designate as negative universalism, the idea of the impossibility of cultural completeness. In the transition period we are in, still dominated by the metonymic and proleptic reason, negative universalism is perhaps best formulated as a residual general theory: a general theory about the impossibility of a general theory.

The idea and feeling of want and incompleteness create motivation for the work of translation. In order to bear fruit, translation must be the crossing of converging motivations with origin in different cultures. The Indian sociologist Shiv Vishvanathan eloquently formulated the notion of want and motivation that I designate as the work of translation. Vishvanathan says: "My problem is, how do I take the best of Indian civilization and at the same time keep my modern, democratic imagination alive?" (2000, 12). If we could imagine an exercise of diatopical hermeneutics conducted by Vishvanathan and a European or North American scientist, it would be possible to think of the latter's motivation for dialogue formulated thus: How can I keep alive in me the best of modern and democratic Western culture, while at the same time recognizing the value of the world that it designated autocratically as uncivilized, ignorant, residual, inferior, or unproductive?

The work of translation may occur either among hegemonic and nonhegemonic knowledges, or among different nonhegemonic knowledges. The importance of this last work of translation is that only through mutual intelligibility and subsequent possibility of aggregation among nonhegemonic knowledges is it possible to construct counterhegemony.

The second type of the work of translation is undertaken among social practices and their agents. All social practices imply knowledge and, as such, they are also knowledge practices. When dealing with practices, however, the work of translation focuses specifically on mutual intelligibility among forms of organization and objectives of action. In other words, the work of translation deals with knowledges as applied knowledges, transformed into practices and materialities. The work of translation between modern biomedicine and traditional medicine is a good illustration of how the work of translation must deal simultaneously with knowledges and the practices into which such knowledges are translated. What distinguishes the two types of translation work is, after all, the emphasis or perspective that informs them. The specificity of the translation work concerning practices and their agents becomes clearer in situations in which the knowledges that inform different practices are less distinguishable than the practices themselves. This happens particularly when the practices take place inside the same cultural universe. Such would be the case of a work of translation between the forms of organization and the objectives of action of two social movements, say, the feminist movement and the labor movement in a Western society.

The relevance of the work of translation as regards practices is due to a double circumstance. On one hand, the sociology of absences and the sociology of emergences permit the stock of available and possible social experiences to be considerably enlarged. On the other, because there is no single principle of social transformation, it is not possible to determine in the abstract the articulations or hierarchies among the different social experiences and their conceptions of social transformation. Only by means of the mutual intelligibility of practices is it possible to evaluate them and identify possible alliances among them. As happens with the work of translation of knowledges, the work of translation of practices is particularly important with regard to nonhegemonic practices, because intelligibility among them is a condition of their reciprocal articulation. The latter is, in turn, a condition of conversion of nonhegemonic into counterhegemonic practices. The antisystemic or counterhegemonic potential of any social movement resides in its capacity to articulate with other movements—their forms of organization and objectives. For these articulations to be possible, the movements must be mutually intelligible.

The work of translation aims to clarify what unites and separates the different movements and practices so as to ascertain the possibilities and limits of articulation and aggregation among them. Because there is no single universal social practice or collective subject to confer meaning and direction to history, the work of translation becomes crucial in defining, in each concrete and historical moment or context, which constellations of nonhegemonic practices carry more counterhegemonic potential. To give a recent example, in March 2001, the Zapatista indigenous movement in Mexico was a privileged, counterhegemonic practice. It was capable of undertaking the work of translation between its objectives and practices (and the objectives and practices of other Mexican social movements) from the civic and labor movements to the feminist movement. That work of translation resulted in Comandante Esther being the Zapatista leader chosen to address the Mexican congress. With their choice, the Zapatistas wanted to signify the articulation between the indigenous movement and the women's liberation movement, and thus deepen the counterhegemonic potential of both.

More recently, the work of translation has become even more important as a new counterhegemonic or antisystemic movement began to take shape. This movement, mistakenly known as the antiglobalization movement, has been proposing an alternative to neoliberal globalization on the basis of transnational networks of local movements. After having first drawn attention to itself in Seattle in November 1999, it reached its global organizational form during the World Social Forum that took place in Porto Alegre in January 2001.[29] The movement of counterhegemonic globalization reveals the increasing visibility and diversity of the social practices that resist neoliberal globalization all over the world. The movement is a constellation of highly diversified movements: on the one hand, local movements and organizations that are not only very different in their practices and objectives but also embedded in different cultures; on the other, transnational organizations, some from the South and some from the North, also differ widely among themselves. The articulation and aggregation among all these different movements and organizations demand a giant effort of translation. What do the participatory budgeting practiced in many Latin American cities and the participatory democratic planning based on *panchayats* in Kerala and West Bengal in India have in common? What can they learn from each other? In what kinds of counterhegemonic global activities can they cooperate? The same questions can be asked about the pacifist and the anarchist movements, or the indigenous and gay movements, the Zapatista movement, the Association pour la Taxation des Transactions financières pour l'Aide aux Citoyens (ATTAC), the landless movement in Brazil, and the Rio Narmada movement in India. These are the questions that the work of translation aims to answer. It is a complex work, not only because the movements and organizations involved are many and diverse, but also because they are embedded in diverse cultures and knowledges. The work of translation must take up knowledges and cultures and their practices and agents. Furthermore, it must identify what both unites and separates them. The points in common represent the possibility of a bottom-up aggregation or combination, the only possible alternative to a top-down aggregation imposed by a grand theory or a privileged social actor.

Conditions and Procedures of Translation

The work of translation supplements the sociology of absences and the sociology of emergences. If the latter expand the number and diversity of available and possible experiences, the work of translation aims to create intelligibility, coherence, and articulation in a world enriched by such multiplicity and diversity. Translation is not a mere technique. Even its obvious technical components, and the way in which they are applied in the course of the translation process, must be the object of democratic deliberation. Translation is an intellectual and a political work at the same time. It has an emotional dimension as well, because it presupposes nonconformity vis-à-vis a want derived from the deficient nature of a given knowledge or practice. Clearly, for these reasons, the conventional social sciences are of little use to the work of translation.[30] Moreover, disciplinary confinement constrained the intelligibility of the reality under analysis, and such constraint is to be blamed for the reduction of reality to hegemonic or canonical realities. For example, to analyze or evaluate swadeshi from the viewpoint of conventional economics would amount to rendering it unintelligible and, hence, untranslatable. The religious and political dimensions of swadeshi, evident in Gandhi's quotation (see p. 180), would be lost in such analysis and evaluation. As in the case of the sociology of absences and the sociology of emergences, the work of translation is a transgressive kind of work that, as the poet teaches, makes its path by walking it.

The work of translation is based on a postulate upon which transcultural consensus must be created: the general theory of the impossibility of a general theory. Without this negative universalism, translation is a colonial kind of work no matter how postcolonial it claims to be. Once such postulate is guaranteed, the conditions and procedures of the work of translation can be elucidated on the basis of the following questions: What to translate? From what and into what to translate? When should translation take place? Who translates? How to translate? Why translate?

What to Translate?

The crucial concept in answering this question is the concept of the *contact zone*.[31] Contact zones are social fields in which different normative life worlds, practices, and knowledges meet, clash, and interact. The two contact zones constitutive of Western modernity are the epistemological zone, where modern science and common knowledge confront each other; and the colonial zone, where the colonizer and the colonized confront each other. These two zones are characterized by the disparity among the realities in contact and by the inequality of the power relations among them.

From these two zones, and in opposition to them, the contact zones reclaimed by cosmopolitan reason must be built. The cosmopolitan contact zone begins with the assumption that it is up to each knowledge or practice to decide what is put in contact with whom. Contact zones are always selective because knowledges and practices exceed what is put in contact. Indeed, what is put in contact is not necessarily what is most relevant or central. On the contrary, the contact zones are frontier zones, borderlands, or no man's lands, where the peripheries or margins of knowledges and practices are the first to emerge. As the work of translation advances, it becomes possible to bring into the contact zone the aspects each knowledge or practice considers more central and relevant.

In multicultural contact zones, it is up to each cultural practice to decide which aspects must be selected for multicultural confrontation. In every culture, there are features deemed too central to be exposed and rendered vulnerable by the confrontation in the contact zone, or aspects deemed inherently untranslatable into another culture. These decisions are part and parcel of the work of translation itself, and are susceptible to revision as the work proceeds. If the work of translation progresses, it is to be expected that more features will be brought to the contact zone, which, in turn, will contribute to further translation progress. In many countries of Latin America, particularly in those in which multicultural constitutionalism has been adopted, the indigenous people have been fighting for the right to control what, in their knowledges and practices, should or should not be the object of translation vis-à-vis the *sociedad mayor*.

The issue of what is translatable is not restricted to the selection criterion adopted by each practice or knowledge in the contact zone. Beyond active selectivity, there is what we might call passive selectivity. It consists of what, in a given culture, has become unpronounceable because of the extreme oppression to which it was subjected over long periods. These are deep absences, made of an emptiness that is impossible to fill—an emptiness that gives shape to the unfathomable identity of the knowledges and practices in question. In the case of long-time absences, it is possible that not even the sociology of absences may make them present. The silences they produce are too unfathomable to become the object of translation.

What to translate stirs another question that is important in contact zones between cultural universes. Cultures are monolithic only when seen from the outside. When looked at from the inside, it is easy to see that they are comprised of various, and often conflicting, versions of the same culture. For example, when I speak of a possible multicultural dialogue about conceptions of human dignity, we can easily see that in Western culture there is more than one conception of human rights. At least two can be identified: a liberal conception that privileges political and civic rights to the detriment of social and economic rights; and a Marxist or socialist conception that stresses social and economic rights as conditions of all the others. By the same token, in Islam, it is possible to identify several conceptions of *umma*. Some more inclusive conceptions go back to the time when the Prophet lived in Mecca. Others, less inclusive, evolved after the construction of the Islamic state in Medina. Likewise, there are many conceptions of *dharma* in Hinduism. The most inclusive versions, which hold a wider circle of reciprocity, are the ones that generate more promising contact zones; they are the most adequate for deepening the work of translation and diatopical hermeneutics.

To Translate from What into What?

The choice of knowledges and practices, among which the work of translation occurs, is always the result of a convergence of experiences of want and nonconformity as well as the motivation to overcome them. It may emerge as a reaction to a colonial or imperial contact zone. For example, biodiversity is today an imperial contact zone between biotechnological knowledge and the knowledge of the shamans, traditional healers, or witch doctors in indigenous or rural communities of Latin America, Africa, Asia, and even Europe. The indigenous movements and allied transnational social movements contest this contact zone and the powers that constitute it, and fight for the creation of other, nonimperial contact zones, where relations among the different knowledges may be more horizontal. This struggle brought a new acuteness to the translation between biomedical and traditional knowledges. To give an example from a totally different field, the labor movement, confronted with an unprecedented crisis, has been opening itself to contact zones with other social movements: namely, civic, feminist, ecological, and migrant workers' movements. In this contact zone, there is an ongoing translation between labor practices, claims, and aspirations, and the objectives of citizenship, protection of the environment, and antidiscrimination against women and ethnic or migrant minorities. Translation has slowly transformed the labor movement as well as other social movements, thus rendering possible constellations of struggles that until a few years ago would have been unthinkable.

When to Translate?

In this case, too, the cosmopolitan contact zone must be the result of a conjugation of times, rhythms, and opportunities. If there is no such conjugation, the contact zone becomes imperial and the work of translation becomes a form of cannibalization. In the last two decades, Western modernity discovered the possibilities and virtues of multiculturalism. Accustomed to the routine of its own hegemony, Western modernity presumed that if it were to open itself to dialogue with cultures it had previously oppressed, the latter would naturally be ready and available to engage in the dialogue, and, indeed, only too eager to do so. Such presupposition has resulted in new forms of cultural imperialism, even when it assumes the form of multiculturalism. I call this reactionary multiculturalism.

Regarding multicultural contact zones, the different temporalities that occur still must be taken into account. As I mentioned previously, one of the principles of the sociology of absences consists of countering the logic of the monoculture of linear time with a pluralist constellation of times and durations in order to free the practices and knowledges that never ruled themselves by linear time from their status as residuum. The objective is to convert the simultaneity provided by the contact zone (as much as possible) into contemporaneity. This is not to say that contemporaneity annuls history. This is an important caveat, particularly with regard to contact zones of knowledges and practices in which extremely unequal relations of power lead to massive production of absences. In such situations, once a previously absent given knowledge or practice is made present, the danger is to believe that the history of that knowledge or practice starts with its presence in the contact zone. This danger has been present in many multicultural dialogues, mainly in those in which indigenous people have participated after their claims and rights started being recognized from the 1980s onward. The contact zone must be monitored by all of the participants to prevent the simultaneity of contact from meaning the collapse of history.

Who Translates?

Knowledges and practices only exist as mobilized by social groups. Hence, the work of translation is always carried out among representatives of those social groups. As argumentative work, the work of translation requires intellectual capacity. Cosmopolitan intellectuals must have a profile similar to that of the philosophical sage identified by Oruka in his quest for African sagacity. They must be deeply embedded in the practices and knowledges they represent, having a profound and critical understanding of both. This critical dimension, which Oruka designates as "didactic" sageness, (1990, 28) grounds the want, the feeling of incompleteness, and the motivation to discover in other knowledges and practices the answers that are not to be found within the limits of a given knowledge or practice. Translators of cultures must be good cosmopolitan intellectuals. They are to be found among both the leaders of social movements and the rank-and-file activists. In the near future, the decision about who translates is likely to become one of the most crucial democratic deliberations in the construction of counterhegemonic globalization.

How to Translate?

The work of translation is argumentative work, based on the cosmopolitan emotion of sharing the world with those who do not share our knowledge or experience. The work of translation encounters multiple difficulties. The first difficulty concerns the premises of argumentation. Argumentation is based on postulates, axioms, rules, and ideas that are not the object of argumentation because they are taken for granted by all those participating in the argumentative circle. In general, they are called *topoi*, or commonplaces, and constitute the basic consensus that makes argumentative dissent possible.[32] The work of translation has no topoi at the outset because the available topoi are the ones appropriate to a given knowledge or culture, hence, not acceptable as evident by another knowledge or culture. In other words, the topoi that each knowledge or practice brings into the contact zone cease to be premises of argumentation and become arguments. As it progresses, the work of translation constructs the topoi adequate to the contact zone and the translating situation. It is demanding work with no safety nets and is ever on the verge of disaster. The ability to construct topoi is one of the most distinctive marks of the quality of the cosmopolitan intellectual or sage.

The second difficulty regards the language used to conduct the argumentation. It is not usual for the knowledges and practices present in contact zones to have a common language or to master the common language equally well. Furthermore, when the cosmopolitan contact zone is multicultural, one of the languages in question is often the language that dominated the colonial or imperial contact zone. The replacement of the latter by a cosmopolitan contact zone may thus be boycotted by this use of the previously dominant language. The issue is not just that the different participants in the argumentative discourse may master the language unequally. It is that the language is responsible for the very inexpressible nature of some of the central aspirations of the knowledges and practices that were oppressed in the colonial contact zone.

The third difficulty concerns the silences. Not the inexpressible, but rather the rhythms with which the different knowledges and social practices articulate words with silences and the different eloquence (or meaning) that is ascribed to silence by the different cultures. To manage and translate silence is one of the most exacting tasks of the work of translation.

Conclusion: Why Translate?

This last question encompasses all the others. It makes sense, therefore, to answer it as a conclusion to the argument presented here. The sociology of absences and the sociology of emergences, together with the work of translation, enable us to develop an alternative to lazy reason: what I call cosmopolitan reason. This alternative is based on the core idea that global social justice is not possible without global cognitive justice.

The work of translation is the procedure we are left with to give meaning to the world after it has lost the automatic meaning and direction that Western modernity claimed to have conferred on it by planning history, society, and nature. The answer to the question—Why translate?—also answers the second question formulated earlier: If we do not know if a better world is possible, what gives us legitimacy or motivation to act as if we do? The need for translation resides in the fact that the problems Western modernity attempted to solve remain unsolved, and the solutions seem more and more urgent. The solutions proposed by the previous paradigm are not available to us, that being the reason for its profound crisis. In other words, in the transition period in which we find ourselves, we are faced with modern problems for which we have no modern solutions.

The work of translation, undertaken on the basis of the sociology of absences and the sociology of emergences, is a work of epistemological and democratic imagination, aiming to construct new and plural conceptions of social emancipation upon the ruins of the automatic social emancipation of the modernist project. There is no guarantee that a better world is possible or that all those who have not given up struggling for it conceive of it in the same way. The oscillation between banality and horror, which intrigued Adorno and Horkheimer, is now turned into the banality of horror. The possibility of disaster begins, today, to be obvious.

The situation of bifurcation mentioned by Prigogine and Wallerstein is the structural situation in which the work of translation takes place. The objective of the translation work is to create constellations of knowledges and practices strong enough to provide credible alternatives to neoliberal globalization, which is no less and no more than a new step of global capitalism toward subjecting the inexhaustible wealth of the world to mercantile logic. We know that it will never succeed in reaching this objective entirely, that being perhaps the only certainty we draw from the collapse of the modernist project. But that does not tell us if a better world is possible or what profile it might have. This is why cosmopolitan reason prefers to imagine the better world from the vantage point of the present. Thus, it proposes the expansion of the present and the contraction of the future. Once the field of experiences is enlarged, it is possible to evaluate the alternatives that are possible and available today. This diversification of experiences aims to re-create the tension between experiences and expectations, but in such a way that they both happen in the present. The new nonconformity results from the verification that it would be possible to live in a much better world today and not tomorrow. After all, Bloch wonders, if we live only in the present, how come it is so fleeting?

Expectations are the possibility of reinventing our experience by confronting the hegemonic experiences imposed upon us with the immense variety of experiences, whose absence is actively produced by metonymic reason, or whose emergence is suppressed by proleptic reason. Therefore, the possibility of a better future lies not in a distant future, but in the reinvention of the present as enlarged by the sociology of absences and the sociology of emergences, and rendered coherent by the work of translation.

The work of translation permits us to create meanings and directions that are precarious but concrete, short-range but radical in their objectives, uncertain but shared. The aim of translation between knowledges is to create cognitive justice from the standpoint of the epistemological imagination. The aim of translation between practices and their agents is to create the conditions for global social justice from the standpoint of the democratic imagination.

The work of translation creates the conditions for concrete social emancipations of concrete social groups in a present whose injustice is legitimated on the basis of a massive waste of experience. The work of translation, based on the sociology of absences and the sociology of emergences, only permits us to reveal or denounce the dimension of such a waste. The kind of social transformation that may be accomplished on the basis of the work of translation requires the constellations of meaning created by it to be transformed into transforming practices. For that, the work of translation must be supplemented by the practice of manifestos.

Notes

1. The project can be currently consulted on the Web. It is available at: www.ces.fe.uc.pt/emancipa.

2. I use metonymy, a figure of speech related to synecdoche, to signify the part for the whole.

3. I use prolepsis, a common narrative device of anticipation, to signify knowledge of the future in the present.

4. Nunes, addressing contemporary debates on this subject, illustrates how the new configuration of knowledges has to go beyond the two cultures (1998/1999).

5. For a first critique of the lazy reason, see my quest for a new commonsense (1995, 2000).

6. In the West, the critique of both metonymic and proleptic reason has a long tradition. In the modern era, it can be traced back to romanticism and appears under different guises in Kierkegaard, Nietzsche, phenomenology, existentialism, and pragmatism. The laziness of the debates lies in that they do not question, in general, the peculiar disembeddedness of reason as something set apart from, and higher than, the rest of reality. This is why, in my view, the most eloquent critique comes from

those for whom metonymic and proleptic reason are not just an intellectual artifact or game, but the generating ideology behind a brutal system of domination, that is, the colonial system. Gandhi and Martí are two outstanding voices. In the colonial context, lazy reason lies behind what Quijano and others call the "coloniality of power," a form of power that, rather than ending with the end of colonialism, has continued to be prevalent in postcolonial societies (Quijano 2000; Lander 2000).

7. Jaspers considers the period between 800 and 200 BCE as an "axial age," a period that lay down "the foundations upon which humanity still subsists today" (1951, 98). In this period, most of "the extraordinary events" that shaped humankind as we know it occurred in the East—in China, India, Persia, and Palestine. The West is represented by Greece and, as we know today, Greek classic antiquity owes much to its African and Eastern roots (Bernal 1987). See also Schluchter (1979).

8. Benjamin thought that World War I had deprived the world of the social relations through which the older generations passed their wisdom onto the younger generations (1972, II, pt. 1, 214). He argued that a new world had emerged after the war, a world dominated by the development of technology, a world in which even education and learning ceased to translate themselves into experience. A new poverty has thus emerged, a lack of experience in the midst of hectic transformation, a new form of barbarism (1972, II, pt. 1, 215). And he concludes his essay in this way:

> We have become poor. Piece by piece have we relinquished the heirloom of humankind, often deposited in a pawnshop for a hundreth of their value, only to get back the small change of the "current balance" [*Aktuelle*]. (My translation, 1972 II: pt. 1, 219)

9. Kafka has two antagonists: the first pushes him from behind, from his birth. The second blocks the road in front of him. He struggles with both. The first supports him in his struggle with the second, for the first wants to push him forward. In the same way, the second supports him in his struggle with the first—the second, of course, is trying to force him back. But this is only theoretically so. For it is not only the two protagonists who are there, but himself as well, and who really knows his intentions? However that may be, he has a dream that some time in an unguarded moment—it would require too, one must admit, a night darker than anything has ever been yet—he will spring out of the fighting line and be promoted, on account of his experience of such warfare, as judge over his struggling antagonists. (Kafka 1960, 298–99)

10. Quijano considers the racialization of power relations an intrinsic feature of capitalism, a feature that he designates as the "coloniality of power" (2000, 374).

11. "The concept of historical progress of mankind cannot be sundered from the concept of its progression through a homogeneous, empty time" (Benjamin 1969, 261). And he counterposes: "The soothsayers who found from time to time what it had in store certainly did not experience time as either homogeneous or empty" (1969, 264).

12. The literature on all of these topics is immense. See, for example, Brush and Stablinsky (1996); Balick et al. (1996); Shiva (1997); Visvanathan (1997); Brush (1999); Escobar (1999); and Posey (1999). Different case studies of conflicts and possible dialogues among knowledges in all of these areas can be read in the project "Reinventing Social Emancipation," mentioned in the introduction of this chapter (consult the themes on multiculturalism and cultural citizenship and biodiversity, rival knowledges and intellectual property rights). The papers can also be read in Santos (2002c, d).

13. On popular economic organizations and alternative production systems, consult the case studies included in the research project "Reinventing Social Emancipation." The papers can also be read in Santos (2002b).

14. On mimimum guaranteed income, see, for example, Van Parijs (1992) and Purdy (1994).

15. See, for example, Blowfield (1999); Renard (1999); Simpson and Rapone (2000).

16. See Compa and Diamond (1996); Trubek et al. (2000).

17. See, for example, Ross (1997); Schoenberger (2000); Bonacich and Appelbaum (2000).

18. Consult the theme of new labor internationalism in the research project "Reinventing Social Emancipation." The papers can also be read in Santos (2002e).

19. A variety of case studies on participatory democracy can be read in the research project "Reinventing Social Emancipation"; consult the theme of participatory democracy. These papers can also be read in Santos (2002a).

20. See Fedozzi (1997); Santos (1998a); Abers (1998); Baiocchi (2001); and Baierle (2001).

21. See Heller (2000) and Desai (2001).

22. See Stavenhagen (1996); Mamdani (1996); Van Cott (1996, 2000); Gentili (1998).

23. See Gonçalves (2000); Fischer (2000); Jamison (2001); Callon et al. (2001).

24. See Ryan (1991); Bagdikian (1992); Hamelink (1994); Herman and McChesney (1997, 1999); McChesney et al. (1998); and Shaw (2001). Many independent media centers can easily be consulted on the Internet.

25. Banuri argues that the development of the "South" has been disadvantageous

> not because of bad policy advice or malicious intent of the advisers, nor because of the disregard of neo-classical wisdom, but rather because the project has constantly forced indigenous people to divert their energies from the *positive* pursuit of indigenously defined social change, to the *negative* goal of resisting cultural, political, and economic domination by the West. (emphasis in the original) (Banuri 1990, 66)

26. On the concept of umma, see Faruki (1979); An-Na'im (1995, 2000) and Hassan (1996). On the Hindu concept of dharma, see Gandhi (1929/1932) and Zaehner (1982).

27. See Gandhi (1967, 1941). On swadeshi, see also, among others, Bipinchandra (1954); Nandy (1987); and Krishna (1994).

28. On sage philosophy, see also Oseghare (1992) and Presbey (1997).

29. On counterhegemonic globalization, there is a growing body of literature. See, among others: Santos (1995, 250–377); Keck and Sikkink (1998); Evans (1999); Brecher et al. (2000); Cohen and Rai (2000).

30. As Immanuel Wallerstein points out, not only did the social sciences evolve from the divorce of the quest for truth and the quest for the good society, but they also banished the enchantment of reason (1999, 137–251).

31. The concept of contact zone has been used by different authors to mean different things. For instance, Mary Louise Pratt defines contact zones as:

> [S]ocial spaces where disparate cultures meet, clash and grapple with each other often in highly asymmetrical relations of domination and subordination—like colonialism, slavery or their aftermaths as they are lived out across the globe today. (1992, 4)

In this formulation, contact zones seem to involve encounters among cultural totalities. This does not have to be the case. The contact zone may involve selected and partial cultural differences, the ones that, in a given time-space, find themselves in competition to provide meaning for a given course of action. Moreover, as I claim in this chapter, unequal exchanges extend today far beyond colonialism and its aftermath, even though colonialism continues to play a much more important role than one is ready to admit.

32. On topoi and rhetoric in general, see Santos (1995, 7–55).

References

Abers, Rebecca. 1998. "From Clientelism to Cooperation: Local Government, Participatory Policy, and Civic Organizing in Porto Alegre, Brazil." *Politics and Society* XXVI, no. 4 (December): 511–37.

An-Na'im, Abdullahi. 2000. "Human Rights and Islamic Identity in France and Uzbekistan: Mediation of the Local and Global." *Human Rights Quarterly* XXII, no. 4 (November): 906–41.

An-Na'im, Abdullahi, ed. 1995. *Human Rights and Religious Values: An Uneasy Relationship?* Amsterdam: Editions Rodopi.

Bagdikian, Ben H. 1992. *The Media Monopoly.* Boston, MA: Beacon Press.

Baierle, Sérgio Gregório. 2001. "OP ao Termidor?" Presented to the seminar O Orçamento Participativo visto pelos seus investigadores (31/05–2/06/2001). Porto Alegre: Prefeitura de Porto Alegre.

Baiocchi, Gianpaolo. 2001. "From Militance to Citizenship: The Workers' Party, Civil Society, and the Politics of Participatory Governance in Porto Alegre, Brazil." Unpublished Ph.D. diss., University of Wisconsin-Madison.

Balick, Michael J., Elaine Elisabetsky, and Sarah A. Laird. 1996. *Medicinal Resources of the Tropical Forest.* New York: Columbia University Press.

Banuri, T. 1990. "Development and the Politics of Knowledge: A Critical Interpretation of the Social Role of Modernization Theories in the Development of the Third World." Pp. 29–72 in *Dominating Knowledge: Development, Culture and Resistance,* eds. F. A. Marglin and S. A. Marglin. Oxford: Clarendon Press.

Benjamin, Walter. 1969. *Illuminations.* New York: Schocken Books.

———. 1972. "Erfahrung und Armut." Pp. 213–19 in *Gesammelte Schriften,* Vol. II, pt. 1., eds. R. Tiedemann and H. Schweppenhäuser. Frankfurt: Suhrkamp.

Bernal, Martin. 1987. *Black Athena: The Afroasiatic Roots of Classical Civilization.* New Brunswick, NJ: Rutgers University Press.

Bipinchandra, Pal. 1954. *Swadeshi & Swaraj (The Rise of New Patriotism).* Calcutta: Yugayatri Prakashak.

Bloch, Ernst. 1995. *The Principle of Hope.* Cambridge, MA: MIT Press.

Blowfield, Mick. 1999. "Ethical Trade: A Review of Developments and Issues." *Third World Quarterly* XX, no. 4 (August): 753–70.

Bonacich, Edna, and Richard P. Appelbaum. 2000. *Behind the Label: Inequality in the Los Angeles Apparel Industry.* Berkeley: University of California Press.

Brecher, Jeremy, Tim Costello, and Brendan Smith. 2000. *Globalization from Below: The Power of Solidarity.* Cambridge, MA: South End Press.

Brockman, John. 1995. *The Third Culture.* New York: Simon & Schuster.

Brush, Stephen. 1999. "Bioprospecting the Public Domain." *Cultural Anthropology* XIV, no. 4 (November): 535–55.

Brush, Stephen B., and Doreen Stablinsky, eds. 1996. *Valuing Local Knowledge: Indigenous Peoples and Intellectual Property Rights.* Washington D.C.: Island Press.

Callon, Michel, Pierre Lascoumes, and Yannick Barthe. 2001. *Agir dans un monde incertain: Essai sur la démocratie technique.* Paris: Seuil.

Cohen, Robin, and Shirin M. Rai. 2000. *Global Social Movements.* London: Athlone Press.

Compa, Lance, and Stephen Diamond. 1996. *Human Rights, Labor Rights and International Trade.* Philadelphia: University of Pennsylvania Press.

Desai, Manali. 2001. "Party Formation, Political Power, and the Capacity for Reform: Comparing Left Parties in Kerala and West Bengal, India." *Social Forces* LXXX, no. 1 (September): 37–60.

Escobar, Arturo. 1999. "After Nature: Steps to an Anti-essentialist Political Ecology." *Current Anthropology* XL, no. 1 (February): 1–30.

Evans, Peter. 1999. "Counter-Hegemonic Globalization: Transnational Networks as Political Tools for Fighting Marginalization." Available at http://sociology .berkeley.edu/faculty/evans/#currentprojects.

Faruki, Kemal A. 1979. *The Constitutional and Legal Role of the Umma.* Karachi: Ma'aref.

Fedozzi, Luciano. 1997. *Orçamento participativo: Reflexões sobre a experiência de Porto Alegre.* Porto Alegre: Tomo Editorial.

Fischer, Frank. 2000. *Citizens, Experts, and the Environment: The Politics of Local Knowledge.* Durham, NC: Duke University Press.

Gandhi, Mahatma. 1929/1932. *The Story of My Experiments with Truth,* 2 vols. Ahmedabad: Navajivan.

———. 1938. *Hind Swaraj.* Ahmedabad: Navajivan.

———. 1941. *The Economics of Khadi.* Ahmedabad: Navajiva.

———. 1951. *Selected Writings of Mahatma Gandhi.* Boston: Beacon.

———. 1960. *Discourses on the Gita.* Ahmedabad: Navajivan.

———. 1967. *The Gospel of Swadeshi.* Bombay: Bharatiya Vidya Bhavan.

———. 1972. *Satyagraha in South Africa.* Ahmedabad: Navajivan.

Gentili, A. M. 1998. *O leão e o caçador: Uma história da África sub-sahariana dos séculos XIX e XX.* Maputo: Arquivo Histórico de Moçambique.

Gonçalves, Maria Eduarda, ed. 2000. *Cultura científica e participação pública.* Oeiras: Celta.

Hamelink, C. J. 1994. *The Politics of World Communication.* London: Sage.

Hassan, Riffat. 1996. "Religious Human Rights and The Qur'an." Pp. 361–86 in *Religious Human Rights in Global Perspective: Religious Perspectives,* eds. J. Witte Jr. and J. D. van der Vyver. The Hague: Martinus Nijhoff Publishers.

Heller, P. 2000. "Degrees of Democracy: Some Comparative Lessons from India." *World Politics* LII, no. 4 (July): 484–519.

Herman, Edward S., and Robert W. McChesney. 1997. *The Global Media: The New Missionaries of Corporate Capitalism.* London: Cassell.

Jamison, Andrew. 2001. *The Making of New Knowledge: Environmental Politics and Cultural Transformation.* Cambridge: Cambridge University Press.

Jaspers, Karl. 1951. *Way to Wisdom: An Introduction to Philosophy.* New Haven: Yale University Press.

———. 1976. *The Origin and Goal of History.* Westport, CT: Greenwood Press.

Kafka, Franz. 1960. "He." Pp. 290–99 in *Description of a Struggle and the Great Wall of China,* trans. T. and J. Stern. London: Secker and Warburg.

Keck, Margaret E., and Kathryn Sikkink. 1998. *Activists Beyond Borders: Advocacy Networks in International Politics.* Ithaca, NY: Cornell University Press.

Koselleck, Reinhart. 1985. *Futures Past: On the Semantics of Historical Time.* Cambridge, MA: MIT Press.

Krishna, Daya. 1994. *Swadeshi View of Globalisation.* New Delhi: Swadeshi Jagaran Manch.

Lander, E., ed. 2000. *La colonialidad del saber: eurocentrismo y ciencias sociales—perspectivas latinoamericanas*. Buenos Aires: CLACSO.

Leibniz, Gottfried Wilhelm. 1985 [1710]. *Theodicy: Essays on the Goodness of God, the Freedom of Man, and the Origin of Evil*. La Salle, IL: Open Court.

Lepenies, Wolf. 1988. *Between Literature and Science: The Rise of Sociology*, trans. by R. J. Hollingdale. Cambridge: Cambridge University Press.

Mamdani, Mahmood. 1996. *Citizen and Subject: Contemporary Africa and the Legacy of Late Colonialism*. Princeton: Princeton University Press.

Marramao, Giacomo. 1995. *Poder e secularização: As categorias do tempo*. San Paulo: Editora da Universidade Estadual Paulista.

Martí, José. 1963. *Obras completas*. Havana: Editorial Nacional de Cuba.

McChesney, Robert Waterman. 1999. *Rich Media, Poor Democracy: Communication Politics in Dubious Times*. Urbana: University of Illinois Press.

McChesney, Robert W., Ellen Meiksins Wood, and John Bellamy Foster, eds. 1998. *Capitalism and the Information Age: The Political Economy of the Global Communication Revolution*. New York: Monthly Review Press.

Nandy, A. 1987. *Traditions, Tyranny and Utopias*. Delhi: Oxford University Press.

Nunes, João Arriscado. 1998/1999. "Para além das 'duas culturas': Tecnociências, tecnoculturas e teoría crítica." *Revista Crítica de Ciências Sociais*, no. 52/53: 15–59.

Oruka, H. Odera. 1990. "Sage-Philosophy: The Basic Questions and Methodology." Pp. 27–40 in *Sage Philosophy: Indigenous Thinkers and Modern Debate on African Philosophy*, ed. H. O. Oruka. Leiden: Brill.

———. 1998. "Grundlegende Fragen der afrikanischen 'Sage-Philosophy.'" Pp. 35–53 in *Vier Fragen zur Philosophie in Afrika, Asien und Lateinamerika*, ed. F. Wimmer. Vienna: Passagen.

Oseghare, Antony S. 1992. "Sagacity and African Philosophy." *International Philosophical Quarterly* XXXII, no. 1 (March): 95–104.

Posey, Darrell Addison, ed. 1999. *Cultural and Spiritual Values of Biodiversity*. London: Intermediate Technology.

Pratt, Mary Louise. 1992. *Imperial Eyes: Travel Writing and Transculturation*. London: Routledge.

Presbey, Gail M. 1997. "Who Counts as a Sage? Problems in the Further Implementation of Sage Philosophy." *Quest: Philosophical Discussions* XI, nos. 1 and 2: 53–65.

Prigogine, Ilya. 1997. *The End of Certainty: Time, Chaos, and the New Laws of Nature*. New York: Free Press.

Purdy, David. 1994. "The Second Marriage of Justice and Efficiency." *New Left Review*, no. 208: 30–48.

Quijano, Aníbal. 2000. "Colonialidad del poder y classificacion social." *Journal of World-Systems Research* VI, no. 2 (Summer/Fall): 342–86. Available at: http://jwsr.ucr.edu.

Renard, Marie. 1999. "The Interstices of Globalization: The Example of Fair Coffee." *Sociologia Ruralis* XXXIX, no. 4: 484–500.

Ross, Andrew, ed. 1997. *No Sweat: Fashion, Free Trade and the Rights of Garment Workers*. London: Verso.

Ryan, Charlotte. 1991. *Prime Time Activism: Media Strategies for Grassroots Organizing*. Boston, MA: South End Press.

Santos, Boaventura de Sousa. 1995. *Toward a New Common Sense: Law, Science and Politics in the Paradigmatic Transition*. New York: Routledge.

————. 1998a. "Participatory Budgeting in Porto Alegre: Toward a Redistributive Democracy." *Politics and Society* XXVI, no. 4 (Winter): 461–510.

————. 1998b. "Oppositional Postmodernim and Globalizations." *Law and Social Inquiry* XXIII, no. 1 (Winter): 121–39.

————. 2000. *A crítica da razão indolente: Contra o desperdício da experiência.* Porto: Afrontamento.

————. 2001a. "Toward an Epistemology of Blindness: Why the New Forms of 'Ceremonial Adequacy' Neither Regulate nor Emancipate." *The European Journal of Social Theory* IV, no. 3: 251–79.

————. 2001b. "Nuestra America: Reinventing a Subaltern Paradigm of Recognition and Redistribution." *Theory Culture and Society* XVIII, no. 1 (February): 2–3.

————, ed. 2002a. *Democratizar a democracia: Os caminhos da democracia participativa.* Rio de Janeiro: Record.

————, ed. 2002b. *Produzir para viver: Os caminhos da produção não capitalista.* Rio de Janeiro: Record.

————, ed. 2002c. *Reconhecer para libertar: Os caminhos do cosmopolitismo multicultural.* Rio de Janeiro: Record.

————, ed. 2002d. *Semear outras soluções: Os caminhos da biodiversidade e dos conhecimentos rivais.* Rio de Janeiro: Record.

————, ed. 2002e. *Trabalhar o mundo: Os caminhos do novo internacionalismo operário.* Rio de Janeiro: Record.

Schluchter, Wolfgang. 1979. *Die Entwicklung des okzidentalen Rationalismus: Analyse von Max Webers Gesellschaftsgeschichte.* Tübingen: Mohr.

Schoenberger, Karl. 2000. *Levi's Children: Coming to Terms with Human Rights in the Global Marketplace.* New York: Grove Press.

Serequeberhan, Tsenay. 1991. "Introduction." Pp. xvii–xxii in *African Philosophy: The Essential Readings,* ed. T. Serequeberhan. New York: Paragon.

Shaw, Randy. 2001. *The Activist's Handbook: A Primer.* Berkeley: University of California Press.

Shiva, Vandana. 1997. *Biopiracy.* Boston: South End Press.

Simpson, Charles, and Anita Rapone. 2000. "Community Development from the Ground Up: Social-Justice Coffee." *Human Ecology Review* VII, no. 1: 46–57.

Snow, C. P. 1959. *The Two Cultures and the Scientific Revolution.* New York: Cambridge University Press.

————. 1964. *The Two Cultures and a Second Look.* Cambridge: Cambridge University Press.

Stavenhagen, Rodolfo. 1996. *Ethnic Conflicts and the Nation-State.* London: Macmillan.

Trubek, David, Jim Mosher, and Jeffrey Rothstein. 2000. "Transnationalism in the Regulation of Labor Relations: International Regimes and Transnational Advocacy Networks." *Law and Social Inquiry* XXV, no. 4 (Fall): 1187–1211.

Van Cott, Donna L. 1996. *Defiant Again: Indigenous Peoples and Latin American Security.* Washington, D.C.: Institute for National Strategic Studies, National Defense University.

————. 2000. *The Friendly Liquidation of the Past: The Politics of Diversity in Latin America.* Pittsburgh: University of Pittsburgh Press.

Van Parijs, Philippe. 1992. *Arguing for Basic Income.* London: Verso.

Visvanathan, Shiv. 1997. *A Carnival of Science: Essays on Science, Technology and Development.* Oxford: Oxford University Press.

———. 2000. "Environmental Values, Policy, and Conflict in India." Unpublished paper presented to the Seminar on Understanding Values: A Comparative Study on Environmental Values in China, India, and the United States (sponsored by Carnegie Council). Available at: www.carnegiecouncil.org/pdf/visvanathan.pdf.

Wallerstein, Immanuel. 1998. *Utopistics, or Historical Choices for the Twenty-first Century.* New York: New Press.

———. 1999. *The End of the World as We Know It: Social Science for the Twenty-first Century.* Minneapolis: University of Minnesota Press.

Wallerstein, Immanuel, and Etienne Balibar. 1991. *Race, Nation, Class: Ambiguous Identities.* New York: Verso.

Weber, Max. 1958. *The Protestant Ethic and the Spirit of Capitalism.* New York: Scribner.

———. 1963. *The Sociology of Religion.* Boston: Beacon Press.

———. 1968. *Economy and Society: An Outline of Interpretive Sociology.* New York: Bedminster Press.

Zaehner, R. C. 1982. *Hinduism.* Oxford: Oxford University Press.

11

Continuing American Provincialism and the Rest of the World

Janet L. Abu-Lughod

I've been struck recently by a growing polarization (or at least obfuscation) around the use of such terms as *global/globalization*, which we "progressives" originally claimed as our special tool of analysis. It is a little frightening. When the annual reports of American transnational corporations marvel at the "new economy" of globalization, and when even the Bush administration throws around such terms as *globalization* and *global leadership* (while reneging on any international agreements not to its liking), we must ask why a concept that had so much promise as a powerful analytic tool has now been preempted by the ruling class. Is there any meaning left? Has it become just another word for hypermodernization in the image of and under the domination of "the West," whatever that may be? What is the relationship between theories of globalization and world-system theories? And since we are interested in antisystemic movements, how do the somewhat inchoate protests against globalization—in the streets of Seattle and other unlikely places—fit in? What are the politics of labeling? Where are all the fancy terms coming from? And why are they surfacing now? Is there a real deprovincialization of American social science or does the new verbiage conceal the same old preoccupation with the United States, this time viewed not in isolation but as the center of its larger empire?

This has made me think back to earlier American usages and approaches to the world. I am old enough to have experienced, over the past half-century, at least four generations of American academic endeavors to take into account what I have long called TROTW (the Rest of the World).[1] Each time, the work of serious scholars has been preempted to serve political and military interests that do not necessarily have the good of poor people and other countries in mind.

The first came in the wake of World War II, when a provincial American academy, stimulated by Truman's Point Four Program, conceptualized almost all areas outside the Atlantic Alliance as "backward" and in need of technological, or even psychiatric, assistance to bring them into the modern world. (At that time, Japan was then unequivocally included in the list of "backward" nations.) It is fascinating to go back to the literature of the late 1940s and early 1950s and to observe the gradual substitution of euphemisms for the original: *backward* changed to *underdeveloped*, then to *developing*, and finally to *late* or *newly industrializing*, and so on. However, even after the language was cleaned up, the theories retained their unidirectional assumption, namely, that the developmental trajectories of such countries would recapitulate those of the West, given the requisite technological and cultural changes that would follow from their incorporation into the larger, that is, Western, world.

A second iteration came in the course of the Cold War (which of course remained "hot" in Asia), accompanied by the extensive movements of decolonization that were convulsing the world scene in the late 1950s and early 1960s. By then, American policy had refocused from the noblesse oblige of Point Four to planning (defensively, to be sure) for the next war. The goal was to involve American scholars more directly in non-Western studies, encouraging their greater contact with and expertise in foreign areas of particularly strategic significance. Viewed as especially threatening to the West were those countries trying to chart paths of autarchic economic development and to form their own lateral alliances. At Bandung in 1955, these actors had called themselves the nonaligned nations (within neither the capitalist nor the communist camps). Only later was this term revised to *Third World*, which eventually came to mean poor. (Japan had slipped out of this latter category and China was virtually ignored, except in relation to the Korean War.)

This was the era during which most American centers of "area studies" were born. Government funding, more or less "laundered," was made available to train students in defense languages and to support overseas research in those regions deemed important to American interests as a world power. Individual centers focusing on Africa, the Middle East, and, to a lesser extent, Asia and Latin America proliferated. But the organization of such area studies was definitely on the "spokes of the wheel" pattern—with direct lines from the U.S. core to multiple, but separately considered, peripheries.

During the late 1960s and early 1970s, a third cycle of reaction could be discerned, as American academics came under increased suspicion in non-Western countries and in Latin America. Many of the guiding ideas in this resistance were actually initiated within the so-called periphery.[2] Third World regions were becoming increasingly disillusioned. They were disappointed that decolonization and autarchy failed to liberate them from the long reach of global (read: core) forces. Dissident theorists began to reconceptualize the problem as the persistence of neocolonialism and dependency. Newly "liberated" colonies came to recognize that their continuing problems were exacerbated by the persistence of neocolonial relations with their former metropoles or, in the case of Latin America where direct foreign rule had long ago disappeared, by the power of the United States to generate dependency. Similar symptoms were being noted on widely divergent continents and common causes were being sought. The time was ripe for a new synthesis, one that undermined the spokes-in-the-wheel approach to area studies by insisting that conditions in the periphery were tied together because of their relative positions vis-à-vis the core regions of capitalism.

It was no accident that this era of paradigm reconceptualization culminated in American scholarship with the publication in 1974 of Immanuel Wallerstein's path-breaking opening volume of *The Modern World-System*. Here, ostensibly, was a theory that treated the entire world—at least large portions of it since the sixteenth century—as a single unit of analysis, and focused on the interconnected spatial economies of a tripartite division into core, semiperiphery, and periphery. While his approach represented an enormous step forward and served as an essential corrective to isolated area studies, it still was not entirely freed from some of the biases of Eurocentrism that had plagued modernization and dependency theories. In more ways than intended, it resulted in a truncated analysis of non-Western areas, attributing many of the conditions in TROTW simply to the manner in which they had been gradually incorporated into the long reach of the core capitalist countries. It was difficult to find their independent agency.

Even though Wallerstein's book does not use the term *global*, I would trace the present academic preoccupation with globalization to that seminal work. The book put social scientists on notice, and legitimately so, that they could no longer treat national, or even regional or urban, histories as if they were independent of one another. Wallerstein argued forcefully that even back to the beginning of modern times in the sixteenth century, there really was only *one unit* of analysis—and that was the world-system. Although by the sixteenth century the core had been firmly situated in Western Europe, that region was already forging linkages to widely scattered semiperipheries and was spreading its tentacles to peripheral zones that hitherto had been relatively isolated from the system.

My own contribution, stimulated by Wallerstein's world-system thinking, was *Before European Hegemony: The World-System AD 1250–1350* (1989), which pressed that analysis farther back in time to the thirteenth century.[3] Then, rather than a single hierarchy of core, semiperiphery, and periphery, a far more complicated system of multiple hierarchies was organized on the basis of large civilizational units—much as there are today. Furthermore, the global system did not operate uniformly within those large culture/regional units but rather through far more circumscribed networks among key urban centers of diverse regions/empires. In my work on the thirteenth century, I borrowed a particularly apt metaphor: the image of an archipelago of urban centers in an enormous sea of spaces relatively untouched by "higher" functions coordinated by multiple core places. By the time we come to the imperialist order of the late nineteenth century, this concept is captured by the port-metropole relationship, tying extractive and control centers in colonies to their colonial rulers. Today, these have come to be known as global cities, which, as I shall develop later, have assumed their own hierarchical system.

Although global functions may be concentrated in these urban centers, it came to be recognized that the *New International Division of Labor* (Fröbel, Heinrichs, and Kreye 1980) entailed the integration of primary producers, the importation of labor, as well as the off-shoring of many manufacturing activities. I'm not sure exactly when the term *global* came to be substituted for *international,* but, during the 1980s, this change became more pervasive. Unhappily, by the 1990s, it had been adopted by all, but by then its meaning was increasingly debased.

The penultimate iteration is upon us. If one peruses contemporary newspapers, magazines, and books, if one reads the advertisements of major telecommunications companies and the brochures distributed by brokers to sell stock or if one listens to the talking heads on television public affairs programs, one recognizes that global babble has now become deafening. I have not done the required content analysis, but it seems to me that the use of the words *global* and *globalization* has been increasing exponentially in the last two decades.[4] These are the buzzwords that are used more and more to frame every issue: economic, political, or cultural. That alone should make us suspicious that we are losing analytic power, that glib ideology is supplanting reality.

In 1989, I first caviled against the loose use of *global/globalization* as an empty slogan (Abu-Lughod 1991). This was toward the beginning of the vogue that has now diffused to all corners of the social sciences, not to mention august chambers of transnational organizations spouting the ideology of liberal (read: unfettered) capitalism. Like the diffusion of polyester pantsuits to Dallas, globalization is everywhere—and by being everywhere, has become nowhere in particular. (When my former colleague, an anti-Marxist-Weberian ex-Jesuit who specializes in the sociology of religion(s), titles his latest lecture "The Globalization of Religion," we know we have reached the end of the line.) Like *modernity/modernization*, the terms have become so eviscerated of their empirical referents that they yield neither theory nor method. They have perhaps become mere slogans in the garbage dump of words about words.

But the issue is more serious than evisceration of meaning. Attitudes toward "One World" have fractured along a variety of political fault lines: north and south, right and left, ideologues of rampant capitalism as well as proponents of conservation environmentalism. Advocates of each of these positions now assume that the restructuring of the world-economy from 1974 on has resulted in a quantum leap of global integration, even though their diagnoses and interpretations of these processes differ. The first "symptom" was the global car (transnational production) or the export of capital and repatriation of product and profits. Then came the import of guest labor, some of it in its third generation by now. Then came arbitrage (the "trade" in money and its derivatives). Along with that came indebtedness, supervised by such international institutions as the World Bank and the International Monetary Fund. Finally, consumption patterns diffused and blended (not only "culture" but also material resources). This new level of entailment is seen as truly meriting the term *global* or *globalization*.

This process, according to the Right at least, climaxed with the fall of the Soviet Union in 1989, which to them proved the superiority of capitalism. The Left did not demur from acknowledging this triumph, even though it has chiefly responded with street protests outside the meetings of dominant international organizations. Proponents on various sides of the fault line, whether left and right or north and south, concurred by adopting the same words and apparently placing similar value on the process. That is when we should have started to worry. Is this truly the end of American provincialism? Or is it a new form of self-congratulatory egoism?

What to do? Can this baby be rescued from the murky bathwater that now threatens to drown it? Can serious scholarship reclaim the analytic power promised by seeing the world-system as the proper unit of study?[5]

It seems to me that there are numerous promising developments in the empirical study of the growing entailment of the world-system that deviate from this debasement of the currency. Studies of commodity flows strike me as one fertile way to proceed, but this same method can be applied to the spread of diseases in humans (i.e., AIDS) and animals (to wit, foot and mouth). Studies of the movement of monetary instruments are another, although these are harder to get at because so many transactions go unrecorded or are hidden. Linkages in social movements are also a fertile field for inquiry.

Let me draw my examples from recent studies of cities, because I am a comparative urbanist rather than an expert on global developments. I see significant progress in recent studies, as the premature generalizations of the 1980s are being overturned or at least fundamentally modified by expansions in time and space.

Two types of correctives are now appearing. The first is an effort to situate the processes of globalization within a deeper historical trend line, recognizing that whereas the details have changed, the role of cities as nodes of international flows preexisted the contemporary era and are continuing, despite rumors of their demise. The second is an effort to decenter the study of global cities away from exclusive preoccupation with Western dominance by examining how the processes of integration affect and are affected by differential reactions to it in both core and noncore regions.[6] My own recent work is moving in these two directions, even though only one has yet seen print.

One of the purposes of my recent book, *New York, Chicago, Los Angeles* (1999), was to introduce a more historically grounded account of the interactions, inter alia, among the three largest metropolitan regions of the United Sates and the changing world-system within which they developed. Taking for granted that international connections always, but only partially, affected their fates, the book traces how these cities were gradually transformed from recipients of European influences and power to control centers for much of the global economy. I argue, however, that the obvious differences among the three cities are attributable to much more than global forces. The book has recently been the object of a wonderful set of critiques,[7] but I would like to add one of my own. In evaluating this attempt in retrospect, I think it suffers from too heavy an emphasis on American exceptionalism. Its failure to compare American urbanization with processes in other parts of the world is a major limitation, so this must be left to another effort.

This brings me to the second type of correction that is now occurring in the literature on global cities, namely, greater attention is being paid to those urban places that are not control centers at all, but instead are being integrated (or rather, reintegrated) into the world-system as new types of subordinates. Several books and articles I have read deal with the question of how global forces are affecting what we used to call "Third World cities." I am thinking here of an article I read recently for a journal (I am unable to recall who the authors are) comparing Mumbai with Accra. There are also some case studies included in a collection edited by planners Peter Marcuse and Ronald Van Kampen (2000). New directions are explored in the work of geographer Kris Olds, who examines agency, power, and the politics of international (read: Western) architectural firms in reconstructing the "global" of the Pacific Rim. His excellent bibliography documents the growing literature in this new vein.[8]

Perhaps these are signs that a new stage of de-provincialization is beginning—one that refocuses attention on the zones that are not cores but that serve ancillary functions in the world-system. As part of this trend, I have been working for the past few years on research comparing two global cities of today's semiperiphery: Cairo and Istanbul. I trace how they are responding in similar ways to their reincorporation into the world-system within the past twenty-five years. Both, of course, are in deep trouble. There are widening gaps in the class structure, "problems" with minority groups, expanding debt under the discipline of international and U.S. funding, inflation, devaluation, and a serious liquidity crisis. Similar problems are visible in their spatial orders. There are new zones for international capital that contrast sharply with expanding "informal" quarters. And there are contrasting cleavages in their social responses: identity tensions between Westernized consumption patterns and the reintroduction and spread of, inter alia, the *hijab* (a scarf to cover the hair).

Although the similarities are readily apparent, I think we are still very far from understanding the role of the World Bank, the International Monetary Fund, and the U.S. military alliances in generating a new class of compradors in Egypt and Turkey, inter alia. The protests being mounted in these countries, as well as in scattered Western cities, depend more upon instinct than detailed analysis. I think this should be of the highest priority in adumbrating the new world-system.

Postscript

This article was written just before September 11, 2001. At the minimum, it requires the addition of a fifth reiteration in the process of continuing provincialism, and must end on a discouraging note. Rather than rewriting entirely, I decided to add this postscript in light of 9/11, when a new tragic chapter in globalization was written. While the casualties were scarcely the most serious consequence, the events and the political/military reaction to them unhappily revealed that almost no progress had been made in de-provincializing the American view of the world.

There was outrage and indignation when the so-called periphery "invaded" the self-righteous core, but there was also an abysmal level of ignorance about Central Asia/Afghanistan and an absolute lack of understanding of Islam and its multiplicity of cultures and sects. Even more appalling was the pervasive failure to grasp the real causes for resentment of U.S. policies in the Middle East. This provincialism was found not only in government agencies (which might have reined in President George W. Bush's cowboy mentality, however unlikely) but in the groves of academia as well. I was shocked to read the letters to the editors that came from so-called area experts and to hear speakers at teach-ins who seemed utterly ignorant of the past, of geography, and of the anthropology of tribal cultures. The reactions of the American government and most scholars to the events of 9/11 have illustrated once again how deficient American knowledge and understanding of the rest of the world remains and how such deficiencies have disastrous consequences in the real world.

In short, it appears that a fifth phase of rediscovery of TROTW is sorely needed. As we have seen, ostensible progress in "paying attention" has always been associated with military campaigns and adventures. This cloud may have a silver lining if it brings into view a fuller perspective on the entailments of global reach and the importance of seeing connections even in places that were casually ignored as parts of the periphery. Perhaps the true message is that no place is truly peripheral anymore. While this recognition may promise improved sophistication in academia, it is unlikely to come in time. The bad news is that public policies are still being made on the basis of the same provincialism that we had hoped was being overcome through history and world-systems analysis.

Notes

1. In 1987, I began giving a graduate seminar at the New School formally titled Change in Global Context, but known more informally as TROTW (The Rest of the World).

2. In most area-studies organizations in the United States, countercultural caucuses were being formed that protested control by traditional scholars and that exposed support for area studies to Central Intelligence Agency (CIA) strategies. Subaltern studies were initiated in a variety of periphery countries, which were then embraced by dissident scholars in the United States. It is hard, however, to separate this trend from other movements of the 1960s, such as the anti-Vietnam war protests, student revolts, and civil rights demands.

3. Other scholars, such as Kajsa Ekholm, drew analogies to even earlier, albeit less extensive, "world-systems," tied to the very origins of urban civilization (see Ekholm 1980).

4. I have seen an unpublished paper by a Northwestern University graduate student in management, reporting the results of his content analysis of articles and press releases in standard financial sources in the United States that use "globalization" as the "frame." Unfortunately, I seem to have lost the title page that bore his name while retaining his tables and charts. (I apologize profoundly!) His findings seem credible and support the conclusion of an exponential explosion in the use of the term between 1984 and 1998. According to his analysis, in period I (1984–1987), the concept emerged and became more common, but largely with reference to the financial industry. During this period, the framing was generally positive and globalization was depicted as inevitable and irreversible. Although the stock market crash of 1987 evidenced a brief setback, in period II (1988–1994), the application of the concept had spread to other industries (airlines, cars, chemicals, food, and telecommunications). The process was still depicted as "natural" and inevitable. In period III (1995–1998 when his study ends), the application of the term *globalization* had spread to many other industries (including the media and sports) and the term had emerged in conjunction with a variety of noneconomic issues, such as citizenship, crime, disease, poverty, culture, and consumption. At this point, although corporate press releases continue to frame globalization in positive terms, a strong negative framing emerges in newspaper articles, just as protests begin.

5. I am particularly distressed by some of the verbiage being generated—neologisms and new taxonomies for abstract forces (e.g., various "scapes") that seem to me to be mere incantations, adopted to avoid detailed analysis of specific mechanisms or active agents.

6. For example, Michael Peter Smith (2001) offers a prescription for embedding theory into actual research practice and draws examples from U.S. and other global cities.

7. First presented at a special session at the meetings of the Association of American Geographers, it has appeared as a "Review Symposium" in *Urban Affairs Review* (Brenner et al. 2001). The commentators included Neil Brenner, Susan Clarke, David Ley, and Anthony King. King's comments came closer to my own critique.

8. See the forthcoming article by Kris Olds and Henry Yeung. See also Olds (2001), which shows agents and agency, rather than abstract processes of globalization.

References

Abu-Lughod, Janet. 1989. *Before European Hegemony: The World-System AD 1250–1350.* New York: Oxford University Press.

———. 1991. "Global Babble." Pp. 131–38 in *Culture, Globalization and the World-System,* ed. A. King. Binghamton, NY: Department of Art and Art History, State University of New York at Binghamton.

———. 1999. *New York, Chicago, Los Angeles: America's Global Cities.* Minneapolis: University of Minnesota Press.

Brenner, Neil, Susan Clarke, David Ley, and Anthony King. 2001. "Review Symposium." *Urban Affairs Review* XXXVII, no. 1 (September): 119–57.

Ekholm, Kajsa. 1980. "On the Limitations of Civilization: The Structure and Dynamics of Global Systems." *Dialectical Anthropology* V, no. 2 (July): 155–66.

Fröbel, Folker, Jürgen Heinrichs, and Otto Kreye. 1980. *New International Division of Labor.* Cambridge: Cambridge University Press.

Marcuse, Peter, and Ronald Van Kampen. 2000. *Globalizing Cities: A New Spatial Order.* London: Blackwell.

Olds, Kris. 2001. *Globalization and Urban Change: Capital, Culture, and Pacific Rim Mega-Projects.* Oxford, UK: Oxford University Press.

Olds, Kris, and Henry Yeung. Forthcoming. "From *The Global City* to Globalizing Cities: Views from a Developmental City-State in Pacific Asia." *Review of International Political Economy.* Paper originally presented at IRDF World Forum on Habitat—International Conference on Urbanizing World and U.N. Human Habitat II. Columbia University, June 4–6, 2001.

Smith, Michael Peter. 2001. *Transnational Urbanism: Locating Globalization.* London: Blackwell.

12

Does One Represent Reality or Does One Explain It?

Maurice Aymard

The word *representation* has invaded the vocabulary of most social sciences during the last two or three decades. As with many words that become fashionable for unclear reasons and are used by many people on every occasion with a plurality of meanings, without any strictly formulated definition, I don't like it, and I do my best to use it as little as possible. But as it exists, we must cope with it, and the best way to cope with such a difficult and emphatic word is to underline from the very beginning that it has several meanings, and, when it is applied to social sciences research and writing, we must combine three main sets of methodological criticisms.

Methodological Criticisms: Set I

The first set of criticisms is against the sources, data, and documents we use, collect, and even build up when they do not exist. We wish them to be something more than individual impressions and to give us a direct or indirect access to reality itself. For a long time, social scientists have given preference to the data that has been produced and elaborated by public or independent private bodies, of which either the census or national statistics or (for "traditional" historians) the official political and diplomatic archives would be the ideal pattern. More recently, the development of research has induced scholars to produce new sets of data, for which they fixed the rules of collection so that they could be used as a basis for scientific analysis. Sociologists started with samples, surveys, and panels, and ethnologists with the systematic registration of their own observations. This approach, which could look in an early stage as possible only for scholars who study the present societies, was reinterpreted and reformulated by archaeologists during the last four decades. As a result of a deep revolution in their discipline, the traditional methods of excavation, oriented to the discovery of art objects or monuments, were abandoned. After making a grid of the field, archaeologists themselves (and not local peasants working under their supervision) excavate in a meticulous way, using a small brush and not a spade, some squares only (so as to keep a clear view of the stratigraphy) one level after the other, and register all the objects they can find, either apparently relevant or not, so as to be able to put them in relation with the other objects of the same level.

Archaeologists were among the first, if not the first, to understand that their collection of data (through excavation) was destroying the field forever, and could not be repeated (as a text may be read again and again in the same, or in a different, way). At the same time, it gave them the possibility to transform the objects they found in documents that could be used and processed in a scientific way. But the fact that the initial study, oriented to the collection of the primary sources, destroys the field that is under study, and cannot be repeated (as an experimentation in a laboratory) is not true only for archaeology: All anthropologists know that the observation of the same human group or village will give different results the second time, because the people who had contact with the first scholar will have an idea of what the second is looking for. But we cannot forget that, exactly as anthropology has tremendously increased the number of societies we know and can now compare, as well as our knowledges about them, archaeology has canceled the distinction between history and pre- or protohistory. History is no longer related to the invention of writing, and historical time has been broadened to a minimum of ten millennia or even more. It is relevant for us, in our context of multiethnic societies, that the apparition of the (new) men of Cro-Magnon has not immediately eliminated the (former) men of Neanderthal, and that, for a long period, the two "races" could coexist peacefully in the same place. This extension of the historical time to the totality of the history of mankind is, for us, the best protection against any kind of biological or sociobiological approach, and invites us to study the development of societies, techniques, arts, and cultures in the longest possible run.

All these procedures of identification, selection, and elaboration of any kind of data for a historical use are destined to give us direct or indirect access to historical "realities": access that has been denounced during the last decades, from an epistemological point of view, as the creation of an illusion of reality. The main argument is that the most apparently objective data are always biased by the criteria of production and of selection by the observer himself. As no experimentation is possible, but only the comparison of data for different places and times, the criteria used today by sociologists, ethnologists, or archaeologists would not be, for this reason, different from the documents produced in different periods of the past by various administrations or by individual observers. Whatever the efforts that may be put forth to reinforce the neutrality of the observation, the data are always socially constructed, and inform us as much or more about the mentality of the observer as about the reality they were supposed to observe. This was the main argument of Michel Foucault in his history of madness during the early modern period, and the conclusion of the studies on popular cultures and religions in the 1970s (Foucault 1988). The social scientist is looking for "objects," but is obliged to deal with "subjects" and subjective approaches, including his own, and always needs to start with a systematic critique of the documents he uses.

Methodological Criticisms: Set II

The second level of criticism would be the direct consequence of the first one, and would be focused on the position of neutrality of the social scientist as an observer. The "distant look" of the anthropologist is not only external to the society he studies. It is always hierarchical, and never quite reciprocal. We can list a few exceptions: for instance, Arjun Appadurai trying to keep a balance in his own life between India and the United States, or the experiment done in the 1980s of "importing" African anthropologists to study different "fields" in France (villages, small cities, factories, etc.). Research could not, from this point of view, reproduce the hierarchies of either in a positive way (the most usual), or in a negative one that is symmetric to the first one, but doesn't give, as such, a real existence to the point of view and *weltanschauung* of the other. This contradiction would be the main difference between natural and social sciences. Natural sciences are able to keep up with the dominant position of the most advanced countries. Social sciences cannot:

Scientific understanding of human societies finds its own limits in a position of domination from which the social scientist can never free himself totally, and that starts with language itself, the "natural language" of the observer being used and proposed to the "observed" as a scientific language.

Methodological Criticisms: Set III

The third criticism is focused on conceptualization and methods. Social sciences never went through the same process of unification that, for instance, mathematics in the 1920s and 1930s did. Even in the West, they continue to use different words and concepts, to refer to different values and problems of interpretation, and to put different questions to the present and to the past, developing specific schools and approaches that do not always communicate between them. It is true that it is easier for, let us say, Indian or a Chinese sociologists to be understood, read, reviewed, and celebrated in the Western scientific world if they speak not only the same language, but ask the same questions and use the same conceptual framework as their Western colleagues. But it is not certain that they are doing the best sociological research on their own society and producing the best material for a comparative discussion. The same was true for historians when they tried to impose, everywhere in the world, their conception of history (linked to the invention of writing, the sedentarization of agricultural societies, and the emergence of new political forms of organization that could be called states); their periodization of time—prehistory, ancient times, medieval, modern, and contemporary periods—and their concepts, state, nation, classes, and class struggles, and so on. All the newly independent countries would teach in their schools their own history as the history of a nation, and find, somewhere in the past, a kingdom or an empire (Bénin, Mali, or Ghana, for example) with which they could identify themselves, or a kind of founding father (for instance, in the 1990s, Tamerlane, who was not and could not be an Uzbek, in Uzbekistan) of their historical existence. But we have to keep in mind the question posed by Ravinder Kumar in his paper, "India: Nation State or Civilization State?" (1993). Would it not be better to write a history that could be adapted to every specific situation, and would not respect the unique pattern of the nation-state? Twenty years ago, the best Indian historians were interested in the transition from feudalism to capitalism, and in the protoindustrialization process. They would fit India in a broader comparative history, and India had to go through the same historical stages that Western countries had experienced. This kind of attitude appears much less relevant today. Indian historians are looking for a history of India for itself, one that would focus on its differences and specificities more than its hypothetical similarities to the rest of the world.

These three criticisms are well founded, even if we may not agree with the conclusions that are commonly derived from them. At this stage, three main points need to be underlined.

The first criticism does not mean the failure of our ambition to reach the historical and social "realities," and to explain and understand them. We are reminded that only the realities we try to study are the societies themselves, and that all we can know about them is the result of a complex social construction that strongly links their construction and our reconstruction. But that does not mean the relativization of any kind of knowledge on societies. It means that we can only have indirect access to the social reality, and, even more, that social reality does not exist as such, independently of its context and its procedures of representation. It is always socially and culturally embedded. The counterpart of Foucault's argument about madness is that we need to study the origins and developments of all social and cultural procedures of classification, inclusion, and exclusion produced by any society. They are basic elements of our cultural history and help us to understand from inside the production and stabilization of cultural representations that will not only produce other representations but also contribute to the reshaping of social reality itself (of which the representations are a component). These can be read in an objective manner. The same could be said about Carlo Ginzburg's *Cheese and the Worms* (1980). Popular culture and religion do not exist as such, but only as produced by procedures of isolation, descriptions, condemnation, marginalization, repression, and imposition of new norms that were carried out by the Catholic church, by ecclesiastic institutions like the Inquisition, and by the cultural élites, from the sixteenth century onward. As the miller Menocchio was the first of his family to be able to read, and does not appear to have trained his own son in reading, we can take a full account of the violent effects of the access to written culture on a man, who was not at all prepared to control, classify, and manage the new information of which he was taking hold, and had to mix together these isolated pieces of information in a cosmogony that was coherent for himself, but not for others, and even less for educated clergymen of the time.

The second criticism reminds us that our scholarly disciplines, at the present stage of their development, are unable to produce a coherent and universally accepted set of rules and concepts. They are the historical product of the European expansion, control, and domination of the world. Most of them went through a long and controversial process of transferring their center of international scientific homologation and organization from Europe to the United States, but that does not mean they succeeded in creating an equality of viewpoints. We must acknowledge that, with the exception of mathematical economy (which is only a part, even if an expanding one, of the economic discipline) and of formalized linguistics—the only two scientific disciplines that were able to reach a sufficient level of formalization—most social sciences are not unified at a world level or even at a Euroamerican one. They continue speaking different natural languages, and not a unique scholarly one, even if English may be used as a language of communication between scholars. Natural languages are the only ones that give their name to concrete social realities, and the difficulties start as soon as we try to translate either the kinship vocabulary of a specific society, the words used by local administrations to describe and classify social and territorial realities, or even the broader and more abstract concepts used by social scientists. *Civilization* has eliminated, in English, the older word *civility*, as *civilisation* did in French for *civilité*. But Italian kept *civiltà*, of which *culture* is only a subsection, while German uses three different words: *Zivilisation*, *Bildung*, and *Kultur*. We all know from our daily experience, that, whatever may be our efforts, translation is always an approximation that leaves out a large, and often the most interesting, part of the original word's meaning. For this very reason, a social scientist needs to know as many languages as possible, and must be able to think (and not only to read) in several. Even if he cannot cut his links to his own culture, he needs to develop a multicultural approach of social analysis, description, and theory.

The third point is directly related to the second, and may be used to fix an agenda for the social sciences during the next decades. Social sciences were "invented" when religion started to be considered as cultural data, rather than as the only principle of its organization. They developed to give each society first a better knowledge of itself and of the other societies, then, up to a certain point, possibilities of intervention to control and reorient its own evolutions, and to resolve its own problems. Social sciences are not technologies that could be easily transferred from one country to another. If their internationalization is both a useful and a necessary process, it does not mean that the same solutions could be used everywhere the problems look the same, nor that the same questions can be put in the same terms to different societies and social realities, nor even that the same words and concepts may be used without any preliminary efforts to describe them. It does not mean that a comparison is impossible. It means it is possible only if the differences and specificities of each society are taken into consideration. Social sciences could live for a long period with the conviction that Western societies were superior to others, that their development fixed the top of the world hierarchy, and that the convergence of all the societies of the world around the Western pattern would be the end of both history and the story.

The situation has clearly changed during the last twenty or twenty-five years. Social scientists became aware that the cultural diversity of the world was valid not only for the past and for the present, but also for the future. Social sciences need to be rebuilt and restructured on the basis of this diversity of cultures and civilizations if they don't want to condemn themselves to becoming a more and more repetitive discourse on a specific set of representations.

But this is only one side of the problem, and I will try to analyze the other side, to answer the question: What could be a scientific discourse on social realities, and up to what point can it pretend to explain them? The answer I propose is very simple: It can do it only if it uses one set of representations, most of them being metaphors, but using them as such (as partial and external), and not as direct expressions of reality. The two examples look to me to best fit the center of which we celebrate the twenty-fifth anniversary, and the name of the center itself, and of its founder. The first is the use by Fernand Braudel of the word *civilization*. The second is the different uses by Immanuel Wallerstein and Braudel of the expressions *world-economy* and *world-system*.

When Braudel started using the word *civilization*, its original meaning had been transformed in the West, between the nineteenth and the first part of the twentieth century, by three main changes in the representation of the world. The first was the awareness, at the very moment when Europe was achieving unification of the world, of the plurality of the civilizations that had coexisted and will continue to coexist, and the fact that each of them had its specificities, cultural logic, history, and a future that would not limit itself to merging in the expanding European civilization, to which only the local elites could have access. The second one, influenced by cultural anthropology, was that every civilization was a coherent unity, of which all the various components were strongly related: A civilization is, in the same time, a representation of the world and a material organization of it. The third one was leading to the redefinition and rethinking of the relations between the different civilizations and was causing a discussion about the hierarchies that had been, in a first stage, accepted or formulated between them: Each civilization is a totality, but very few (and maybe none of them) live totally isolated from the others. All civilizations are engaged in a long process of exchange and circulation of cultural goods.

Braudel was never interested in the study of one civilization for itself—from the very beginning, when in Algiers and then in São Paulo, he was confronted with the coexistence of different civilizations both in the Mediterranean and in Brazil. The conclusion he reached was the first definition—not static and isolated, but dynamic and relational—he wrote in 1949, in the first edition of the *Méditerranée*, and which he maintained in the second edition:

> A living civilization must be able not only to give but to receive and to borrow. . . . But a great civilization can also be recognized by its refusal to borrow, by its resistance to certain alignments, by its resolute selection among the foreign influences offered to it and which would no doubt be forced upon it if they were not met by vigilance or, more simply, by incompatibility of temper and appetite. (Braudel 1976, II, 764)

Today everyone, with a few exceptions like Fukuyama and other advocates of one global civilization, would agree with an assertion that was not in the mainstream fifty years ago. In 1963, in a handbook he had accepted as a challenge to write for French high schools on the contemporary world, he extended the application of the same idea to the totality of the world and underlined, even more strongly, the basic role of religion. His contribution was reprinted in 1987 after his death, with the new title of *Grammaire de Civilisations* (the English title is *A History of Civilizations*). But, writing about Christianity and Islam, he asserted:

> Each of these new religions seized upon the body of a civilization already in place, in each case breathing a soul into it. Each was able to draw upon a rich inheritance—a past, a living present, and already— a future. . . . As Christianity inherited from the Roman Empire of which it was a prolongation, so Islam instantly took hold of the Near East, perhaps the world's oldest cross-roads of civilized humanity. (Braudel 1993, 41)

Both were able to extend their influence outside the area they had inherited: Christianity in the direction of Northern and Eastern Europe, then Siberia and across the Atlantic; Islam both east (up to central and Southeast Asia) and south (across the Sahara).

What is important at this stage for Braudel is the identification of a level of coherence of geographical areas that is both spatial and human, and may be used to represent and explain not only the existence of long-run borders but also of circulations between the different civilizations. The limit between Catholic and Protestant Europe will finally, after more than a century of war, coincide with the old frontier of the Roman Empire. The limit between Eastern and Western Christendom corresponds, in the Mediterranean area, to the limit between the two parts, Greek and

Latin, of the same Roman Empire: a limit that Christianization has extended to Northern Europe up to the Baltic Sea. But in both cases, the frontiers are, on one side, much anterior to Christianity, and, on the other, have active consequences in other fields even today. For instance, the breakup of former Yugoslavia, with Catholic Slavonia and Croatia on one side and Orthodox Serbia on the other. Or even the process of extension of the European Union to the East: The only Orthodox country that is a member of the Union is Greece (to which the doors were opened in 1974 for political reasons after the fall of the colonels' dictatorship). The first five countries to be accepted in the following years are Catholic (with, for Hungary, a strong Protestant minority), and they are asked to reinforce, on their eastern border, the control of immigration coming from Orthodox countries. Seen from this point of view, the word *civilization* may be used by Braudel as a key word for an intellectual operation that combines representation and explanation. So he can write in the same book that civilizations are geographical areas, societies, economies, ways of thought (*mentalités collectives*), and continuities (Braudel 1993, chs. 2, 3). They allow the scholar to join with one word Braudel's conceptualization of historical long-run consequences and evolutions, and what has been, up to today, a representation of the historical actors themselves. Civilization functions, in the Braudel intellectual representation, as a metaphor. He uses it to propose a set of logical interrelations between different categories of factors that are, most of the time, presented and described as independent one from the other, but that, at the same time, mean something for the societies for which their belonging to one specific civilization is still today the factor of their own identity and self-identification. The rule he proposes is broad enough to have exceptions: Hebraism will be introduced in the second edition of the *Méditerranée* (1966) as the exception that confirms the rule, that is, as a civilization that has survived after it lost its own space. But all Mediterranean civilizations are given an autonomous existence as heroes of the historical stage directed by Braudel. On this stage, all the individual actions may be not only represented or summarized around emblematic characters, they can also be understood and, to a certain point, foreseen, although they are never totally predetermined. The past explains only a part of the present.

The same could be said of the two expressions *world-economy* and *world-system*, and of their different uses by Braudel and Wallerstein. Braudel had translated the first from the German *Weltwirtschaft* to apply it to the Mediterranean: an economy for itself that gives existence to a world for itself, that is only a part of the world. Wallerstein's contribution was to extend the application of the expression to a no more static, but dynamic context: the European world-economy of the early modern period, with its capacity both for spatial organization and for economic expansion. And he gave a twin brother to it: the world-system. It is interesting to see that Braudel always prefers the first expression to the second, which he usually refrains from using. But even for the first one, he underlines the existence, before the fifteenth century and during all of the early modern period, of other world-economies that could exist before and coexist with the new European world-economy. Whatever the expansion of the European world-economy, the world remains a plurality and cannot be identified with a unique coherent system. As he says in his own language, "the world-economy [is] an order among other orders" (Braudel 1984, 45). It is never the only one. It may help to explain the reality only if it is accepted first as a representation—albeit a beautiful and scholarly one—that allows the scholar to join together the different pieces of the reality.

The social scientist, as Braudel understands his role, is a kind of demiurge that would be at the same time a poet. His power, through the words he borrows from the natural languages and the way he invests a scientific meaning, is to put together and assemble (in a coherent unity) the fragmented pieces of the social reality. But the same words are only images of the world, not the world itself. We can call them, in the best meaning of the word, representations. Can we do more? I don't know. But if we succeed, it will be a wonderful achievement.

References

Braudel, Fernand. 1949. *La Méditerranée et le monde Méditerranéen à l'époque de Phillipe II*, 1st ed. Paris: A. Colin.
———. 1966. *La Méditerranée et le monde Méditerranéen à l'époque de Phillipe II*, 2nd ed., 2 vol. Paris: A. Colin.
———. 1976. *The Mediterranean and the Mediterranean World in the Age of Philip II*. 2 vol. New York: Harper Torchbooks.
———. 1984. *Capitalism and Civilization, 15th–18th Century*, III: *The Perspective of the World*. New York: Harper & Row.
———. 1993. *A History of Civilizations*. New York: Penguin. Originally published as *Grammaire de Civilisations*. Paris: Arthaud-Flammarion, 1987.
Foucault, Michel. 1988. *Madness and Civilization: A History of Insanity in the Age of Reason*, trans. by R. Howard. New York: Vintage Books.
Ginzburg, Carlo. 1980. *The Cheese and the Worms: The Cosmos of a Sixteenth-Century Miller*. Baltimore: The Johns Hopkins University Press.
Kumar, Ravinder. 1993. "India: Nation-State or Civilization-State?" Centre for Contemporary Studies, Nehru Memorial Museum and Library, Teen Murti House, New Delhi, Occasional Papers on Indian Perspectives in Indian Development, VIII.

13

The Scholarly Mainstream and Reality: Are We at a Turning Point?

Immanuel Wallerstein

In his essay on "civilization," Lucien Febvre said: "[I]t is never a waste of time to write the history of a word" (1962, 481). I wish to amend the injunction slightly since I think it is equally true that it is never a waste of time to write the history of shifts in word usage and the centrality of particular concepts. I will trace the different words we have been using to analyze the contemporary world since 1945. Since neither I nor anyone else has done the kind of content analysis necessary to document this, I will do it in the form of an impressionistic mental experiment. What terms have been most frequently used in the titles of the extremely large number of colloquia and conferences held throughout the world during this period? What terms have been used in the titles of papers for these conferences? Furthermore, what are the principal social science concepts that have been adopted and used by politicians and journalists?

Coming out of World War II, and with the defeat of the fascist powers, there were two urgent issues for world social science: First, to explain how Nazism/fascism had been possible (not a subject much discussed before war broke out); and second, to describe the postwar world. The most popular explanatory concept for the immediate past was launched by Theodore Adorno, a leading figure in the Frankfurt School, with his book, *The Authoritarian Personality* (1950). With its emphasis on personality traits (measured by the so-called F-scale), it implied that authoritarians could be found anywhere, but did not give a very good explanation as to why such persons managed to come to power in a particular country.

Others were more concerned with making sure that the misdeeds of Nazism would not be repeated. This led to emphasizing two major concepts. One was instituted by the United Nations in its adoption of the term *genocide*, to describe what the Nazi regime had done to Jews and Roma.[1] The second achieved prominence when UNESCO undertook, as one of its initial intellectual tasks, the publishing of a series of pamphlets on "The Race Question in Modern Science." These pamphlets essentially intended to provide evidence for the absence of any scientific justification for racial inequalities.[2] This may seem banal today, but we have to remember how much of world social science before 1945 had asserted the scientific basis of primordial racial inequality.

Still, fascism was quickly forgotten as a theme in light of the Cold War, which took center stage. Authoritarianism became transposed into totalitarianism (Friedrich and Brzezinski 1956), a concept that was invented in order to bracket Nazism and Communism under the same category, and thus damn them equally.[3] Of course, this represented the U.S. side of the Cold War. Reciprocal concepts were put forward by the Soviet Union and its scholars. They saw the world divided into a "socialist camp" of nations (including the "popular democracies") versus a capitalist/imperialist camp. In this rhetoric, socialism was defined as a stage of social development posterior to capitalism but prior to communism, a usage of the term that became widespread only after 1945.

The discomfort felt in the Western world in general, and in the United States in particular, as a result of the Cold War and of perceived popular support for political forces that were considered hostile to liberal parliamentary regimes, led to a good deal of social psychological analyzing that went beyond the narrow concept of an authoritarian personality. Early writings often featured discussions of "mass society," a new social form that was presumably found in industrialized states (Kornhauser 1959). Another version of this, quite popular in the 1950s, was the distinction between other-directed persons (of the present) and inner-directed persons (of the past) (Riesman 1950),[4] the latter being exemplars of the Protestant ethic, another concept which became popular at this moment (Weber 1952).[5] The concept of mass society was not unrelated to the concept of mass media which now also entered the general vocabulary and indeed fostered the creation of a whole new discipline, communication studies. It should be noted that before 1945, the term *masses* had generally been considered to be left-wing political terminology with positive connotations for those who used it. In the new usage of the adjective *mass*, the general tone was on the negative side—elitist, and distinctly antipopulist.

While East-West issues clearly dominated the initial post-1945 discussions, persistent political upheavals in Asia, the Middle East, Africa, and Latin America began to attract scholarly attention. The term *Third World* was invented in 1954 by a French economist to describe these zones collectively.[6] The use of the word *third* had several connotations. One was the assertion that these countries were not part of the first two worlds (from which one could draw the conclusion that they were or should be neutral [or later nonaligned] in the Cold War). But the term also contained an allusion to the role of the Third Estate in the French Revolution (hence implying their role as the subject of future history). The term had widespread acceptance in the 1960s and 1970s and even later (see Wallerstein 2000a).

Faced with the political reality of the Third World, the ideological contestants in the Cold War developed two separate vocabularies to deal with it. In the West, in analyzing the Third World, one talked of development, modernization, take-off, and of the obstacles posed by traditional societies with primordial values (at a time that the United States and eventually western Europe were said to be entering into a "post-industrial" society within a world defined by the "end of ideology") (Bell 1960, 1973). In the East/Second World/Communist bloc/socialist camp, this entire vocabulary was rejected. In that zone one spoke instead of the imperialism of capitalist powers and of the construction of socialism, both within the context of something called the scientific-technological revolution (Inozemtsev 1982). And in the Third World itself, one preferred to talk of dependency, revolution, and national liberation (Cardoso and Faletto 1967; Dos Santos et al. 1969). Of course, it was not impossible to engage in translation between these rival vocabularies.

Somewhere in the 1960s, and more strongly in the 1970s, the discussion about the political economy of the world-system led to a renewed concern with epistemological questions. The early post-1945 period was a period when science as mantra, hope, expectation, and virtue was at its maximum, and this was true in all the zones of the world-system. It thus came as somewhat of a shock when a young scientist, turned historian of science, invented the concept of the paradigm (Kuhn 1962). Kuhn's concept spawned an enormous new knowledge industry, and has led in paths that he himself repudiated or at least into assertions with which he felt uncomfortable. But his book, taken up widely by social scientists, permitted a wide discussion about the social structure of scientific activity that had been limited to a specialized group before this.

At about the same time, within the world of relatively orthodox Marxist thought, what seemed an esoteric discussion, one about the nature and reality of something called the Asiatic mode of production, was to act as a solvent of the rigidities of analysis encrusted during the Stalinist period for Marxists within and outside the socialist camp (Krader 1975; Tokai 1979; Bailey and Llobera 1981; Foursov 1997). Basically, the Asiatic mode of production had been Marx's unsuccessful attempt to explain the differences between the Western world and the non-Western world. It had been officially put into quarantine by Stalin in the 1930s because of what it implied about Russia. Bringing it out of quarantine after Stalin's death (something done primarily by Hungarians plus Italians and other Western Marxists) produced literature of passing importance, except that it attracted attention once again to the utility of the concept of the modes of production. This led to a bastard compromise in the 1970s and 1980s, the concept of articulation of modes of production, a now forgotten way of handling the social specificities of the Third World (Hindess and Hirst 1977; Wolpe 1980).

In the Third World itself, Raúl Prebisch and the UN Economic Commission for Latin America launched the concept of "core-periphery" as a mode of describing the structuring of the world-economy. And this conceptual language spread very quickly from its Latin American origins.[7] Meanwhile, in France, Fernand Braudel was putting forth, with considerable influence, the importance of the *longue durée* (1958, 725–58) and the concept of the *économie-monde* as a "universe in itself" (1966 [1949], 354), as ways of explaining structural continuities and change in early modern Europe. And within the camp of Marxism, there was an extended discussion of the transition from feudalism to capitalism, which revealed rather basic cleavages in modes of interpreting European history (Hilton 1976).

When I published volume I of *The Modern World-System* in 1974, conceptually what I was doing was putting together the core-periphery antinomy with Braudel's longue durée and économie-monde, and linking it to the Paul M. Sweezy pole of the transition debate. In the post-1968 atmosphere, when Braudel's work was available for the first time in English, world-systems analysis gained a foothold amid the competing conceptual apparatuses that were circulating and debating each other.

There was one other important conceptual fashion in the 1960s, structuralism. It came to prominence out of the effort of Claude Lévi-Strauss to create a new, more scientific way, of treating the West/non-West antinomy, as opposed to the traditional ethnographies of the anthropologists (Lévi-Strauss 1955; 1958). Of course, as Braudel would point out, this was essentially a way of getting on the nomothetic bandwagon of science triumphant (Braudel 1958). Still, structuralism as conceptual language had a heady career in many other fields: linguistics (Chomsky), psychoanalysis (Lacan), Marxist political economy (Althusser), and many others (Dosse 1991).

The world revolution of 1968 had a major impact on all these vocabularies, virtually bringing to an end the attractiveness of modernization theory, orthodox Marxism, and structuralism in one fell swoop. It led to the emergence of three new languages. Within the natural sciences, and spreading from there to the social sciences, the language of the sciences of complexity came to the fore in the 1970s and 1980s. We began to hear of chaos, bifurcations, and the arrow of time.[8] Above all, we began to hear growing skepticism about the long-standing Newtonian truths, a knowledge movement which met significant resistance, and led to the so-called science wars (Ross 1996; Segerstråle 2000).

Within the humanities, and spreading from there to the social sciences, we began to hear of culture, agency, deconstruction, and the multiple "post-" doctrines, a knowledge movement which also met significant resistance, and led to the so-called culture wars (Bolton 1992; Gerson 1996; Bennett 1991). And there emerged a new trinity of terms—class, race, and gender—the result primarily of social movements that had specifically denounced the neglect of race and gender issues in prior social science.

The 1970s, which the United Nations had rashly proclaimed in the 1960s would be the "decade of development," turned out to be instead the decade of the collapse of developmentalist illusions, first in the Third World, and then in the Second World, culminating in the collapse of the communisms in 1989–1991. The so-called Washington Consensus emerged as a way of taking intellectual and political advantage of the changed geopolitical situation. And with it, we got new conceptual language. There were three major sets of terms that were offered to organize our understanding of the contemporary world.

One was that of globalization. This was introduced as the alternative to developmentalism, and premised on a presumed social science imperative known as TINA (there is no alternative). Along with it came a lesser-included concept, governance, which was a way of acknowledging (and presumably dealing with) the sociopolitical fallout of globalization.

Governance turned out to be a greater problem than was initially thought, as states fell apart. In the 1970s, the concept of human rights first emerged as a sort of left-of-center pressure on the U.S. government and its policies. In the 1980s, it became a tool to be used against the

Soviet Union. In the 1990s, it became the weapon of the so-called international civil society to assert its right to intervene whenever what was now called *ethnic cleansing* occurred, in order to prevent new *holocausts* (a term that itself had only become popular in the 1970s) as a mode of sustaining Israel (Novick 1999), and whose exclusive usage with reference to the Nazi genocide was contested by Armenians and many others (Fein 1993; Tatz 1997).

A third set of terms used to describe unrest in what was no longer called the Third World (and only occasionally its successor term, *the South*). It was applied most especially to the Islamic countries. The terms were *fundamentalism, terrorism,* and the now notorious *clash of civilizations* (Huntington 1996). The events of September 11, 2001, have caused this third set of 1990s terms to drown all the others, and they may turn out to be the death knell of the languages of both globalization and human rights.

What this quick survey is intended to show is the fickleness of social science concepts, which have been following the headlines and attaining momentary glory but, by and large, have not shown too much explanatory power. The question is whether we can come up with less fleeting concepts, ones that have more ability to give us insight into the realities of the contemporary world situation. I have argued in some detail, and on several occasions, about why globalization is an unhelpful rhetoric and that we should think of the current period of the past twenty years and the next thirty to forty years as a time of transition, a chaotic and dark time, from our present historical system (a capitalist world-economy) which is, in my view, in a process of disintegration toward an unpredictable future system which will emerge from the multiple social actions of a virtually infinite number of actors (Wallerstein 2000b). I shall not repeat those arguments here.

Two things in this panorama that I have given you offer some optimism that we shall be able to come up with the intellectual tools adequate for understanding and acting in this time of transition. One is the emergence of the two new knowledge movements from the 1970s on— the sciences of complexity and cultural studies. What should be underlined about this pair of movements is that they both challenge the concept of the two cultures, a concept that has dominated world thought for two centuries now, although it only received its name in the immediate post-1945 period (Snow 1959).

The concept of the two cultures involved seeing knowledge as made up of two competing epistemologies, scientific empiricism and humanistic hermeneutics, which pulled apart from each other and were essentially irreconcilable. The social sciences, in-between, were torn apart by this division. The new knowledge movements reverse this situation. They are centripetal rather than centrifugal, moving in the direction of a new unified epistemology of knowledge construction, in which the social sciences, far from being pulled apart, will be a central unifying locus. This reconciliation may not occur, or may not fully occur, but if it does (and only if it does), will we be able to be lucid about the reality in which we live as well as capable of constructing the kind of historical system in which we want to live.

The second cause for optimism is, perversely, the events of September 11, 2001. They are, of course, precisely a reflection of the kind of anarchy in the world-system of which I have been speaking. But they have constituted an intellectual shock of the first order, and that especially to the knowledge centers of the world-system. I have heard repeatedly, in the aftermath of 9/11, scholar after scholar say that he or she had to reflect now on the relevance of what he or she has been doing against the reality they are now at last aware of living. Here again, we cannot be sure what conclusions the intellectuals of the world will reach, but after some fifty, if not several hundred, years of relative rigidity and false or useless conceptualizations, such a shock is salutary and may be helpful.

So, yes, of course we are at a turning point. Let us hope and try to arrange that we turn in the right direction.

Notes

1. The UN Convention on the Prevention and Punishment of the Crime of Genocide was adopted by Resolution 260 (III) A of the UN General Assembly on December 9, 1948. It defines genocide as various acts "committed with intent to destroy, in whole or in part, a national, ethnical, racial, or religious group."

2. In 1950, a group of eight prominent anthropologists from around the world drafted a statement on the race concept. This statement was then revised after consultation with thirteen other experts, and subsequently commented upon and largely endorsed by ninety-six physical anthropologists and geneticists. The statement begins by saying that "scientists have reached general agreement in recognizing that mankind is one; that all men belong to the same species." It recommends dropping the term *races* and replacing it with *ethnic groups*. It says, among other things, that "according to present knowledge there is no proof that the groups of mankind differ in their innate mental characteristics, whether in respect of intelligence or temperament." The text of this statement, of comments on this statement, and of a subsequent 1951 statement may be found in *The Race Concept: Results of an Inquiry*, No. 9 (UNESCO, 1952). UNESCO published a parallel series, *The Race Question and Modern Thought* (1953), which sought to survey the views of various religions, as distinct from the views of scientists.

3. Indeed, in the 1970s, authoritarianism began to be used politically as different from, and less morally reprehensible than, totalitarianism, thereby justifying U.S. government support of "authoritarian" or "traditional autocratic" regimes against the

true enemy, "totalitarian" regimes. See Jeane J. Kirkpatrick: "There are, however, *systemic* differences between traditional and revolutionary autocracies. . . . Generally speaking, traditional autocrats tolerate social inequities, brutality, and poverty, whereas revolutionary autocracies create them" (1982, 49).

4. The book was written about the United States, and clearly ignored the non-Western world entirely.

5. Of course the book had originally been translated into English in 1930 but was not widely read in the United States until after 1945. It had been discussed in Europe since its original appearance in German at the beginning of the twentieth century. But, before 1945, the concept was under discussion only by a narrow group of specialists and had not entered the general domain of the scholarly world, either in the United States or Europe.

6. Alfred Sauvy used it in an article he wrote for *France-Observateur*. It then became the title of a book edited by Georges Balandier (with a preface by Sauvy), *Le "tiers monde," sous-développement et développement* (1956).

7. Actually, Prebisch took the concept from what were obscure German writings of the 1920s, and his ideas were quite similar to those that evolved in Romania in the 1920s and 1930s. But it was only with Prebisch, and only in the 1960s, that these ideas took hold. See Prebisch (1982) and Joseph L. Love (1988).

8. There are now many surveys available, as well as journals devoted to the topic. For one history of the ideas, along with a presentation of one version of the arguments, see Ilya Prigogine (1996).

References

Adorno, T. W., et al. 1950. *The Authoritarian Personality*, 1st ed. New York: Harper.

Bailey, Anne M., and Josep P. Llobera, eds. 1981. *The Asiatic Mode of Production: Science and Politics*. London: Routledge & Kegan Paul.

Balandier, Georges. 1956. *Le "tiers monde," sous-développement et développement*. Paris: Presses universitaires de France.

Bell, Daniel. 1960. *The End of Ideology: On the Exhaustion of Political Ideas in the Fifties*. Glencoe, IL: Free Press.

———. 1973. *The Coming of Post-Industrial Society: A Venture in Social Forecasting*. New York: Basic Books.

Bennett, William J. 1991. *The War over Culture in Education*. Washington, D.C.: Heritage Foundation.

Bolton, Richard, ed. 1992. *Culture Wars: Documents from the Recent Controversies in the Arts*. New York: New Press.

Braudel, Fernand. 1958. "Histoire et la longue durée." *Annales E.S.C.* XIII, no. 4 (October–December): 725–53.

———. 1966. *La Méditerranée et le monde méditerranéen à l'époque de Philippe II*, 2nd rev. ed. Paris: Lib. Armand Colin (orig. 1949).

Cardoso, Fernando Henrique, and Enzo Faletto. 1967. *Dependencia y desarrollo en América latina*. Lima: Instituto de Estudios Peruanos.

Dobb, Maurice. 1946. *Studies in the Development of Capitalism*. London: Routledge & Kegal Paul.

Dos Santos, Theotônio, et al. 1969. *La crisis del desarollismo y la nueva dependencia*. Lima: Moncloa-Campodónico.

Dosse, François. 1991/1992. *Histoire du structuralisme,* 2 vol. Paris: Découverte.

Febvre, Lucien. 1962. "Civilisation: Évolution d'un mot et d'un groupe d'idées," in *Pour une histoire à part entière.* Paris: SEVPEN, 481–528.

Fein, Helen. 1993. *Genocide: A Sociological Perspective.* Newbury Park, CA: Sage.

Foursov, Andrei. 1997. "Social Times, Social Spaces, and Their Dilemmas: Ideology 'in One Country.'" *Review* XX, nos. 3 and 4 (Sum./Fall): 345–420.

Friedrich, Carl J., and Zbigniew Brzezinski. 1956. *Totalitarian Dictatorship and Autocracy.* Cambridge: Harvard University Press.

Gerson, Mark. 1996. *The Neoconservative Vision: From the Cold War to the Culture Wars.* Lernham, MD: Madison Books.

Hilton, R. H., ed. 1976. *The Transition from Feudalism to Capitalism.* London: New Left Books.

Hindess, Barry, and Paul Hirst. 1977. *Modes of Production and Social Formation: An Auto-Critique of Precapitalist Modes of Production.* London: Macmillan.

Huntington, Samuel P. 1996. *The Clash of Civilizations and the Remaking of World Order.* New York: Simon & Schuster.

Inozemtsev, N. N., ed. 1982. *The Scientific-Technological Revolution and the Contradictions of Capitalism.* Moscow: Progress.

Kirkpatrick, Jeane J. 1982. *Dictatorships and Double Standards: Rationalism and Reason in Politics.* New York: Simon & Schuster.

Kornhauser, William. 1959. *The Politics of Mass Society.* Glencoe, IL: Free Press.

Krader, Lawrence. 1975. *The Asiatic Mode of Production: Sources, Development and Critique in the Writings of Karl Marx.* Assen: van Gorcum.

Kuhn, Thomas S. 1962. *Structure of Scientific Revolutions.* Chicago: University of Chicago Press.

Lévi-Strauss, Claude. 1955. *Tristes tropiques.* Paris: Plon.

———. 1958. *Anthropologie structurale.* Paris: Plon.

Love, Joseph L. 1988. "Theorizing Underdevelopment: Latin America and Romania, 1869–1950." *Review* XI, no. 4 (Fall): 453–96.

Novick, Peter. 1999. *The Holocaust in American Life.* Boston: Houghton Mifflin.

Prebisch, Raúl. 1982. *La obra de Prebisch en la CEPAL,* selections by Adolfo Gurrieri. México: Fondo de Cultura Económica.

Prigogine, Ilya. 1996. *La fin des certitudes.* Paris: Ed. Odile Jacob [in English: *The End of Certainty,* New York: Free Press, 1997].

Riesman, David, in collaboration with Reuel Denney and Nathan Glazer. 1950. *The Lonely Crowd: A Study of Changing American Character.* New Haven, CT: Yale University Press.

Ross, Andrew, ed. 1996. *Science Wars.* Durham, NC: Duke University Press.

Segerstråle, Ullica. 2000. *Defenders of the Truth: The Battle for Science in the Sociobiology Debate and Beyond.* New York: Oxford University Press.

Snow, C. P. 1959. *The Two Cultures and the Scientific Revolution.* New York: Cambridge University Press.

Tatz, Colin, ed. 1997. *Genocide Perspectives.* Sydney: Center for Comparative Genocide Studies, Macquarie University.

Tokai, Ferenc. 1979. *Essays on the Asiatic Mode of Production.* Budapest: Akademiai Kiado.

UNESCO. 1952. *The Race Question in Modern Science.* Paris: UNESCO.

UNESCO. 1953. *The Race Question and Modern Thought.* Paris: UNESCO.

Wallerstein, Immanuel. 2000a. "C'était quoi, le tiers-monde?" *Le monde diplomatique* (August): 18–19.

Wallerstein, Immanuel. 2000b. "Globalization or an Age of Transition? A Long-Term View of the Trajectory of the World-System." *International Sociology* XV, no. 2 (June): 249–65.

Weber, Max. 1952. *The Protestant Ethic and the Spirit of Capitalism,* trans. Talcott Parsons, with a foreword by R. H. Tawney. New York: Scribner's.

Wolpe, Harold, ed. 1980. *The Articulation of Modes of Production: Essays from Economy and Society.* London: Routledge & Kegan Paul.

14

The North Atlantic Universals

Michel-Rolph Trouillot

I'd like to engage you in a conversation about the *longue durée* of concepts in the modern world-system by emphasizing a family of words that I call "North Atlantic universals." I don't like to use the word *West*, which we all know is a misnomer, and by North Atlantic I mean what some of us most often call the West. As Martinican writer Edouard Glissant puts it, "The West is not a place, it is a project" (1997). Or to paraphrase a character in Alain Resnais's movie, *Mon Oncle d'Amérique* (1980), "The West does not exist. I know. I've been there."

To locate the West as a project, a geography of imagination is indispensable in understanding the nature, functions, and issues inherent in the longue durée of North Atlantic universals. My insistence on North Atlantic is not simply a quibble with terminology. It is a rhetorical and didactic move toward localizing, or better, parochializing a particular experience. For indeed, North Atlantic universals are words that project the North Atlantic experience on a universal scale that they themselves have to create. I don't like overusing the word *dialectic*, but what I have in mind is indeed a dialectical relation. North Atlantic universals are particulars that have gained a degree of universality, chunks of presized human history that have become historical standards. I suggest that we

may divide North Atlantic universals into somewhat overlapping categories: what I would call *substantive universals,* words that have to do
with content somehow and classificatory universals. The division is largely heuristic, but I hope we will agree on its methodological and political
relevance as I go on.

In the first set, that of substantive universals, I place universals that
claim to project content. Words such as *modernity, development, progress,*
and *democracy* are exemplary members of that already extended family
that contrasts or expands according to context and interlocutors. Belonging to that category of substantive universals does not depend on a fixed
meaning. It is a matter of struggle, contest about and around these universals and the world they claim to describe. There are two examples
that come to mind as candidates for substantive universals: *globalization*
and the *international community.* I love the *international community* in
particular because I think of it as a sort of Greek chorus of contemporary
politics. Nobody has ever seen it, but it is singing in the background and
everybody is playing to it. So it's very interesting that a new universal is
growing right beneath our nose.

North Atlantic universals, so defined, even when assisting or addressing content, are therefore not merely descriptive or referential. They
do not only describe the world, they offer visions of the world. They
appear to refer to things as they exist. But rooted as they are in a particular history, they are evocative of multiple sensibilities, persuasions, and
cultural and ideological choices tied to that localized history. In other
words, I'm suggesting that the words that can be used to describe the
world and the projects themselves as universal must be located. They
come to us loaded with aesthetic stylistic sensibilities, religious and
philosophical persuasions, cultural assumptions ranging from what it
means to be a human being to the proper relationship between humans
and nature, and ideological choices ranging from the nature of the political to its possibilities of transformation.

To be sure, there is no unanimity within the North Atlantic itself on
any of these issues, but there is a shared history of how these issues can
or should be debated. And these words carry that history. Yet, since they
are projected as universals, they deny their localization—especially the
sensibility and the history from which they spring. These North Atlantic
universals are always prescriptive, inasmuch as they always suggest,
even if only implicitly, the correct state of affairs—what is good, just,
sublime, desirable—not only what is, but what should be. Indeed, that
prescription is inherent in the very projection of a historically limited
experience: that of the North Atlantic on the world stage.

In other words, North Atlantic universals do not only prescribe,
they seduce. Indeed, they are always seductive, at times even irresist-

ible, exactly because they manage, in their projection, to hide their specific localized and thus partial history. This power of seduction is further enhanced by a capacity to project affect without ever claiming so. We all think of these words as having no affect, so to speak. And I'm suggesting that part of their seduction is that they come to us with full affect, but with the pretense that they don't carry any emotional charge. To be sure, all ideas come with affect, but a successful universal tends to hide the affect it projects behind the claim of rationality.

I think what makes North Atlantic universals successful is exactly the fact that they come to us clean of history, and of any charge, positive or negative. It makes sense to be modern. How can one not be modern? It is good to be modern. Similarly, how could anyone not want to join the international community? These propositions mean different things to different people. At the same time, the numbers of divergent voices that use and abuse these words verify their attraction. Their capacity of meaning many things to different people is also part of the seduction. One might go as far as saying that the capacity to seduce, by hiding their own history, is inherent in North Atlantic universals. The ability to project transhistorical relevance while hiding the particulars of their marks and origins, including their affective load, makes North Atlantic universals, as hard to conceptualize as they are seductive to use. Indeed, the more seductive these words become the harder it is to specify what they actually stand for.

Part of their seduction resides in the capacity to project clarity while remaining ambiguous. Even if we believe that concepts are words, a very questionable assumption, a quick perusal of the popular press in any European language demonstrates that North Atlantic universals are murky references. They evoke rather than define. Just do an Internet search on words like *democracy, international community,* or *globalization* and you'll understand what I'm suggesting. In this sense, popular evocations of North Atlantic universals work best in negative forms. We have a stronger sense of what modernity may mean when we point to the naysayers, such as the Taliban of Afghanistan, a tribe in the Amazon, or whatever figure temporarily plays the good or bad savage. We do not have a clear idea of what it actually means to be modern, only what it means to reject the modern. Again, seduction and confusion are related. Dreams of a democratic future, practices and institutions of democracy at work, and claims to join or defend international community vary in time and space. More seriously, attempts to conceptualize North Atlantic universals in the scholarly literature reveal little unanimity about their scope, let alone their denotation. It's fascinating to see how long academics have been disagreeing about what modernity may or may not be.

So far, I have insisted on the relativity of substantive universals and on the fact that they mask as much as they reveal. I suspect that most academics, especially most academics who see themselves as progressive or as part of the Left, are willing to accept this relativity, are willing to accept that concepts such as modernity, development, and modernization should be relativized and that they have a particular history. The extent to which politically progressive scholars may question North Atlantic universals depends, however, too much on immediate political sensibilities. That is, we are willing to question progress, development, modernization, or modernity as objective transhistorical categories largely because they come to us within a political package already held under suspicion. Our immediate instinct is to question these categories exactly because of the political package. But if development can (and should be) historicized, why not property? If property, why not money? This is the move that Marx starts to make in *The Poverty of Philosophy*.

> Economists express the relations of bourgeois production, the division of labor, credit, money, etc. as fixed, immutable, eternal categories. . . . Economists explain how production takes place in the above-mentioned relations, but what they do not explain is how these relations themselves are produced, that is, the historical movement that gave them birth. . . . [T]hese categories are as little eternal as the relations they express. *They are historical and transitory products.* (Marx 1955 [1847], 104, 110)

I will make three remarks about these passages. First, I wrote that Marx starts making this move in *The Poverty of Philosophy* because at least one reading of the entire Marx corpus is that all his theoretical work is a continuation of that project which culminates in *Capital*. Remember that the subtitle of this work is *"A Critique of Political Economy."* Second, from the beginning, although Marx's attention is fixed on what I call substantive universals, notably property and money (which are the two major categories about which he questioned Proudhon's views in *The Poverty of Philosophy*), the list and the analysis both include categories that are obviously relational, such as the division of labor or credit. Third, the categories that receive the fullest treatment are those that are substantive rather than relational, such as property, which Marx wished to convert into a relational category, but that is for another discussion.

Clearly, most academics do not go as far as Marx went in relativizing categories. Yet, I want to be provocative and ask: Why should we stop where Marx stopped? Should we not extend a critical evaluation to relational categories, something he did not do, and therefore the words that I call *classificatory universals* starting with the classificatory universal that he himself helped to develop the best—class? That is, if property, why not class? If class, why not race? If race, why not gender? In the chapter on ground rent in *The Poverty of Philosophy* Marx writes these lines:

> In each historical epoch, property has developed differently and under a set of entirely different social relations. . . . To try to give a definition of property as of an independent relation, a category apart, an abstract and eternal idea, can be nothing but an illusion of metaphysics or jurisprudence. (Marx 1955 [1847], 154)

What I suggest today is that we turn the program that Marx applied only to the categories of classical political economy to all North Atlantic universals and all categories that pretend to describe the world. Furthermore, I insist that we pay particular attention to classificatory universals—class, race, and gender.

Why do they matter perhaps more than property? My answer is simple: Classificatory universals have an impact on methodology, and thus on the production of knowledge about the world in a greater, yet more difficult, way than substantive universals. Why? I'm going to take a quick detour, provide some background, and make a few basic claims with which you may or may not agree. I contend that the social sciences, notwithstanding the claims of individual authors, are underpinned by a naive empiricism derived from their congenital tendency to mimic the natural sciences, or more correctly, to mimic a certain vision of the natural sciences held by social scientists. The strategies of expansion, even expansion of perspective, often primarily rely on the alleged discovery of new objects and new topics. This tendency is present even in France, where it's largely taken for granted that the object of study has to be constructed and cannot be reduced to the object of observation. This unfortunate tendency reaches its apex in the Anglophone world where the influence of empiricism is more prevalent and where the object of study is often reduced to the object of observation. What you see is what you get. Anybody trained in history, economics, or anthropology, particularly in the United States, has a sense of what I'm talking about.

What does this have to do with the study of the world-system in the age of so-called globalization? It has a lot to do with it if we consider the longue durée of concepts. One consequence is that we often take the empirical expansion of our material for theoretical growth. That is, when we want to become global, or better yet, universal, we add facts and figures from elsewhere, empirical data from outside the North Atlantic. But is adding facts about the rest of the world the same as studying the world? I'm not even sure that it's the same as studying the rest of the world, let alone studying the world.

Is not the issue how we theorize the world and produce greater knowledge about that world, and how we do research within this theoretical framework? In that sense, I am sorry to say that I do not share the optimism of others. To borrow Bruno Latour's famous title, "We Have Never Been Modern," I will counter that we have never been universal. At least, we have rarely been universal, and, appearances to the contrary, we try quite hard not to be universal. Janet Abu-Lughod commented in chapter 11 of this volume (quite rightly, in my view) that one of Immanuel Wallerstein's most significant contributions in *The Modern World-System* was his insistence upon the world as a fundamental unit of analysis. It is telling that this aspect of his contribution may have generated less discussion than other aspects of that work. The methodological consequences of that claim have not been exposed or explored, at least not to my knowledge, outside the rather limited circle of world-systems analysts. It seems to me that if we want to be global, let alone universal, which are not necessarily the same thing, methodology broadly conceived (I'm not talking about research techniques, which I don't think of as methodology), that is, the construction of the relation between the object of study and the object of observation becomes crucial. Therefore, classificatory universals need to be problematized, which of course brings me back to race, class, and gender.

Wallerstein noted that these three words gained prominence in mainstream social science in the 1970s. But look at their career since then. Although inherently classificatory, they quite quickly became essential and fixed in their contents. They started as concepts and they quickly became topics. But even this is a generous description to the extent that class, certainly in the United States, was quickly ignored, even as a topic. There have been a few studies of the lower classes, but they have been exotic, and thus quickly severed from the very relations that make the class concept meaningful—that is, a relevant classificatory category in the first place. But if class quickly became irrelevant, race or gender did not necessarily fare better. Both became topics, solidifying respectively in Black studies and women's studies. They became, to use Marx's words, "fixed, immutable, eternal categories" (Marx and Engels 1967 [1859]).

Just as Marx says of property, one only has to identify their manifestations. If you look at the majority of mainstream women's studies, we're looking for either gender or something actually less than gender to the extent that it's not relativized at all in particular societies. This is what I mean by empiricist strategies. Or we're going to look at race in Brazil basically to satisfy ourselves that the Brazilians are either more or less racist than the Americans, end of story. This is, of course, a silly exercise if it weren't for the hegemony that it keeps reproducing. I argue that we should actually historicize these very classificatory categories, although I'm not entirely sure how to do it.

I'll end by sketching not even a history of the race concept in its deployment, but what such a history could look for. I don't think I have reached a point where I can do this work, but I'll tease you with a few points of a longue-durée analysis of the concept of race. Interestingly, there is no widespread concept of race, and here I'm summarizing several ideas. There is no widespread concept of race in the Renaissance, that is, at the beginning of the secularization process that gave birth to social theory as we know it. It's not that the word was not there: The word is there, but it's not an essential word in conceptualizing social theory. It takes one in, as Sepúlveda did in arching back to Aristotle to justify enslavement of the Indians giving us the first hint of race as a social theory category. But even in the debate between Sepúlveda and Las Casas, the concept has no explanatory value, neither for Las Casas on the one side nor Sepúlveda on the other. This is, in part, because polygenesis is the strong ideology of the day, so there is no need to separate races. They were created somehow differently in the mind of Latin Christendom. But even then, the emphasis was on peoplehood in a sense, different peoplehood. That's the spirit of Montaigne's letters and his treatment of cannibalism among the Incas. That's the spirit of Montesquieu. Montesquieu doesn't need a concept of race, in that sense. With the African slave trade, and the first description of the Antilles, race starts having explanatory value. In fact, I argue against dominant international history that it's in the Caribbean and the southern plantations of the United States that scientific racism was born—not in Europe. It was then shipped back as a newer product to Europe, via the practices of plantation slavery.

This brings to mind what Brackette Williams calls the "overlap" between the intellectual, political, and lay life of concepts (1991). It seems to me that if we need to historicize categories, we need to keep in mind the fact that they are never just academic categories. They always have lives outside of academia, and their life in academia overlaps with their life outside of academia. With the African slave trade and the first description of the Antilles, race starts having explanatory value. If you read Labat, Du Tertre, or any of the early visitors of the plantation slavery in the Caribbean, you can see how race started to have explanatory value. The Blacks do it this way, the mulattos do it this way, the Europeans do it this way. It's a very different kind of thing from what you see barely a century earlier, for instance, in Jean de Léry's voyage through the land of Brazil (otherwise known as America), where de Léry describes the beginning (in a sense of what Du Tertre calls the "first technological text" (1667–1671) and where de Léry describes the life of savages in the Amazon (1975 [1580]). He doesn't need a concept of race, he doesn't need race to do it; he can do it without racialization. By the time the first French and Spanish travelers, and later, British travelers, describe the Antilles in the late 1690s, they need a concept of race for the description to work.

Therefore, the increase of race is couched as phenotype. It has explanatory value, but it is phenotype. It doesn't rest on biology; it rests on appearance. It will take the work of biologists (or better said, naturalists of the time) to biologize race, at the very same time that the rise of a category of "mulatto" both in what is now the South of the United States and also in Brazil and the Caribbean genderizes race. So, I also argue, that it's not as if we can take race and gender and put them together. We need to look at the ways in which these categories intertwine.

These increased features are going to be objectified by scientific racism in the eighteenth century. Race is fully biologized in the eighteenth century and the beginning of the nineteenth century. It has now become a scientific concept that reenters academia, supposedly with the weight or value of biology. By the late nineteenth century, biological inheritance, rather than simply race, becomes an explanation of behavior across group boundaries—not just in the Americas, not just in Europe, but throughout the world. You can see this shift. I'm arguing that race is not always race. The concept of race has different kinds of contents and different kinds of modes of production. The concept of race as biological inheritance of behavior is dated in the mid- to late-nineteenth century. But then it takes on a life of its own, particularly with racism and the Reconstruction in the United States.

This is the way in which Franz Boas is going to discover race as the concept of biological inheritance and build the foundation of American cultural anthropology on the questioning of that concept of race. Boas does not attack any concept of race; he attacks the concept of race as biological inheritance of behavior. In response to this concept of race as the biological inheritance of behavior, American anthropology invents a concept of race as culture. I argue that part of what the concept of culture in American anthropology does is to allow American anthropologists to have their cake and eat it too. That is, they can talk about behavior without challenging racism, because the race-as-culture concept is actually an anticoncept.

To understand the emphasis on culture in the United States, you have to understand the impossibility of having a serious and open debate about U.S. racism. What we call multiculturalism, for instance, has nothing to do with culture. The idea that somehow a Black, inner-city Chicago kid is closer culturally to a Kalahari Bushman than to his northern White, middle-class counterpart is nonsense. But this nonsense allows us to be polite and avoid talk about racism. In this sense, culture is an anticoncept. It doesn't have any validity from within, but it allows us to escape another kind of conversation.

In the longue durée of the world-system, what worries me is that this culture, built upon the boundaries solidified by biology, is now being exported to the rest of the world from the United States with the "globalization" of consumer culture, particularly the movie and sports industries. We're selling Michael Jordan as culture to the rest of the world, from Brazil to Nigeria to South Africa, and I'm not sure it's a good thing. I suggest that concepts matter—in particular, contexts of deployment. These contexts of deployment require (I'm taking Immanuel Wallerstein very seriously) that we think of the world as a unit of analysis. To think of the world as a unit of analysis does not mean that we can't conduct particular studies, such as studying how the concept of race and culture intertwine in Boas and anthropology. But if we do this, we need to do it within the context of a deployment which itself is historical and universal in the sense of universal history. To treat race, gender, and even class as historicized categorical universals is, in Marx's own words, to fall into an "illusion of metaphysics or jurisprudence" (1955, 154).

References

Du Tertre, Jean Baptiste. 1667–1671. *Histoire générale des Antilles habitées par les Français*. Paris: T. Iolly

Glissant, Edouard. 1997. *The Poetics of Relation*. Ann Arbor: University of Michigan Press.

Latour, Bruno. 1993. *We Have Never Been Modern*. Cambridge, MA: Harvard University Press.

Léry, Jean de. 1975 [1580]. *Histoire d'un voyage fait en la terre du Brésil*. Geneva: Droz.

Marx, Karl. 1955 [1847]. *The Poverty of Philosophy*. New York: International Publishers.

Marx, Karl, and Friedrich Engels. 1967 [1859]. *Capital: A Critique of Political Economy*. New York: International Publishers.

Williams, Brackette. 1991. *Stains on My Name, War in My Veins: Guyana and the Politics of Cultural Struggle*. Durham, NC: Duke University Press.

Index

About the Contributors

Immanuel Wallerstein	Director, Fernand Braudel Center, Binghamton University; Senior Research Scholar, Yale University
Samir Amin	Director, Forum du Tiers-Monde, Dakar
Christopher Chase-Dunn	Director, Institute for Research on World-Systems, University of California, Riverside
Bart Tromp	Political Science, Leiden University
Claudia von Werlhof	Political Science, University of Innsbruck
Giovanni Arrighi	Director, Institute for Global Studies in Culture, Power and History, Johns Hopkins University
Pablo González Casanova	Instituto de Investigaciones Sociales, Universidad Nacional Autónoma de México
Marcel van der Linden	Director, Internationaal Institut voor Sociale Geschiednis, Amsterdam
Randall Collins	Sociology, University of Pennsylvania
Mahmood Mamdani	Institute of African Studies, Columbia University
Boaventura de Sousa Santos	Director, Centro de Estudos Sociais, University of Coimbra
Janet L. Abu-Lughod	Sociology, New School University, Emerita
Maurice Aymard	Administrator, Maison des Sciences de l'Homme, Paris
Michel-Rolph Trouillot	Anthropology, University of Chicago